THE NEW RUM

THE
NEW
RUM

A MODERN GUIDE TO
THE SPIRIT OF THE AMERICAS

BRYCE T. BAUER

The Countryman Press
A division of W. W. Norton & Company
Independent Publishers Since 1923

This book expands on "Rum's Revenge," by Bryce T. Bauer, published on September 17, 2015, in *Craftsmanship Quarterly* (https://craftsmanship.net/rums-revenge/).

Image Credits:
Page 23: Courtesy of Library of Congress
Page 60: Courtesy of Demerara Distillers Limited
Page 257: Courtesy of Citizen Spirits, LLC
Page 265: Courtesy of Facundo Rum Collection
Page 294: © 2018 Real McCoy Spirits, Corp
Page 300: Courtesy of Haus Alpenz
Page 302: Courtesy of Gani Piñero Photography, LLC
Additional interior graphics provided by Shutterstock.

For information about permission to reproduce selections from this book, write to Permissions, The Countryman Press, 500 Fifth Avenue, New York, NY 10110

For information about special discounts for bulk purchases, please contact W. W. Norton Special Sales at specialsales@wwnorton.com or 800-233-4830

Manufacturing by Versa Press
Book design by Faceout Studio
Production manager: Devon Zahn

The Countryman Press
www.countrymanpress.com

A division of W. W. Norton & Company, Inc.
500 Fifth Avenue, New York, NY 10110
www.wwnorton.com

978-1-68268-000-1

10 9 8 7 6 5 4 3 2 1

TO MY PARENTS,
FOR NURTURING INDEPENDENCE
AND WANDERLUST.

CONTENTS

▼
INTRODUCTION

It's cliché to retail stories about rum that turn on collegiate binges of neon juice and cheap rum and resolve, after the regrets, with a commitment to never touch the stuff again. Read enough rum articles and talk to enough rum producers and you may even become convinced that the frat house punch bowl represents a truly existential threat. But I am not going to start there. Instead, I'm going to start with a story about why I think rum is—pinch your ears tight, spirits partisans—the world's best spirit and why, despite that, it is vastly underappreciated.

You see, when it came to rum in college, I was lucky. At some point early on, a friend, who in retrospect I've decided must have taken up the practice during his summers among the nautical in Nantucket, convinced me that if I was going to drink rum, then the rum I ought to drink was a rum from Barbados with the name of Mount Gay. While it would be a decade before I actually knew it as one of the world's great rums, I followed his advice. At the time I just knew it tasted decent and was, for the mildly pretentious set one would expect a budding booze writer to run in, affordable enough.

Eventually I graduated from mixing my rum with soda—this was when everyone was convinced high fructose corn syrup was an existential threat—to drinking it in lazy, high-summer mojitos on my cousin's patio, with mint scoured from the farmers' market when we were lucky and those terrible herb clamshells when we weren't. For a few years that was good enough.

What happened next reflects the real peril facing rum makers, though: I moved on. When my drinking became, well, more serious, I turned to wine, with its intricate taxonomies and well-articulated hierarchies, and to whiskey, with its craftsmanship heritage and its lodestars at scotch and bourbon. Before I ever got back to rum, I even turned to mezcal, a spirit that, in just a couple of years, managed to dump its association with a dead worm and skeezy gringos and take the mantle as arguably the world's most "authentic" spirit, that elusive property that is our era's most important marker of quality.

Rum, for the most part, seemed to be an afterthought. A good mojito is an exquisite thing, but I figured that had more to do with the mint and the sugar and the fact that on a hot day, it would seem the only thing better than chilled soda water is chilled soda water with mint, sugar, and alcohol. As for rum outside of a mojito, well what was there? There was rum named after pirates. There was rum named after what I think are beaches. There was rum flavored with more varieties of fruit than there is available in Manhattan's Chinatown. But no one's a connoisseur of those things. That much I knew about rum. Rum, I figured, was made from sugarcane, which gives us cheap, ubiquitous, almost-the-definition-of-a-commodity white table sugar, so therefore it must just not have a noble lineage. You know where this is going: I was woefully mistaken.

Nonetheless, for nearly a decade the woe held, until just a few years ago. Then an editor sent me out to explore the burgeoning American craft rum scene. I trekked down cobblestone streets in Red Hook, Brooklyn, and weaved among the warehouses of East Williamsburg. I came back with a lot of questions and really only one answer, which was that it wasn't really that unusual to be making rum in New York City, far though it was from the tropics, where sugarcane was first turned into rum. On one level, the reason for that has to do with the intricate social, political, and economic history in which rum, as a fundamental strand of the European colonial story in the Western Hemisphere, is entwined. But on another it was a reflection of an even greater quality of the spirit.

You see, in rum there is something wonderful. Let me explain:

As I write this there are six glasses set in front of me. In each is a different beverage that, in at least some part of the world, is called rum.

The first is Appleton Estate 21 Year Old, a rich Jamaican rum with deep wood notes, but accompanying them are also clearly identifiable funky and fruity flavors that make the island's rum so unique. Next to it is Brugal 1888, another long-aged rum, but this one from the Dominican Republic and made in a much different style, with a long, complex finish of spice and toffee and oak barrel flavors. The third is Diplomático Mantuano from Venezuela, which compared to the other two has a distinctly sweet body and a much softer mouthfeel. The fourth, the rum that I can't actually open and pour until I am ready to taste because its nose of tropical fruits is so intense, is Rum Fire, also from Jamaica. It hasn't seen a lick of wood, and yet it is almost sippable, despite being 126 proof, with a body that's also best described as funky and fruity, though this is a different funk and a somewhat different cornucopia of fruits than the Appleton. The fifth is Damoiseau XO, from the French island of Guadeloupe. Like the other aged rums, it has clear notes of spice from the oak barrel but is far brighter and more vibrant than either the Appleton or Brugal and has its own clearly detectable strangeness. The final, from Brazil, is a bottle of what is known as "cachaça" from the producer Leblon. It is also made from sugarcane, but you'd be forgiven for thinking otherwise—what is in this bottle of clear spirit takes me back to my childhood, when I lived on a farm with a lawn. In the spring, when the grass was wet and lush and my chore was to mow it, I would find myself immersed in its redolence and that of the gasoline I could never quite pour into the mower's tank without spilling. That's what this bottle tastes like, followed suddenly by the clear note of the flavor—but not the sweetness—of sugarcane.

No other spirit can achieve such a range. As one rum expert, Jeff "Beach-bum" Berry, the tiki wizard behind New Orleans's Latitude 29 bar and a number of essential cocktailing books on the style, told me, the only comparison for rum's diversity that makes sense is wine.

"A pinot noir and a Chablis are as different as night and day. They are different colors, they don't taste anything like each other, but they are both wine. Same thing with rum," he said.

In that diversity, however, is rum's challenge. Say "rum" and one person thinks of Bacardí Carta Blanca, light, a little harsh, and calling out for lime and a little sugar, while another thinks of Appleton Rare, lush, tropical, with a little bit of that funk that Jamaican rums are famous for, and in need of nothing but a glass.

Wine confronted that challenge by divvying its world up into categories and qualifiers that can be layered to intricacy. As such, wine has "Sonoma Coast syrahs" and "Australian Shirazes," "Napa chardonnays" and bottles of "Chablis." You may not know exactly what you are going to get with each of those, but at least you know you won't be getting white Zinfandel.

Nomenclature is descriptive and partially defensive. I'm "Bryce" and that schmuck over there is not, and if he tries to trade on my accreted goodwill by pretending he is, I get to clobber him. I suspect the Bordelais would do the same thing to you if you decided to squish some supermarket red grapes up in your Milwaukee apartment and sell that as "Bordeaux."

Rum has none of that. Owing perhaps to the fact that it is produced in so many often small, often poor countries that frequently are still tangling with the legacy of colonial sugar slavery—and made by distillers who in many cases produced almost entirely for the bulk rum market—rum, instead, has little more than "white," "gold," and "dark" categories that are only helpful if you have a hue fetish. It's the equivalent of gathering up the Bordelais and the Chablisians and the Californians and even a few charlatans and telling them they have to compete, but they have to do so all under the same name.

So instead, when you order rum, the only reliable thing you know is that you'll get alcohol. Fine, perhaps, if your goal is to grab a frozen daiquiri and stumble down Bourbon Street, but not so great if you're contemplating spending $60 on something you want to savor. Perhaps it's for this reason that rum has yet to follow wine or whiskey into the highest echelons of connoisseurship. This is a tragedy, because the world is full of great rums, some that deserve as much reverence as the best bottles of whiskey and wine, or more perhaps, when you consider the conditions under which this product of one of the more volatile, less developed regions of the world is made.

For the purposes of this book, I am going to operate on the belief that variety and experimentation are good, and the unique, even if it comes at the cost of efficiency, is something worth preserving. If those don't sound like particularly radical principles, that's only because in the past decade, decade and a half, a renewed interest in small-scale, local, artisan production has reshaped everything from cabinetry to coffee, booze included. But for most of rum's nearly four hundred years of existence, the world was primarily on a drive to efficiency. In categories amenable to manufacturing for mass consumption—and rum is one—the producers' goal was more likely to be standardization, homogenization, and the leveraging of economies of scale. Often that rum was sold generic or shunted off to brands to be repackaged to whatever market segment someone could figure out how to sell to, which seems to have mostly been the now much-maligned midcult looking for something sweet, fruity, and fun. This heritage of rum—and I'm using "heritage" here in the literal sense, not as it's used as marketing gloss—has crashed into what economists have come to call the "experience economy," predicated on the selling of authenticity.

Absent finer categorization, such as those for scotch, bourbon, and cognac, and the standard-making regimes that spring up once a group with a mutual interest in creating value for its products is created, rum is left as a wildly diverse category with many competing interests, all of which are trying to cram into just those three letters. It's no wonder, then, that some industry followers, in their more enraged moments of pique, can muster little more defense for r-u-m than to say it's all but meaningless.

But adventures in rum, it turns out, are boundless as well, and the story of rum is too long to fit even into a book. So here I've focused primarily on the Caribbean, because that is where rum originates, and primarily on the former English and Spanish colonies therein, because that's what has defined rum for Americans. But when I took those first few serious sips of rum in Brooklyn, I knew none of that. Instead I just got hooked, and I knew I would never be able to shake the curiosity unless I could figure out what was behind them. So I bought $70 worth of sunscreen, acquired a double prescription of Malarone, and headed off in search of the source of those first few faint memories of the spirit I had from college.

MOJITO

The mojito gets a bad rap, in part because to make it well takes a bit of time and a bit of effort, so it's often made poorly. But done well it competes with the daiquiri—which I'll rhapsodize on later—as the cocktail equivalent of the sublime. The key is good fresh mint, patient muddling, and balance. The first is so hardy and vigorous that there are few excuses not to just grow it yourself. If it survived my windowsill, I can't imagine it'll perish on yours. The latter two come with practice and devotion, two things the drink strongly encourages. Then it just comes down to rum. After my college ritual I still have an affinity for Mount Gay Eclipse, but any dry, well-made rum will do. (What's dry and well made? Well, take a sip. If it's sweet or you want to spit it out, find something else.)

2 ounces rum

0.75 ounce fresh lime juice

6 mint leaves

1 teaspoon fine sugar (sugars like castor sugar dissolve easier in cocktails)

Soda water

Put lime juice, mint leaves, and sugar in a tall glass. Muddle the mint. Add rum and ice and top with soda water.

CHAPTER 1

They Call It Kill-Devil

I set off for Barbados at the beginning of August—nearly the height of the already steamy average-temperature chart and right around when Caribbean hurricane season starts churning. Google "Barbados in August" and mostly what's returned are TripAdvisor forum threads started by people asking whether they should. The general consensus seems to be that it's fine unless you mind afternoon rain, uncomfortable highs, and climatic unpredictability—most people seeking a beach getaway do mind. But dirty little secret: I don't particularly care for beach getaways. On the one hand there's the sand, which in most other circumstances is considered what it is, a gritty irritant; on the other is the water, which primarily causes drowning. So I was happy to have an excuse to not bring a beach towel. Besides, leaving it behind would mean that I'd have more time for my real task at hand anyway: drinking rum.

To that end, a few days after my arrival on a desperately freezing Jet-Blue flight from New York's JFK airport, I grabbed an early-morning bus to Speightstown, which I'd come to understand was the second-largest town in Barbados and, more importantly, the closest point of easy public transit disembarkation to the fount of the fondest of my earliest rum memories. As my bus wended its way up Highway 1—the 15-mile trip from the apartment I was renting in the south coast village of Hastings to Speightstown took a full hour—we passed through Barbados's Platinum (née Gold) Coast, past mansions perched right along the water and the Gucci and Louis Vuitton shops of Holetown's Limegrove Lifestyle Centre, which in terms less worked over by the world's land-slinging class would have been called a mall.

What I was expecting when I got to Speightstown was a slightly less bustling version of Barbados's capital of Bridgetown, the narrow, balcony-lined downtown streets of which I had been walking for the previous few days, dodging the wares of the trinket shops spilling out onto the sidewalk and the trinket shoppers rummaging through them. On the sweaty verge of heatstroke from a midday sun that sent more rational people to seek cover, like the woman who stopped me on the sidewalk one afternoon to make the suggestion that I take the bus, I could almost imagine that I was in a time several centuries prior, when this city and this island were the pinnacle of Western civilization in the Western Hemisphere. During the middle of the seventeenth century, it was the most densely populated bit of anglophone soil in the world.

That fantasy quickly fell apart when our bus reached Speightstown. While I can't say that the place definitively is *not* Barbados's second-largest town—the facts seem quite solid on that point—I quickly realized what would have been apparent had I bothered to look the place up on Wikipedia: it may happen to be Barbados's second-largest town, but it also happens to be one-thirtieth the size of Bridgetown. Bustling second city, at a population of 3,630, this was not. After wandering around town for a bit, hoping that I had just gotten off too early and was simply on the outskirts of the city, I resigned myself to the fact that I was not going to be spending my morning amid busy port crowds, so I walked along the waterfront instead. Eventually I reached a small grove of trees growing in the sand at the edge of the Almond Beach Resort. An oval sign was stapled to one. Because the red print was fading and the daylight was muted from heavy clouds that occasionally burst to deliver several minutes of downpour, I had to walk up close to make it out. It read CAUTION: ALL TREES WITH RED BANDS PRODUCE SMALL GREEN APPLES, WHICH ARE POISONOUS. DO NOT HANDLE OR EAT THESE APPLES, ALSO PLEASE DO NOT STAND UNDER THESE TREES WHEN IT IS RAINING AS THE WATER FROM THE TREES MAY CAUSE BLISTERING. THANK YOU.

Say what you want about overdevelopment, but nature, it seems, doesn't surrender easily.

I'd come up here to in essence take a trip back in time, to chase the origins of rum. All good stories need a beginning, but rum, like most good spirits, has no such story to tell. Where it came from, who first made it, when that first drop sputtered its way off the first batch of mash, swirled through some sort of condenser, and dripped out the other end as the newest of the world's great distilled drinks is unknown.

But there were perhaps few places closer to the beginning of that story—and unfortunately "perhaps" is the best we are going to get here—than the northern tip of this 167-square-mile chunk of coral in the eastern Caribbean that not too many centuries ago was the gilded center of the Western world.

Resigned to the fact that I'd come a few centuries too late to see much of the wealth that once made this place so valuable and gave cause to bring distillation to the island in the first place, I took a cab to my final destination, a half-dozen miles away in the parish of St. Lucy (the only one of Barbados's 11 parishes, each of which is named after a saint, to be named for a woman), to the Mount Gay Distillery. As I did, the scenery became increasingly less like that of the quintessential Caribbean cliché. As we made our way inland, Barbados's famous white-sand beaches faded away and with them the resorts and palm trees and open-air bars that made up the new, somewhat gilded, always a bit too precariously subjected to the whims of international finance raison d'être of the place today. Replacing them was a bumpy, expansive landscape, one that had been the fount of Barbados's wealth and prestige.

Mount Gay proudly proclaims on its label that it was established in 1703. That, however, is wrong, as I had learned the day before when I stopped by the Mount Gay Visitors' Centre and Bottling Plant, a separate facility from the distillery in St. Lucy. The reason for the separation of the two facilities, which were once owned by separate companies, may date back to an old Barbadian law that forbade rum to be bottled at the same place it was produced. Today, however, the plant is located just north of Bridgetown and, crucially, a mile from the cruise ship terminal. In addition to being a bottling plant, it serves as an attraction for the tourists thirsty for yet another rum drink. And the visitor center staff knows their audience well: the cocktail-making class and competition Mount Gay invited me to, and in the spirit of intrepid journalism I had absolutely no intention of refusing, included such introductory tips as throwing out the jigger—measurement certainly not being the mantra anyone wants to espouse on a Caribbean vacation.

But the facility isn't all kitsch and enthusiastic consumption. Like most booze brands, Mount Gay is keen to tell its story, so the tour starts with, well, a tour, walking visitors through the legends and methods of the brand. Judging from the density of selfies taken, the most popular item on the tour—after the actual booze, of course—was a display of all of the bottles in the Mount Gay portfolio lined up, ready to serve as a photo backdrop for dutiful group after dutiful group of my fellow visitors. On one of the walls hangs a document backing up that 1703 date in the form of a deed from that year describing the transfer of property, including that for rum making, from one generation to the next.

But 1703 is not really Mount Gay's birthdate. It must be older for there to have been anything to document on the day in 1703 when that deed was drawn. In an industry where heritage is often touted as everything—even when it is nothing—Mount Gay doesn't crow the actual date of their birth because they don't know it. Anyway, the 1703 date is still old enough for Mount Gay to claim to be the oldest rum brand in the world.

When I arrived at the distillery in St. Lucy, I was met by Raphael Grisoni, an exuberant Frenchman who serves as the distillery's managing director (Mount Gay is today owned by the French liquor conglomerate Rémy Cointreau), and Darrio Prescod, the brand ambassador, for a drive through the property surrounding the distillery, which Mount Gay recently acquired with the hope of increasing domestic molasses production. At one point we stopped at the shell of an old stone windmill perched at the top of a hill— the "mount" of Mount Gay (unlike the many other Caribbean islands, which are volcanic protrusions, Barbados is flat and actually lies in the Atlantic, making it, to a geographic stickler, not even part of the Caribbean). The afternoon was drizzly and the land that fell away around us was tranquil and muted and covered with short stocks of young sugarcane, a reminder of the teeming landscape this would have been three hundred years prior.

Sugarcane took root in the West Indies in 1493, when Christopher Columbus, on his second voyage west, planted a stalk in the soil of Hispaniola, the island shared today by Haiti and the Dominican Republic. He thought it a better place to grow cane than any other in the world. While sugarcane would eventually flourish on that island, the Spanish at the time had little interest in growing what would come to take on that appellative for anything valuable of a particular color: "white gold." In reality, they had little interest in growing any agricultural product whatsoever. It was *actual* gold that they'd come for, and though the Caribbean islands had little, they intended to get all that they could, impressing the island's native inhabitants to mine it for them—an operation that consumed the indigenous Americans at a rate of several thousand a year until the gold, and the natives, were virtually expended.

As Spain was pillaging the Americas, sugar cultivation fell to the Portuguese, English, and French colonists, who set up plantations on their own land well before the Spanish started theirs—a delay that led not only to an early underdevelopment of the Spanish sugar industry, but also gave the Spaniards a late start in what would prove to be another crucial plantation product: rum.

Saccharum officinarum, as sugarcane is known formally, is a type of grass that had been cultivated for centuries before European settlement of the Western Hemisphere began. Nonetheless, when Columbus set sail, it was still a rare commodity in Europe. Most likely domesticated in Papua New Guinea, sugarcane enticed consumers—though not necessarily in the dry, granular form we know it today—through China and India before eventually spreading into North Africa, the Mediterranean, and onto Madeira, São Tomé, Principe, and the Canary Islands as the Spanish and the Portuguese took them over, which was likely how Columbus was acquainted with the plant in the first place: his wife's family was involved in the trade.

It was the Portuguese, in the sixteenth century, who were the first to set up a thriving sugar industry in the New World in what is today the states of Pernambuco on Brazil's bulbous knuckle and Bahia. While sugarcane had many uses by then—as a spice and medicine, as building material, and likely by some as a low-alcohol fermented beverage, a sugarcane wine in essence—rum was not among them, though a spirit named cachaça may

Sugarcane production emerged in the Caribbean soon after European discovery. Laborious, unpleasant, and dangerous, cane cultivation and processing was forced upon a coerced labor force. As sugar production took over the West Indies, it fueled the transatlantic slave trade and all its attendant horrors. In this 1749 illustration by John Hinton, workers press cane to extract juice and boil the juice to begin concentrating the sugar. Emerging as it did on the cusp of the industrial era, the operation appears to rely on gravity to make the cane juice flow downhill to the boilers.

have been. It'd be another century before reliable reports emerged of a distilled beverage made from sugarcane in what are today the traditional rum islands. In the intervening time, the sugar plant jumped, coming from Brazil to the new English colony of Barbados, where it quickly displaced what had been smallholdings growing an assortment of crops, including cotton, ginger, indigo, and tobacco, the last considered to be of such vile quality that many of the farmers growing it spent a portion of their earnings on imported tobacco for their own personal consumption. Barbados was colonized by the English in 1625, and by 1652 about 80 percent of the island's arable land had been impressed into sugarcane cultivation, which eventually consumed the effort of 90 percent of its labor force. (It also led to massive deforestation, like it did on many of the other Caribbean islands; the heavily forested landscape that greeted many of the early visitors was unknown to those of just a few decades later who, like visitors today, know the islands as a largely treeless expanse). The sugarcane boom, meanwhile, wasn't confined just to the New World. Concomitant with the grass's transformation of the landscape of the places it flourished, like Barbados, was a transformation of the diets of the Europeans who stayed back home.

At the beginning of Spanish colonization of the New World, sugar made scarcely a mark on the diet of any but the wealthiest Europeans, who used it primarily in minute quantities, as a spice like pepper, nutmeg, and saffron. However from that point on, its consumption rose like an exponential growth curve on, well, a sugar high (needless to say, the crash has yet to come). By the start of the eighteenth century, the English, who had Europe's sweetest tooth, were consuming four pounds of sugar per person per year. By the nineteenth century they were eating more than quadruple that, at eighteen pounds per capita annually. Over the course of yet another century, consumption quintupled again. Even those dramatic statistics, however, obscure just how quickly sugar caught on: As Sidney Mintz shows in his stellar study of the rise of sugar production, *Sweetness and Power*, these earlier statistics are rough and a little misleading—in the 1700s, and to a lesser extent the 1800s, most people were consuming no sugar, so the per capita consumption of those wealthy enough to afford sugar was likely considerably greater than the numbers would suggest. Sugar's transformation from a luxury for the spice cabinets of the rich into a pantry staple for all ushered in, or at least accompanied, a host of changes to the British table. As Europe's cooks concocted new recipes to impress their guests, the concept of sweetness changed from that of an exotic flavor to a point on the

Sugarcane being harvested for Ron Barceló in the Dominican Republic. While mechanical sugarcane harvesting is common, in many places cane is still cut by hand.

tetrahedron of primary tastes—along with bitterness, sourness, and saltiness. In its incursion it had allies in a slate of rapidly popularizing products also coming in from the outposts of the European colonial world.

"Much of the new demand was the result of other new tropical products coming onto the English market," Matthew Parker writes in *The Sugar Barons*. "London's first coffeehouse opened in 1652. Tea imported from China by the East India Company started gaining popularity at around the same time, and for the rich, chocolate from cacao became fashionable. All three needed, in most people's opinion, sugar to make them drinkable."

Unlike previous staple commodities, starches primarily, the sugar Europe was consuming only made it to the table after a long chain of industrial processing. The sugar in sugarcane—sucrose—is locked in a fibrous stalk that looks much like ginger root. When crushed, it streams out in a light green juice with a moderately sweet and vegetal flavor and a mouthfeel not unlike that of coconut water. While sugarcane juice is sometimes drunk locally, it is highly unstable, and juice pressed in the morning in a tropical climate will have started fermenting naturally by the end of the day. To get the sugar that Europe was consuming, planters would crystalize the juice's sucrose to produce a wide array of various grades of dry sugar. But the crystalizing process was never complete, and as a result it produced considerable amounts of liquid, sucrose-laden molasses that could be processed no further.

The common narrative on rum is that for decades planters were scrambling to dispose of all the excess molasses Europe's sweet tooth was leaving behind in the Caribbean. As the story went, they fed it to their livestock, and then to their slaves, and then they spread it across their fields as fertilizer, and when all of those outlets had their fill and the molasses continued to accumulate, they simply dumped it into the ocean. That was until one day, when a colonist of veritably unrivaled intelligence fermented a bit of that molasses, fired up a still, and birthed a new discovery destined for the world's compendium of Greatest Ideas. Behold: rum.

It's a story that sounds logical enough and one that's useful, in particular, to distillers who use some other type of sugar derivative for their rum and are, because of that fact, fond of referring to molasses as "industrial waste." I'm convinced this is in the hope of evoking in their rival's product an image of some kind of toxic bubbling effluent issued from the bowels of a hellish factory and diverted, just seconds before otherwise being dumped into its rightful place in a dark pit for unmentionable discards, to that drink you now hold in your hand and are so eager to take a sip of. It is, as we will see, an image not entirely devoid of accuracies (a few may quibble, but "hellish" for one seems like a pretty accurate description of a sugar mill to me). But the story of rum's emergence from the sugarcane fields of the Caribbean is quite a bit more complicated.

There was no sudden rum epiphany. Instead there were many things in the ferment of the early colonial world that lead up to a boom in rum, not unlike the one that had preceded it in sugar (and in tea, coffee, chocolate, tobacco, and opium—all precious foreign substances that, many have pointed out, possess mood-altering properties and addictive potentialities).

For most of sugarcane's history, throughout its rise in the Arab world, the Mediterranean, and what would eventually become Brazil, it seemed to not have been distilled, at least not in any significant amount. However, it was fermented to create drinks known as *guarapo* by the Spanish and *grappe* by the French, which helped satisfy the thirst early colonists and slaves brought over from pre-industrial Europe and Africa. But that isn't to say no one was producing distilled spirits.

The most accepted evidence suggests the technique has its roots in ancient alchemy, that attempt to turn common metals into gold, something later Europeans found easier performed if the metal was in the more traditional form of ore and the transmutation was effectuated by enslaved indigenous Americans. However, alcohol production from a semi-modern still traces back to a man named Taddeo Alderotti in Bologna in the late thirteenth century. He documented a method of creating what he called *aqua vita*—"the water of life"—as Adam Rogers writes in his book *Proof*, which tells the story of humanity's pursuit of intoxicating drinks. Crucially, however, Alderotti was a physician, not a beverage slinger, and it doesn't appear he was gunning for a career change.

Of his invention, Rogers writes, "Word began to spread. Whatever this liquid was, it seemed to cure diseases, relieve pain, fix bad breath, purify spoiled wine, preserve meat, and draw out the essences of plants." Miraculous sure, but also uses which require only small quantities to make you feel better or to keep the things you were going to eat and drink from making you feel worse. Distilled spirits to be used in large quantities to make you think you feel better, and later perhaps make you feel quite a bit worse, wouldn't appear for a few hundred more years—right about the time a few farmers on Barbados were looking to get out of the game of growing fusty tobacco.

In fact, anthropologist Frederick H. Smith, in *Caribbean Rum*, his study of the rise of West Indies rum production, points to some evidence that sugarcane first came to Barbados for the purpose of producing alcohol, albeit in fermented form. As it is, no one knows who distilled the first drop of rum, or whether they did it in Barbados. (The Brazilians claim fermented sugarcane distillation first took place in their country in the middle of the sixteenth century, but whether, if it did, that means they can rightfully claim the title as the first producers of rum is a question that will be taken up in later chapters.) However, the first definitive reference to the existence of what would come to be known as "rum" traces firmly to the island. It comes from a British author and wayward sugarcane planter named Richard Ligon, who lived in Barbados for several years in the middle of the seventeenth century and later published a book about his time there.

In his account, he lists several locally produced drinks available to Barbadians, including one made from fermented potatoes and another from cassava root, which was made by Indians, who first chewed the cassava and then spit it out, a process found throughout the Americas. This sets off fermentation, eventually producing an alcoholic beverage which "tastes the likest to English beer of any drink we have there," he wrote. While Ligon was tepid on the tastiness of those root-based beverages (of the one from cassava, which was called *perino*, the best he could muster was that it was "not altogether so pleasant"), he saved his greatest scorn for a beverage made from the "skimming of sugar."

He found it to be "infinitely strong," "not very pleasant in taste," and prone to such overconsumption on the island that its drinkers could often be found passed out on the ground, which was, he concluded, "a very unwholesome lodging."

As for the name of such an illustrious beverage, the Barbadians, he wrote, called it "Kill-Devil."

Ligon's was just one of the early commentaries on rum (another, from around the same time, called it "a hott hellish and terrible liquor"), and "kill-devil" was just one of the early names for the product. But in time drinkers across the Caribbean settled on calling the stuff rum, which was most likely an abbreviation of the word *rumbullion*, a term, back in the English West Country, where many of Barbados's settlers originated, that meant "a great tumult," Smith writes.

It wasn't exactly progress on the reputation front. But then early colonists didn't seem to be paying much attention to their interlocutor's assessments, anyway.

Over the next century or two, rum followed sugar as it spread throughout the Caribbean, showing up in the French Caribbean, where it was called *rhum*, and the Spanish, where it came to be known as *ron*. And its production wasn't just a convenient source of befuddlement for the islands' populations—though it certainly was that too—it also quickly turned into a key best practice of sugar-estate management. Though early records are sparse, those that do exist show successful planters incorporating skimmings from boiling pots used to produce sugar; molasses; the discards of previous distillations, called dunder; and sugarcane juice that couldn't otherwise be transformed into sugar into the wash from which they produced rum. All told, rum production could provide anywhere from 15 to 40 percent of a sugar estate's revenue by midcentury, Smith's analysis shows.

As Ligon's commentary suggests, the destination for all the rum the sugar estates were producing, at least in the earlier years, wasn't exactly a mystery—it was mostly going down islanders' throats. By the last half of the seventeenth century, planters on Barbados were likely capable of producing upward of one million gallons of rum per year; however, only a few hundred thousand gallons of that seems to have been exported during that time. Instead, compendiums could be filled with anecdotes of the excesses of Caribbean drinking—one of the most famous coming from the table of James Drax, one of the island's foremost sugarcane planters, who threw a feast for the visit of Ligon that included, in addition to kill-devil, brandy, sherry, several types of imported wine, and several more of locally produced drinks.

Meanwhile, another of Barbados's planters, Christopher Codrington, who went on to found Barbados's Codrington College, was so fond of drink—and ostentation—that he sent a commission back home to England to produce what may be the world's largest covered punch bowl, which was a foot and a half high and nearly as wide ("covered" being the operative word here, as plenty of the uncovered type have been made larger). While the islands' elite may have been particularly showy about their drinking, the appetite for alcohol cut across all classes and groups. According to figures provided by Ligon, per capita consumption of rum alone by sugar estate workers may have been around nine gallons a year, a figure which would be roughly double the total per capital alcohol consumption in the United States today.

The causes of such excessive consumption were likely plural, but a significant driver of it, Smith argues, was from the stress and challenges of living in the colonial Atlantic world. While the life of a sugar planter was extravagant, it was also isolating and monotonous, lacking few peers with whom to socialize and little opportunity for entertainment other than boozing and feasting. Most sugar estate owners intended to stay in the West Indies only as long as they could acquire enough wealth to enter the ranks of the elite back in England. For the poorer populations and the slaves on the island, life was to varying degrees oppressive and lacking opportunity, which sent them to seek solace in drink as well. On top of that, life was deadly.

Throughout the first few colonial centuries, "There had been similar emigration from Europe to the Caribbean and to North America—about half a million; but in 1776 there were only 50,000 whites in the British Caribbean compared to two million in the Thirteen Colonies," Parker writes in *The Sugar Barons*. In Jamaica, which Parker classified as the deadliest place for white Europeans in the world at the time except West Africa, nearly a quarter of Kingston's population died every single year, a death rate equivalent to London's at the height of the Great Plague. The city's infant mortality rate was similarly horrendous, ranging on either side of 50 percent during that time. As grim as those statistics were, they nonetheless represented a triumph of sorts: after all, to die in the Caribbean meant that at least the person had managed to survive the voyage over, an exceptionally deadly endeavor in its own right.

Living up to the reputation of their trade, the hucksters of the day sought to turn these negatives into a selling point, advertising that though a Caribbean migrant might not live as long as his brethren who stayed home, he was surely to have lived much more, indulging as he could in the fast and loose life of the West Indies. It was a pitch that apparently fell short. Such was the reputation of the Caribbean and demands for labor therein that some Europeans—prisoners of war, the poor, the drunk—feared being kidnapped and sent there against their will, something that came to be known as being "Barbadosed."

Against all these stresses, alcohol served as a palliative and rum quickly entered the Caribbean pharmacopeia. Not only was the drink used to purify often-tainted water, but in the four-humorist system of the time, islanders believed rum could counterbalance coldness by heating up the body and temper excessive body heat because it was itself fiery. So crucial was alcohol believed to be to good health, British soldiers viewed sobriety as insalubrious—a gangplank, of sorts, to illness—and endeavored to be intoxicated as consistently as possible. To help them remain so, the Royal Navy, in keeping with practice of other navies of the day, mandated in 1731 that each sailor be entitled to a gallon of beer or a half-pint of rum or other spirits a day. It was a custom that, owing to the increasing power of the West Indies lobby in Parliament, was eventually narrowed to just rum and one which held for over two hundred years, until it was abolished on Black Tot Day, July 31, 1970, when the last dram was taken and the remaining shipboard barrels and glassware were tossed into the ocean. (If you're looking to relive high-seas revelry, you can buy a bottle of Black Tot, a rum filled from what were the remaining landside stocks, at a stunning $1,000 a bottle; you'll have to take care of the malaria and the five-masted ship yourself, though.)

As rum drinking became more routine in Caribbean culture, and as those who caught a taste for it while transiting the region spread that taste elsewhere, rum became an increasingly popular tipple far from the tropics. By the beginning of the eighteenth century, North American colonists were buying hundreds of thousands of gallons of rum a year from Barbados. At the time, their population was less than a half million, but even then, that supply apparently wasn't enough to slake their thirst, for they were also buying massive quantities of molasses—some four million gallons at the very least fifty years later, and likely significantly more, by which point the colonies' population had more than quadrupled. A few wholesome bakers might have been turning a bit of that into brown bread, but the vast majority was headed for the rum distilleries that dotted the Eastern Seaboard, where some cities had dozens. From them issued hundreds of thousands, sometimes upward of one million additional gallons of rum annually, though not all of it was consumed by the colonists.

Similarly, rum made an incursion into the drinking cultures of the European nations from whence the colonists came, albeit with uneven results. As they had done with sugar, the British slurped down this latest colonial export with particular verve. Though they got off to a temperate start, importing just 2,000 gallons of rum a year into England and Wales at the start of the eighteenth century, their thirst increased quickly after that. So much so, in fact, that within three-quarters of a century, they were importing nearly three times that much per day. For sugar barons on the islands of the Caribbean's two other main colonial powers, Spain and France, the rum boom proved less lucrative, however. For them, the spirit kill-devil ran into opposition back home. The reason had nothing to do with lousy reviews carried home by drinkers or abhorrence of tales of besotted colonists. Instead it was a product of a far more endemic force, special interest politics. Unlike Britain, Spain and France had a long and entrenched history of booze production and, as a result, a long, entrenched, and powerful lobbying force to protect it. And those traditional alcohol producers weren't going to let arriviste rum steal drinkers' gullets away from wine and brandy.

In France, as those producers castigated rum as an unhealthy drink, the government banned its import into the mainland. Spain, meanwhile, banned production outright in her colonies—a move aimed at not only protecting the market at home but also as a way to preserve buyers for mainland booze among her colonists abroad. (The British West Indies lobby, perhaps taking a cue from this spirits selectivism, successfully convinced their government in 1808 to in turn ban the production of liquor from corn, squashing a local source of alcohol in favor of a foreign one.)

Because of the perishability of sugarcane and the desire of its European consumers to receive the product in such a radically different form than how it emerged from the ground thousands of miles away in the Caribbean, sugar estates were usually tied to sugar mills in a single operation. The scale was dictated by operating efficiency and indivisible below a certain point; typically, they were much larger than the smallholdings of yeoman settlers elsewhere, including on the islands before the arrival of sugar. Beyond just growing it, sugar estate workers also processed the sugarcane—pressing the freshly cut cane, boiling and crystalizing the resultant juice, and distilling the molasses into rum.

The organization that such a complex system of labor (some of which was skilled), equipment, provisions, and capital required resembled that of a proto-factory, albeit one out on the farm rather than in the city. In this way, some scholars have argued, sugarcane cultivation in the West Indies presaged the Industrial Revolution, and the Caribbean landscape came to be dominated, two centuries before England's, by the "dark satanic mills" that were that era's hallmark, as Parker writes in *The Sugar Barons*.

The quote Parker is using is William Blake's, but the point is elementary. What made those mills churn, producing the sugar and rum that issued from them, the wealth that paid for the planters' extravagant feasts, and the capital that funded the modern era, is a story taught to every grade-school student, often in front of a map centered on the Atlantic Ocean and overlaid with three swooping arrows: the famous triangular trade, which abetted one of humanity's most heinous and prolonged crimes. Rum, particularly high-proof rum distilled in New England from Caribbean molasses, played an essential role in the slave trade. Inextricable from the story of European colonization of the Caribbean and the sugar revolution, and therefore inextricable from the story of rum, is the story of slavery.

"In this instance, millions of human beings were treated as commodities. To obtain them, products were shipped to Africa; by their labor power, wealth was created in the Americas. The wealth they created mostly returned to Britain; the products they made were consumed in Britain; and the products made by Britons—cloth, tools, torture instruments— were consumed by slaves who were themselves consumed in the creation of wealth," Mintz writes in *Sweetness and Power*.

The succinctness of Mintz's last point shrouds a particularly jarring point: slaves were seen as depreciable assets, expensive to purchase but destined to be worn out, like the copper in a still, bit by bit sacrificing itself for a product to be enjoyed by others. In this chattel view, slaves who ran away or killed themselves could be construed as having stolen themselves from their master.

Altogether, for the more than three-century-long era of Western Hemisphere plantation slavery, some eleven million slaves were brought to the New World, with more than half of them destined for the sugar fields of the Caribbean, South and Central America, and the area that would become the southern US. Their arrival, coupled with—or perhaps driven by—the spread of sugar monoculture, transformed the demographics of islands like Barbados, which lost tens of thousands of its early European settlers in the thirty years after 1630, while the slave population increased more than sixfold. In many colonies the slave population far outnumbered the free, a situation that caused further anxiety and isolation for the planter class and their paid employees, and which they used to justify particularly cruel punishments for even minor offenses out of fear that laxity would encourage insurrection. Even though they were frequently underfed, occasionally starved, and on some plantations expected to simply steal the food they needed to survive from neighboring plantations, a slave caught eating cane could still be whipped. Jamaican records document slaves being urinated or defecated on by another slave as punishment for an infraction or mutilated for attempting to escape; if they were thought to be plotting against their master, they could be tortured to death. If they survived to old age and became too elderly to work, they could be "cynically" manumitted, freed and left to beg out their final days "in the very last stage of human misery, naked, famished, diseased and forlorn," wrote the contemporary abolitionist William Dickson. All of that was in addition to the ever-present threat of dismemberment or death that accompanied the dangerous work on the plantation.

Sugar didn't originate slavery, but slavery seems to have been with sugar since the beginning—the Arabs, who brought cane into the Mediterranean, also developed the African slave trade, and the two systems fit exquisitely.

As Parker explains: "The institution of slavery requires the suppression of spirit, intelligence, and initiative on the part of its victim. Sugar, with its mind-numbing, simple but repetitive and physically exhausting tasks, demanded exactly the same thing." Caribbean and New World sugar production, with its own tremendous scale, was, moreover, slavery's breakout application, giving the institution a scale, intensity, and utter cruelty never before seen—and one that almost from the beginning launched calls for its abolition. It would be generations before those calls would be successful; in the meantime, slavery was perpetuated and justified in ways that, centuries later, of course don't justify it. Some argued that African slavery was a way to protect the native people, who had already been worked nearly to extinction. Some said that slaves were better off under the civilizing society of European culture and its Christian tradition. Others simply argued that sugar would be too expensive without it.

The real reason, of course, was one captured by English slave trader William Wood, who wrote in 1718 that the "labour of negroes is the principal foundation of our riches from the plantations. The African trade . . . is the spring and parent whence the others flow."

As slavery proliferated across the sugar colonies, rum, as it had for the early white settlers, came to play an increasingly intricate role in the lives of enslaved Africans. Far more than merely producing the raw material for it, on many plantations slaves were distillers themselves—a role for which female slaves were considered particularly well suited, because planters thought they'd be less likely to drink on the job. When new slaves arrived on a planation from their voyage across the Atlantic, the Middle Passage that routinely claimed the lives of more than 10 percent of them, rum was used to "season" them to the Caribbean and their oppressive new situation. When slaves performed a particular task well or completed a particularly difficult task, some plantation owners would use rum as a reward, as they also did when the slaves had finished bringing in the harvest—a time known as crop over, which lends its name to a festival on Barbados still. Rum was also used by some plantation overseers in exchange for sex from their female slaves.

Altogether, the trans-Atlantic trade, fueled by sugar, molasses, and alcohol from the colonies, basic goods for the plantations and extravagances for the planters, and slaves from Africa, transformed economies on both sides of the ocean. In the Caribbean, islands were transmuted from uninhabited masses of coral, like Barbados, and wild ancient volcanos stretching from the seafloor, like Jamaica, to veritable pearls on the necklace of Europe in just a few short decades. By 1650, just twenty-five years after the British first settled Barbados, it was already the richest place in the English colonial world, and Bridgetown had quickly swelled to become the second-largest port in all of the Americas, after Boston. It was a pattern that repeated throughout the sugar islands.

"The gentry here doth live far better than ours do in England," a man named Henry Whistler concluded when he visited in the middle of the seventeenth century. One hundred years later, in Jamaica, which Whistler would go on to help conquer, per-capita income approached £1,000, or nearly twenty-five times that back home in England.

It was enviable hazard pay, perhaps, but those back home in Europe had little need to feel left out—wealth from all that conspicuous consumption accreted on the other side of the Atlantic as well, as much as tripling economic activity there by one estimate.

"The plantation-based trading area," writes economic historian Richard B. Sheridan, "became a remarkable engine of economic growth, as it drew into its orbit the resources of four continents and scattered islands in the Atlantic basin."

It was, of course, a boom like all booms: one that could not last. Had I peered out from the mount of Mount Gay two and a half centuries earlier, at the island's late-eighteenth-century zenith, I could have peered across some five hundred sugar estates, most with their own little windmills spinning and their own stills boiling. It was a scene I could have seen repeated across many of the Caribbean islands and in the sugar-growing regions of South, Central, and North America as well. On each of those, rum, as it did in Barbados, accompanied sugar production, but owing to the veering contours of history, the meandering flows of trade, the vagaries of taste and custom and happenstance, the rum on each would have been different. In some places that difference would be by just degrees, on others the comparison could make you swear you're drinking a different spirit entirely.

But I saw little of that. Because of an archipelago of factors, including the inevitable exhaustion of the soil that comes from intensive sugarcane monoculture, emancipation of slaves, and changes in world supply and demand, by the time I arrived the sugar islands produced just a tiny fraction of the amount of sugar they did in their heyday, and many had ceased production altogether. Like the Caribbean sugar industry, the Caribbean rum industry, on the sole basis of number of producers, had diminished as well.

After we'd finished surveying the cane fields, Raphael Grisoni, Darrio Prescod, and I hopped into Grisoni's Subaru to head back to the distillery so I could begin learning how rum was made and how its production has changed and is changing—a story that I still had to chase through several more countries in the Caribbean to truly understand. From there Prescod gave me a ride back to the bus station in Speightstown. As the bus headed down Highway 1, along Barbados's west coast toward Bridgetown, the day's clouds broke into torrents. The trees swayed in the wind, blister water cascading off some of them. The tourists probably took refuge at the bar. In the half millennia since European settlement of the Western Hemisphere, the image of the Caribbean has changed radically. Rum, however, is still an integral part of it and there are still many phenomenal producers to visit in the region.

RUM PUNCH

I don't know how long something has to be around before it gets embodied in rhyme, but punch has been around for a long time—coming not only before there were "mixologists" bringing back the classic cocktails of yore, but before there were even classic cocktails of yore. Many punches today are terrible, the juice too sweet and the alcohol too cheap. But a great punch can be flavorful, complex, and go down a little too easy. Infinitely scalable and quickly replicable, it's also the way to do booze for parties. You can thank the Bajans for one more quality that makes punch well-suited to imbibing: they also made the recipe easy to remember. All you need is their little rhyme: "One of sour, two of sweet, three of strong, four of weak." To wit:

1 part citrus (fresh lime juice, typically)

2 parts sweetener (simple syrup works well)

3 parts rum (don't skimp; go with something flavorful such as a Bajan or Jamaican rum)

4 parts water or other "weak," such as juice or tea

Mix ingredients in a bowl with ice. Add spices such as nutmeg, anise, cinnamon, or cardamom as desired.

CHAPTER 2

Rivers of Molasses and Rum

"One can learn much about British Guiana from the air," wrote the Trinidad-born author V. S. Naipaul in *The Middle Passage*, his travelogue of a journey through the Caribbean at the beginning of the 1960s, just a few years before the country dropped British rule and its British appellation, becoming what is today just Guyana. When Naipaul wrote that, I don't think he could have imagined how literally I would experience his observation.

I'd departed for Guyana aboard a Boeing 767-300, arranged in the typical two-three-two seating setup, that looked to be about twenty years old and was operated by an airline called Fly Jamaica, which I learned was itself only five years old. At the head of each row was a flat-screen television. The two smaller ones on the side, in front of the narrower rows, were "deactivated," according to the labels affixed to them, but the one larger television in the middle worked, as I learned about an hour into our flight, when it flipped on after the flight attendants had come by to pass out those little headphone adapters that were required for the two-prong armrest ports popular on planes of a certain vintage. At first I hardly took notice, caught up instead in the decision of whether to order gin—my typical in-flight tipple—or rum, which seemed the requisite, given the purview of my research. It proved a moot conundrum. They had no gin. Apparently, I'd crossed beyond the Bombay Sapphire meridian.

As I settled in, I was curious to see what, exactly, a nascent shoestring airline would choose as collective in-flight entertainment for a load of travelers from one touristless Caribbean capital to another. Perhaps a local rom-com, hot and sweaty with, I imagined, rum. I could hope.

What flashed up instead was a photo of a pond. Then, four seconds later, another photo of another pond; then, four seconds later, another photo of another pond; then, four seconds later, a college campus; then, four seconds later, a primary school tucked amid the jungle; then, four seconds later, an aerial shot of some neighborhood; then, four seconds later, some people milling about, dressed for a festival; then . . . I fished out my notebook, ordered another rum, and settled in, realizing I must have booked myself a ninth-row seat to the fever dream of some functionary in the Guyanese tourism agency. For the next two hours it continued: an aerial shot of some streets, which seemed merely to confirm that the Guyanese capital of Georgetown had streets; an expanse of sugarcane under cultivation; a refueling station on the Pomeroon

River; something called the "South Dakota Circuit," which looked like a freeway interchange but was later clarified to be a track used for go-carting; a fish pond; some kids paddling to school on the Mazaruni River; the Eping Falls; the Maipuri Falls; the Kumarau Falls; a second view of Kumarau Falls; a third view of Kumarau Falls; a rodeo; a cattle herd; a squinty-eyed frog; a harvestman; a wolf spider; an emerald boa; a tarantula; a skeleton-leg tarantula; a giant bird-eating tarantula; a "pray mantis"; the Mazaruni Prison; the Shanklands resort; an airfield cut in the middle of the jungle; a giant red scar from a strip mine cut in the middle of the jungle; a giant centipede; a legless lizard; the variety of moth known as a "white peacock"; a caiman crossing a dirt road, captioned, "Stop! Caiman Crossing!"; a turkey vulture picking up carrion, captioned, "Cargo pickup." It continued, never repeating, as far as I could tell, until the last few minutes—a relentless and quotidian traveler's slide show of the worst order and pre-excursion. It almost seemed to make redundant the "Welcome to Guyana" plantscape that greeted me when I stepped off the airplane and walked across the tarmac to the airport, a low-ceilinged affair of white wood paneling that reminded me of one of the livestock sales barns I would occasionally visit with my father as a child. As I cleared customs, I wondered whether the slideshow was intended as a message to go home, something akin to: "You've seen everything. Now you can return back to whatever paradise you mistakenly left."

During Naipaul's own visit, when he landed he found a poor, raw country located on the northeastern coast of South America that was vast, thick, untamed, and malarial. It's a place that, because of its similarly tortured colonial legacy of plantations and sugarcane slavery, many people consider part of the Caribbean. But the comparison would seem to end at the coast—once past the cane fields there, it was a place almost bare of people, save for a few Amerindians, a few ranchers, a few miners of gold and diamonds, and a few traders from across the border in Brazil, all of whom functioned far removed from the state.

"When one thinks of Guiana one thinks of a country whose inadequate resources are strained in every way, a country whose geography imposes on it an administration and a programme of public works out of all proportion to its revenue and population. One thinks of the sea-wall, for ever being breached and repaired; the dikes made of mud for want of money; the dirt roads and their occasional experimental surfacing; the roads that are necessary but not yet made," Naipual wrote at the time. It would seem little has changed since then.

Guyana's legacy is that of contention. Originally formed in the seventeenth century as the colonies Demerara, Berbice, and Essequibo of the Dutch, a colonizer whose record of administering slavery Naipaul writes "is even blacker than the French," Guyana was a treasure item to be volleyed around in the contests of Europe two hundred years later, before being purchased by the British at the beginning of the nineteenth century. When slavery ended in the British colonies in 1834, the system was replaced by indentureship, its analog in virtually every way, except the workers were from India rather than Africa and consigned to work for only a set period of time, conditions the planters exploited by pitting the two groups against each other and by trying to squeeze as much labor out of workers in whom they had only a short-term interest. Today Guyana is perhaps most famous in the North American mind for its association with Jonestown, the jungle outpost of cultist Jim Jones's Peoples Temple that ended with the death of more than nine hundred people by ingestion of cyanide and gunshot wounds, an event that coined the phrase "to drink the Kool-Aid."

Before my arrival, I had already heard a lot about Guyana, most of it in the form of caution. The capital, Georgetown, once a beautiful colonial town—"the most beautiful city in the West Indies," Naipaul wrote— had slid into disrepair and crime, I was told. So far in my tour of the rum archipelago, I had been bouncing around guest houses and apartments rented on Airbnb, trying to avoid, as much as possible, the slushy cocktails and aggressive leisure of the Caribbean tourist districts, which wear fast for me. In other places with a reputation for being unsafe, the risk was generally considered marginal; the refrain, cheery: just don't wander down the street with a wad of Benjamins spilling from your pocket and you'll find yourself in a vibrant culture. It was an easy edict to follow. I didn't have any wads of Benjamins. The warnings that came for Georgetown, however, came with the sternness of a parent delivering those few pieces of life advice they actually expect you to follow (for my father, this was: "Son, wear a condom."). So I booked myself into the Pegasus hotel, the second-most revered property in Georgetown, after the slightly pricier Marriott, which sits on an adjacent plot of land. With TripAdvisor reviewers consistently balancing their complaints with praise for the place's vigilant security, the Pegasus is something of a bunker for visitors who have $150 a night to spend in a place where the per capita GDP is just over $4,000.

Cheddi Jagan International Airport, named after the politician and future president of independent Guyana who Naipaul deemed modest and hardworking during his own visit, sits on a site that was originally known as Atkinson Field, an air base built by the United States during the Second World War. As the Department of Defense's primary mission was protecting the region's bauxite mines and Venezuelan oil-tanker traffic, rather than providing civil aviation convenient access to the capital, the airport is nearly an hour's drive from Georgetown.

All I could see from the car's window as I passed along it was a Guyana thrumming in the hot, Saturday night; the nightlife, groups of young Guyanese walking to and from outside bars that were practically pushing themselves onto the roadway. The effect was to create the sense of a country confidently on the make, of lively suburbs spiraling out from the capital. Unfortunately, it was a facade. When Naipaul was traveling through

Guyana, it was just readying to leave colonial rule; when I arrived it was just finishing its Golden Jubilee—its celebration of 50 years of independence.

In the intervening time, other than the Peoples Temple, the country has largely stayed out of the international news. Search the databases and most articles that come back, four decades later, are about that event or about the release of World Health Organization statistics showing Guyana leading the world in suicides, at nearly four times the world average. (The situation has improved somewhat in the most recent set of statistics, with Guyana dropping to second place for aggregate suicides among both genders.)

As it was, had I been able to zoom out on my way from the airport into town, as if I were peering down from Google Maps' satellite view, I would have seen that the buzzing energy along the highway was in truth just a few streets deep. Beyond it were the remnants of the sugarcane estates that had made this place something to fight over two hundred years ago, when there were nearly four hundred of them.

As sugar's dominance of the Caribbean waned, the estates steadily closed. In 1976 there were six remaining, all nationalized under a government entity called the Guyana Sugar Corporation, commonly referred to as GuySuCo. After settling into my hotel, I got in a cab and headed out to one of the remaining estates to see the transformation of sugarcane into granulated sugar and rum's precursor, molasses.

The Uitvlugt Sugar Estate, named after the original Dutch owner of the planation where it sits and pronounced something akin to "iFlood," as if Apple had written the Book of Genesis, is located on the west bank of the Demerara River, the Amazon silt–filled waters of which I could see plunging into the Atlantic from my hotel room, turning the ocean water mocha-brown for nearly a mile from the coast. To get there we had to cross the Demerara Harbour Bridge, a 1¼-mile-long expanse of floating metal plates, then wind our way through the little villages that run along the ocean to the factory.

Sugarcane at the Appleton Estate in Jamaica. A reedy grass, reminiscent of bamboo, sugarcane is harvested about five times before it is replanted.

Sugar starts as a grass, though a particularly tall, reedy one that resembles bamboo. Depending on the conditions of where it is grown and a place's harvest cycles, it can take up to eighteen months to mature, and each planting can be harvested about five times before it becomes more efficient to replant, which is done by cutting a stalk into sections demarcated by the periodic thick growth bands, from which new roots will sprout when planted.

In Guyana, the sugarcane fields are located on the flat alluvial plains that run toward the coast and are crisscrossed with canals, originally built by the Dutch.

Having grown up on a corn and soybean farm in the American Midwest, I still had a lingering assumption of agriculture primarily being the growing and the plucking out of the ground of something that looks, generally, like how it will ultimately be used. (In the time before ethanol and high fructose corn syrup entered the public lexicon, I thought of corn as destined primarily for cattle feed, which of course didn't seem too far away from steaks.) Sugarcane, however, has no ears full of bleach-white sugar grains.

The process of transforming sugarcane to sugar crystals begins with the harvest. In many sugarcane-growing regions, the cane fields, prior to harvest, would traditionally be burned to remove the razor-sharp leaves that grow the length of the sugarcane stalk and to help clear the fields of rodents and snakes. Though the practice is waning, it is still prevalent, including in Guyana. Once the sugarcane is cut, by hand or by machine, a virtual timer begins. Sugarcane deteriorates quickly and therefore must be processed within several hours, or else it will spoil. The result is that the cane fields need to be near a sugar factory, and the fields and the factory usually work as one economic unit—sugarcane processing, in essence, being just another step in sugarcane growing.

At Uitvlugt the sugar processing happens in several worn buildings built out of corrugated sheet metal, the main one of which is a sprawling structure several stories tall run through with conveyors and topped by thick smokestacks—the markers of sugarcane processing's essential goals of crushing the stalks to extract their juice and removing all the water until the sucrose in it has crystalized into something resembling the sugar we're used to buying at the store. In short, it's a process that's accomplished through the application of a lot of heavy machinery and steam.

Once I was issued a hard hat, I was introduced to Puran Dhanraj, a young Guyanese man who had worked at Uitvlugt for about two years, starting out by rotating through each of the production stations before taking a job in management. I never asked Dhanraj how many tours he'd given, but when we stepped into the factory, I suspected the number was slight. After spending weeks visiting rum distilleries, with their defined tourist protocol and noticeable deference to the specter of a personal-

The molasses used to make rum is the product of a long process of sugarcane processing that also results in crystallized sugar. At the Uitvlugt Estate in Guyana, cut cane arrives on barges to a sugar factory.

After being chopped, sugarcane is pressed to extract a sucrose-rich juice. The Uitvlugt Estate, Guyana.

injury lawsuit, walking with Dhanraj through Uitvlugt was a shock. The catwalks that weave through the facility passed next to, over, and around massive rollers, choppers, and boilers and were often slippery with condensation. To make matters worse, the whole place was booming—so much so that Dhanraj often had to tug lightly at my shirt if I was walking ahead of him and headed in the wrong direction. Except for the moments when we stepped into an office or a control room, our conversation was limited to staccato shouts.

Fresh-cut cane arrives six tons at a time from the fields that supply Uitvlugt, piled on long, low metal barges that float down through the canals to the factory, where they are then hoisted up one by one out of the water in a contraption that looks like a giant cradle. From there the cane is washed and chopped into smaller pieces, a process that also begins to break the cell walls and release the sugarcane juice. Once the cane is down to the

Once extracted and filtered, sugarcane juice is boiled down to concentrate the sucrose. The Uitvlugt Estate, Guyana.

consistency of garden mulch, it's passed through four giant, grooved rollers to extract the juice, which runs out as a translucent liquid that's slightly green from the stalks' chlorophyll. The juice is then heated to kill any bacteria and quickly cooled in a process they call "flash down," to settle sediments out of it. Flocculants often are added to help in this process. This settled "mud" is then washed to flush out any sugarcane juice that remains before being discarded.

Sugar concentration is measured in a unit known as "brix," which equates to one gram of sugar, in the form of sucrose, the primary form it is in in sugarcane, per one hundred grams of liquid. After pressing, the resulting sugarcane juice at Uitvlugt is about twelve brix.

As Dhanraj and I walked through the factory, an odiferous amalgam of dirt and earth, fuel, hot vegetal sugar, and molasses was pervasive, though the dominant scent would vary depending on whatever process was going on nearby. Almost constantly in sight were the giant steam boilers that powered the facility, which were themselves fired with cane trash left over from the extraction of the juice, a substance known as "bagasse." The factory was, in essence, feeding itself.

Whenever we passed a worker, Dhanraj would stop him—they were mostly men—and have him explain what he was responsible for, from how the boiler worked to the crystallization vats, which they seemed eager to do. Frequently they even shut down bits of their stations to give me a better sense of how the whole process worked.

Once the sugarcane juice is ready, it's heated to boil off the water, a process which steadily increases the concentration of sugar in the liquid until there is more sucrose than water remaining to dissolve it all, a state

As the sugarcane juice is further concentrated through boiling, sugar crystals begin to form within a liquid that will become molasses. The Uitvlugt Estate, Guyana.

your chemistry teacher would have told you is known as "supersaturation." If your chemistry education was anything like mine, you learned what happens next sometime in high school. At this part in the lesson, you probably had your own supersaturated liquid, or you were supposed to, but it didn't look any different from an unsaturated solution. Depending on what you thought of your teacher, you were either worried that your lab group had messed up—yet again, if you were in my lab group—or your teacher didn't know what he was talking about and you were getting a bum education. Then your teacher passed around a bit of whatever it was that supposedly had been supersaturated in your liquid and told you to sprinkle a little bit into your solution. Once you did—voilà!—crystals or precipitate started forming. Sugar factories use a similar process. As the sugarcane juice is boiled down to about seventy-five brix, when the sugar will start to crystalize, a tiny bit of seed sugar, as it is known, is added to promote proper crystallization.

They then continue to boil the sugar solution, at Uitvlugt for a few hours more, to grow the crystals. To see how it was progressing that day, Dhanraj and I stopped by one of the large boiling columns, which had a narrow slat of a viewing window in it. Behind it we could see a viscous liquid. Then Dhanraj grabbed onto something that looked like an antique brass faucet handle and tugged, drawing out a long metal pole that resembled a barrel thief and contained a notch running its length. It was cradling some of the sugar solution, which Dhanraj smeared across a glass microscope slide and held up to the light. He then did the same thing at another column farther along in the process. Between the two stages, the sugar crystals nearly tripled in size, from being barely visible to the naked eye to being quite distinctive. By this point the solution had also caramelized to a rich, brown color—the color, in fact, of molasses. But we weren't ready to make rum yet.

No matter how long the sugar makers let their liquid boil, they'll never get pure sugar. Instead it'll remain locked in that brown, viscous sludge.

To extract the crystals, the factory workers transfer the mixture to centrifuges. When one of these centrifuges finished at Uitvlugt, the operator opened up the top, scooped out a handful of sugar, and put some in my palm. The crystals were warm and a light golden brown. Some of them would be sold in this form, but normally the sugar is sent on to be purified and whitened further at facilities called sugar refineries, which are frequently located in major consuming countries, far away from where the sugar was actually grown. For something as quotidian as sugar, I was surprised at the amazement I felt over what I held. In my hands were a few ounces of the well over ten thousand kilograms of sugar the facility can produce an hour. Just a few hours earlier it had been a stalk of sugarcane in one Uitvlugt's several thousand acres of fields.

The sugar from the first batch removed from the sugarcane juice is called the A-strike. Because not all of the sugar comes out the first time, the remaining molasses, called the A-molasses, is then sent back through the crystallization and centrifuge process twice more, creating two more "strikes" of sugar, the B- and C-strikes, and two more eponymous grades of molasses. After that point, it becomes too expensive for a sugar factory to try to crystalize and pull out any additional sugar. Because of this, the "final," or "blackstrap," or occasionally "third boil" molasses is sometimes denigrated as "industrial waste," but it is far from spent. Depending on the efficiency of the factory, it can contain 50 percent sugar, or slightly more, and is still quite sweet, as I found out when Dhanraj pointed out a veritable Demerara River in miniature of the stuff flowing through a channel behind me. Invariably, in the Caribbean, whenever there was molasses or sugarcane juice around, I was invited to take a taste. Invariably, whether I'd washed my hands recently or not, I'd dip a finger in. The molasses at Uitvlugt was warm, like the freshly crystalized sugarcane, and when I licked it off my finger it was rich and smoky and bitter. (Earlier in Barbados, when I'd had a chance to try a bit of local molasses that had just arrived at the

Once the sugar crystals are sufficiently formed within the molasses, they are extracted with a centrifuge, producing crystalized sugar of a slightly off-white color; white table sugar undergoes further refinement at sugar refineries. The Uitvlugt Estate, Guyana.

Mount Gay distillery, Raphael Grisoni, the managing director, pointed out the distinct licorice flavor, which I hadn't noticed. But it didn't surprise me when I later learned that blackstrap molasses is frequently used in licorice candy.) The flavor came from the fact that molasses contains a range of other components besides sucrose, including minerals and B vitamins.

Technically a distiller can make rum from any of the products created during the sugar-making process—from the sugarcane juice to a concentrated sugarcane syrup, from molasses from the first or second boil, or even from the crystallized sugar itself. Traditionally, however, rum in most parts of the world has been made from that final molasses as a way to increase the value of what was otherwise a bulky and little-desired product. (As the sugar industry has modernized, it's worth noting the nature

A tanker full of molasses slowly unloads at the Mount Gay rum distillery in Barbados. Once a sugar factory has extracted as much crystalized sugar as economically feasible, the leftover material, often known as blackstrap or final molasses, is sold to rum producers for distillation.

of the final molasses has changed, however, with sugar producers being able to extract more sugar from cane than they could at the founding of the Caribbean sugar islands five hundred years ago. In the beginning, production records also suggest distillers would produce rum from a mixture of byproducts from various stages of the sugar-making process that they, for one reason or another, had no better use for, and that the base material would change throughout the season.)

Historically, that was how it was done at Uitvlugt as well. However, no matter how many steamy, slick catwalks I passed through in buildings so hot they made Guyana's outside tropical midday temperature feel cool, I was never going to find a rum still in action.

Today, the molasses from Uitvlugt and the other sugar estates in Guyana goes instead to a facility at what was once the Diamond Sugar Estate located back on the east bank of the Demerara River, a few miles from Georgetown. It is run by a company called Demerara Distillers Limited, frequently referred to as DDL, and it's a hard place to explain. It's perhaps most visibly known as the distillery that makes the El Dorado range of rums. To many rum aficionados it is also some of the holiest ground in the cane spirits world. But even before the company opened its Rum Heritage Centre in 2007, it was also something of a museum, albeit one of the living history variety.

When Guyana's sugar production was at its peak, the hundreds of sugar plantations located along its three rivers meant that the country, consequently, also had hundreds of rum producers. In the main, each had its own still and its own slightly different style, but collectively they became known worldwide under the moniker of Demerara rums, a style that became famous for being deep, smoky, and exceptionally flavorful. Throughout the eighteenth and nineteenth centuries Demerara rum producers vied with those in Jamaica for the title of the biggest exporter of rum within the British West Indies and often fell just behind Martinique as the biggest in the world. At some point, their rum came to dominate the blend that the Royal Navy would eventually issue to tens of thousands of sailors every day.

Nonetheless, rum in Guyana, as elsewhere, was still an adjunct to the sugar industry, and as Guyana's sugar estates consolidated or shut down, the number of distilleries dwindled as well.

Broadly speaking, the stills distilleries use to make any type of liquor can be split into two types: pot stills and column stills. When you think of distilling, especially if you think of craft distilleries or scotch whisky makers, you are probably thinking of a pot still. They are the original still, reminiscent of those used by alchemists thousands of years ago, with a bulbous base—the "pot"—that sprouts a tapering tube that's tall and bends until it's horizontal, a path that might have a bit of swoop in it—often called a gooseneck. Some pot stills can be quite small, capable of producing just a few gallons of liquor per run, and you could set one on your stove to whip up some homemade hooch if you wanted (and whisk it away to a convenient hiding place when the federal agents come, because bootlegging is still illegal in America and most other countries). Others are comparatively massive, with outputs more in the range of a few hundred gallons, but they'd probably still fit in your garage, provided you cut a hole in the roof.

A column still, which you'll definitely have to cut a hole in your roof to install, looks like, well, a column—a vertical tube of metal. In their more diminutive iterations, they look a lot like a several-foot-long section of culvert tubing stood on end, while at their largest and most advanced they can take on the form of a large facility that resembles an oil refinery. In the latter version, one column can contain several parts one would call a column; some people refer to this as a "multicolumn still." (Confusingly, though, column stills that people don't consider "multicolumn" can also contain multiple parts that look like a column; the difference will become clearer as we talk about more of these things.) Credit for the first widely used column still for booze making goes to an Irishman named Aeneas Coffey, who invented his version in the thoroughly modern year—at least for our topic at hand—of 1830. By 1880 the Coffey still, as the design is still known today, was in use in the Caribbean.

Across these broad categories there are a number of still variations, some subtle, others more dramatic; some distillers, especially new craft distillers, even use what's called a "hybrid" still, which is basically a small column still stuck on top of, or linked with piping to, a pot still, generally with valves that allow a distiller to adjust between running the still more like a pot or more like a column.

Though a distillery may have several of one kind of still, most have no more than one, maybe two, kinds of stills. Demerara Distillers has a remarkable nine, including some of the rarest stills in the world.

The Diamond Distillery, located back on East Bank Public Road, which runs from the airport to Georgetown, is one of the larger distilleries in the Caribbean, capable of producing tens of millions of liters of alcohol a year, or considerably more than all of the distilleries on Barbados combined. Unlike most other rum distilleries, Demerara Distillers is also a highly diversified company, producing, in addition to rum, an array of food products such as jams and jellies, vinegar, and soda carbonated with waste CO_2 produced by the plant. When I arrived, I found myself at a gate and guardhouse rather than a gussied-up visitor center for cruise ship tourists (though the distillery does welcome tourists). There I was met by Darryl Manichand, the distillery production manager, who may very well be the most energetic and thorough tour guide in the Caribbean.

As Manichand led me around, he showed me where the distillery grows its starter yeast, feeding it molasses and aerating it in a bubbly, frothy process that looks as though someone is blowing a straw into a large vat of chocolate milk, a process called propagation. We then climbed up to some access platforms for a sweeping view over the Demerara River Valley and the cane fields below, source of the 220 tons of molasses the distillery uses every day. It arrives in a steady stream of trucks, thirteen tons at a time, and Manichand said the plant consumes 100,000 liters of wash every four hours, operating around the clock for 330 days a year.

Since distilleries all operate on the same principles, it's rare to see in them anything truly unexpected, at least as it relates to distillation; liquor production at its essence is an industrial process. It's a little like visiting apparel factories—one may be making Madison Avenue luxury, the other off-the-rack basics, but it's all bolts of fabric and sewing machines. In booze making, most of what distinguishes one product from another, more or less, is what happens in the distiller's head. (I'm distilling the point considerably myself here, but it's what a liquor maker does with the tools that matters primarily, rather than the tools themselves, though the tools matter.)

What I saw in front of me when Manichand and I walked into the Diamond Distillery still house, however, was something I am unlikely to see anywhere else again.

"Is that the wooden pot still?" I asked Manichand a little incredulously.

One of the reasons I'd come to Guyana was to see the thing now in front of me. It looked like two giant, covered vats made of reddish-brown wood staves, banded together. Each had a stubby, wide gooseneck sticking out that was a dark slate gray streaked through with the turquoise of copper patina, and one of the goosenecks connected one of the vats to the other. While I was there, liquid was cascading off the still, almost as if it had produced so much rum that it was overflowing. When I asked what was

While most stills are now made out of metal, over a century ago, many were made of wood. A few of the last surviving wooden stills that are still being used for spirits production are at Demerara Distillers Limited in Guyana. They include this wooden Coffey still.

going on, Manichand explained that the water was there to keep the wood moist, so that it wouldn't dry out, shrink, and leak steam.

Demerara Distilleries is famous not just for the fact that it has so many different types of stills, but that three of those are made from something almost unheard of: wood—a technology most producers abandoned over a century ago in favor of metal.

The double wooden pot still I was looking at is known as the PM still because it originally came from the Port Mourant sugar estate, which is now run by GuySuCo and is located near the Berbice River (it was also

Cheddi Jagan's birthplace). It was made from greenheart, an Amazonian hardwood frequently used in shipbuilding because it is one of the most dense in the world and is resistant to marine borers. (When I researched it later, I learned it also has the bizarre quality of occasionally "exploding" when milled because the cut pieces have a tendency to come apart with so much force.) The still is ostensibly more than 250 years old. However, even greenheart wears eventually, and occasionally individual staves have to be replaced, something that brings to mind the classic philosophical paradox of identity and Plutarch's Ship of Theseus, in which Plutarch writes about the ship Theseus returned to Athens in after his exploits. Once back, the Athenians, so taken with the relic's preservation, replaced its decayed timbers one by one until they were all changed, creating, Plutarch writes, "a standing example among the philosophers, for the logical question of things that grow; one side holding that the ship remained the same, and the other contending that it was not the same." It's perhaps a point that goes past pedanticism, and Manichand told me that the gooseneck is at least original, but it is one that I heard trotted out occasionally by others in the rum industry who wanted to land a punch against a rival.

The other two wooden stills at DDL are a single pot wooden still, similar to the double pots, from what was once the Versailles estate and known as VSG, and a wooden Coffey column still from an estate known as Enmore, which is referred to as the EHP for Enmore's founder, Edward Henry Porter. The latter is a blocky contraption, painted a deep red, which reminded me of Herzog & de Meuron's 56 Leonard Street, the residential tower in Manhattan's Tribeca neighborhood built of offset cantilevers that has come to be known affectionately as the Jenga building.

The goal of every still is the same: to take a mixture—the "wash" in rum making—and separate the stuff that you want—primarily but not exclusively ethanol, or drinking alcohol—from the stuff that you don't—primarily but not exclusively water—by exploiting the differences in the boiling points of the various substances. Water boils—turns from a liquid to a gas—at 212 degrees Fahrenheit. Ethanol does so at 173. Because of that difference, if you take a mixture containing ethanol and water and heat it up, the ethanol will boil off first, leaving the water behind. To get a strong drink, then, all you need to do is build a device to capture that ethanol vapor and recondense it, to cool it down to below its boiling point, in other words. Given that bit of information, if I stranded you on an uninhabited island and let the desperation fester for long enough, I bet you could even figure out a crude still yourself. But let's not risk it: all you'd have to do is set a pot of fermented liquid over a fire, throw a piece of cloth on top, and periodically wring it out until you'd vaporized all the lower-boiling-point alcohol. *Hooch couture*, you could call it.

But if you want a *good* drink, things get a bit more complicated. That's because floating around in that wash are all sorts of other chemicals, many of which are volatile enough to turn into vapor during ethanol distillation, and many of which also have what are called "organoleptic" properties—taste, aroma, or the ability to create the sensation known as mouthfeel. In booze making these chemicals are called congeners. Some of them are tantalizing, some are repulsive, and a few, such as methanol, are even deadly. Getting them in the right combination is what separates a delicious dram from the dreck. (It's worth making a quick reference to the old adage of "the dose makes the poison" here, because many of the chemicals that give a spirit taste or aroma will kill you if you consume enough of them, though in the concentrations found in distilled spirits the ethanol is going to kill you long before they do. Meanwhile, even methanol, when the dose is too low to be deadly, like the tiny concentrations at which it appears in wine, lends some organoleptic properties that alcoholic beverage producers have occasionally found desirable, particularly bootleggers eager to convince consumers their product packs a punch.)

In pot distillation, the liquid that comes out of the still is separated into the "heads," "hearts," and "tails." Each contains a variety of volatile compounds that originated in the "wash" of fermented molasses or some other sugarcane product. Here samples have been taken from the three stages of distillation at the Novo Fogo (also known as Porto Morettes) cachaça distillery in Brazil. The hearts are what you want to drink. They are where most of the ethanol comes through.

"I tell everyone that distillation is really just a glorified filter," Andrew Hassell, the managing director of the West Indies Rum Distillery in Barbados, which produces rum for Cockspur and a number of other brands, told me when I visited him. "The art of distillation is keeping the stuff you want to keep and getting rid of the stuff you don't. How well you do that and how efficiently you do that is what separates you from everybody else."

Pot stills and column stills filter their liquid in different ways, however. Pot stills run in a batch. For them, you prepare some wash, fill up the pot, turn the thing on, and wait until all your rum has come through. You then rinse and repeat for your next batch. Column stills, on the other hand, are designed so that they can operate continuously. For them, you feed in a constant stream of mash and steam to heat it up, and out comes a constant stream of rum and wash leftovers.

To filter out the desirable congeners from the undesirable ones in a pot still, a distiller makes "cuts" at various moments during the course of distillation. A typical pot still run is divided into three main sections: the heads, the hearts, and the tails. The heads consist of the first liquids to come off a still, which are typically undesirable and include things such as acetone and any methanol in the wash. (Some distillers call the first part of the heads where these chemicals concentrate the "foreshots," and they are always discarded.) After that comes the hearts, which, as the name suggests, is the liquid the distiller is after. It's where a significant part of the ethanol is and where the undesirable chemicals mostly are not. Finally out comes the tails, which consist significantly of what's known as "fusel alcohol" or "fusel oil." That *fusel* is the German word for "bad liquor" or "rotgut" tells you about as much as you need to know about their qualities. Except not quite. Though distillation is by and large science, taste is not, and the congeners throughout the run help create the flavor of the finished product. Moreover, with a pot still, the breaks between what substances are coming out aren't exact. It's not that at first all the methanol comes out, then all the ethanol, then all the water. Instead the distribution is blended: some of the ethanol comes out and so does some of the water. In fact, one distillation is rarely enough—distillers using pot stills will often run their liquid through a second or third time or have equipment on their stills that effectively does the same thing. In rum distilleries, particularly those in the English-speaking Caribbean, that extra equipment is often in the form of two of what are called "retorts." They look, essentially, like two copper tanks. The gooseneck from the pot still feeds into the first one and a pipe from the first one feeds into the second, and together they help boost alcohol concentration and pull out more impurities.

Given all that—and a number of other variations on still design that are way too esoteric for our purposes here—there are no hard rules on where the heads end and the hearts begin and when to start dumping the tails. Those decisions are all up to the distiller.

In a column still, the separation happens differently. Instead of waiting for the wash to slowly rise through various temperatures and capturing what comes off at the appropriate point in the process, as in a pot still, in a column still a steady stream of wash is injected and broken up into its constituent parts on the fly and removed. This works because the temperature in the column varies through its length. Therefore, in a properly calibrated still—and calibration here is key, as Hassell told me, "It is not called a still for no reason; a still means that once you have it correct, you don't eff with it"—the components with higher boiling points condense at the bottom and are removed there, while those with a lower boiling point, like ethanol, come off as vapor at the top, from where they are then re-condensed into liquid. Column stills often have perforated plates inside to help further separate the components of the liquid, and those with additional columns can more precisely filter it, creating a purer product, a process called rectification.

The reason not every distillery uses the same type of still, the reason they haven't all come together and figured out which one is the best while simultaneously saving readers of booze books some lengthy discussion of chemistry they already learned in high school, when they were too young to licitly take advantage of it, is because not every type of still is best for creating every type of booze. Generally, pot stills tend to produce a "heavier" distillate with more congeners and more flavor from the wash. But they are also less efficient. Column stills, meanwhile, excel at efficiency and purity; however, they tend to produce a "lighter" distillate that is not as deep and rich off the still. When you get down to the individual stills themselves, the differences tend to be much more complex and more subtle.

In addition to the three wooden pot stills, the Diamond Distillery houses copper pot stills; Coffey stills; a French Savalle still, a common design in the Caribbean that is named after its original Dutch manufacturer; a several-story-high modern multicolumn still; and a gin still.

The story of how all of the stills ended up at the Diamond Distillery stems from the consolidation of the sugar industry and subsequent closing of sugar factories in the late nineteenth and early twentieth century, a trend that came to a head in 1930, Demerara Distillers's Lennox Shaun Caleb told me.

"There was a realization that we were down to nine distilleries, so at some point, if there were further consolidation, more history would be lost," he said. "It was a milestone for what it represented: a decision to keep the stills."

Caleb is the master distiller at DDL. After my tour with Manichand, we met to talk about what it was like to work with all of those different stills at the El Dorado Rum Heritage Centre, a tasting room and museum that surveys Guyana's rum history and showcases several model stills.

With all of this equipment, what Demerara Distillers is trying to achieve, in essence, is time travel. Their destination: the world of Guyanese rum making circa 1930, when the country had many more sugar estates and therefore many more rum distilleries, each producing unique rums. At DDL the distillers see it as their duty to faithfully re-create what was available back then, Caleb told me. To do so, they produce distillate in approximately two dozen different varieties, which in rum distilling are called "marks" or "marques," depending on your linguistic heritage. (When I checked the figure with him, the most specific response he gave was "thereabouts, thereabouts," echoing distillers elsewhere, who typically consider the precise figure here a trade secret.) That variety is achieved by the fact that each still produces a different product and some stills can be configured to produce several different varieties of rum.

For the wooden stills, it's the unique conductive properties—or rather lack of conductivity—of the wood versus metal that help create the unique rums they produce. Most pot stills today are heated by steam coils that spiral through the base of the still, some are heated by a steam jacket that wraps around it and holds the steam, a very few are heated directly by fire, like a water kettle on a gas stove, because an open flame is not the safest thing to have next to a device that's designed to concentrate alcohol beyond the point of flammability and because the flame can scald the wash. The wooden pot stills at DDL, however, are heated by direct steam injection, as they always have been, a process that also adds a bit of water to the wash during the distilling cycle. Overall, the wooden stills can take up to sixteen hours to distill a batch of wash, producing a very full-bodied, aromatic rum with a potent flavor.

"One can imagine with that amount of time there will be a lot more reactions taking place during the process, and so lighter components combine to form heavier components, and so the overall weight of the product increases accordingly," Caleb said.

The wood stills also lack something else that has a considerable impact on the resulting spirit: abundant copper.

Burnished copper stills, with their gleaming golden hue and shiny steel controls in contrasting silver aren't chosen just for the beauty they lend to an incredible tonnage of rum (and whiskey and cognac) marketing material. They are also a crucial component in the palatability of the spirit they produce.

Most ingredients used to create liquor, molasses included, contain sulphur, that element that goes on to form compounds with odors like rotten eggs, including those which your energy utility decided would be offensive enough to get you to run outside and immediately report a natural gas leak. No spirits company wants you to run outside and phone the fire department as soon as you pop the cap on one of their products, so they want most of that sulphur out. Luckily copper bonds with sulphur during distillation to create copper sulfide, which then flakes off as a slate gray solid. This is why, in the dramatic way distillers sometimes talk about their stills, the copper is referred to as being "sacrificial." It's also why, DDL's Stills of Theseus aside, even old distilleries tend to have relatively new pot stills—with consistent use, they have to be replaced every few decades. Newer column stills, however, are usually made of stainless steel with replaceable copper packing or parts, so they last longer.

Demerara Distillers's two metal column stills, the Coffey and the Savalle, also produce different distillates. Caleb explained that between those two types, the Coffey, which is smaller, tends to produce rums that are fruitier and more floral because fewer of the organoleptic components are extracted before the rum comes out the other end. Meanwhile, the Savalle gives the operator tremendous flexibility to manipulate what is produced.

"The Savalle, because there are four columns, because we can operate it several different ways—two, three, or four columns—and even within those combinations, the way we feed, the way we extract impurities, the process conditions can be further manipulated to give us as many as nine different products, whereas with the Coffey you essentially only get one shot," he said.

One of the marks the more precise Savalle still allows Demerara Distillers to produce, for example, is a light rum that nonetheless has a signature, striking nose of "creamy, chocolatey coconut," Caleb said. Chemical analysis showed the aroma comes from the interaction of three or four congeners in minute quantities, on the order of about ten parts per million.

"If we want to keep it we would not operate the third column because the third column extracts a lot of that product," he explained. Whereas if you want a cleaner product, that third column is in operation, so those notes are stripped away."

More impressive, from a technological standpoint at least, is that some of the more advanced, modern column stills even have taps at the plates at various points along the column. When the still is stable and these plates stay at a consistent temperature, the distiller can then pull out whatever chemicals are condensing there. It's not a perfect system—a distiller can't target individual compounds if there are multiple ones in the wash with the same boiling points—but in essence this allows distillers to begin to see their wash as a storehouse of all sorts of different aromas, flavors, and textures waiting to be extracted in any combination they desire, then remixed as they see fit into the final rum.

"The analogy I give people is when you have the wash from the fermentation, imagine that in there you have a basketball, a tennis ball, a football, whatever. They are all mixed together. You then put this in your column still and adjust it until you have just the right ball coming to the correct height that it goes out a particular hole. Say it's the tennis ball. You come and say you want some baseball with tennis ball, we will then collect the baseball and blend it," Hassell said. "The old-fashioned thing to do was to try to adjust the column to have both of those balls coming out at the same time, but it's a lot easier, if you want to have good organoleptic balance, to separate because once we have the baseball separate from the tennis ball, we then know how strong those baseballs are and we can then blend it back exactly how you want."

From the beginning, the mission of Hassell's West Indies Rum Distillery was to be at the forefront of distilling technology—when it was founded toward the end of the nineteenth century, it had one of the first column stills in the Caribbean. But even DDL, despite an identity firmly rooted in Guyana's centuries-long rum-making heritage, has embraced advanced distillation techniques. As Manichand and I were walking through the company's giant multicolumn plant we passed a tap, which he opened, sending a stream of distillate into a small container. He held it up for me to take a whiff. It was distinctive of little other than ethanol. He said it was

96.5 percent alcohol by volume, which is a higher concentration then most stills can achieve.

Moreover, the distillery, like many others, has begun to use techniques like gas chromatography and mass spectrometry to peer into their liquids and get a better understanding of where, exactly, their flavors are coming from.

"We have tried to understand at a much more fundamental level all of the twenty-four marks," Caleb said. "Quite apart from the sensory profiles that each are noted for, we have tried to dig deeper into what are the chemical profiles that contribute to that, what particular compounds must be present in what quantities, what synergies exist, what are the outer limits beyond which the profile changes."

Certainly, before the emergence of the modern production technology available today, distillers had dramatically improved their craft from rum's beginnings. As rum historian Wayne Curtis writes in his book, *And a Bottle of Rum*, from rum's earliest decades no "account has surfaced that has anything nice to say about the taste of kill-devil." Much of the knowledge they used to make those improvements has become the crucial property and key to the identity of distilleries. Manichand told me that when they bought the stills they also had to make sure to hire the operators to acquire their embedded knowledge of the intricacies that make each machine unique as well. New technology doesn't necessarily change that craft—old-style stills exist throughout the rum archipelago. But the use of modern production techniques has sparked a debate about how tradition in the rum world should be valued and described, and at what point rum no longer is considered a rum, particularly when it's produced by a distillery that can create something delicious for a fraction of the cost of someone using an ancient, or ancient-style, still.

The 300-year gamut of distilling history packed into DDL's plant made these questions particularly stark, and I turned them over in my head as I rode back to the Pegasus hotel. But I had no new answers when I was back. My attention instead shifted to something more immediate. I quickly dropped my things in my room and called down to the front desk to see if the package I'd been waiting for had arrived. When they told me it had, I scurried down to pick it up.

My first day in Guyana, I'd gone down to the restaurant for dinner right as a local band was coming onstage. The patio where I was sitting was packed, and a few minutes later a group of three sat down in the extra chairs at my table.

In between sets of poorly rendered and stale American Top 40 interspersed with some great reggae and soca, my unexpected dinner companions introduced themselves. One was a Guyanese-born New Yorker, the second a government official from somewhere in the interior, and the third the New Yorker's aunt, who has started a business making gift baskets since retiring. After chiding me for not planning a trip to Kaieteur Falls, famous as one of the most powerful waterfalls in the world, she promised to send over a welcome gift.

The feast that arrived, of plantain chips, tamarind balls, guava cheese, and prune tarts, girded me for the trip back to Cheddi Jagan airport the next day, reminding me that pleasure and hospitality can flourish even in rough places.

When I arrived I dropped my bag on the scanner, walked through the magnetometer, and was about ready to grab it when the security officer on the other side stopped me.

"Excuse me, sir, but do you have a jar of coffee in there?" she said.

I did. There are some things you just don't leave to chance.

"Will you take it out?" she asked.

I dug down and pulled it out. As I did, I remembered yet another tip someone gave me about traveling in the country: to avoid becoming an unwitting drug mule, I should absolutely not accept any packages from any strangers. I'd bought the coffee myself, but the idea that a coffee-sized jar of coke might be something one would try to smuggle out of the country was, well, jarring. When I turned the label toward her she said, "Oh," with a smirk of surprise before adding, "Have a nice flight."

EL DORADO MAI TAI

In addition to being favored by the Royal Navy, Demerara rums have enticed drinkers for centuries, but they found particular purchase in the cocktails of the tiki era, where their deep, rich flavors could survive being mixed with the plethora of ingredients typical in such cocktails. One of the classics, the Mai Tai, was invented by one of the tiki's impressarios Victor Bergeron, who went by the name "Trader Vic" and ran the collection of Trader Vic's restaurants (a fuller story of tiki and rum can be found in Chapter 7). This version is not the original recipe, but instead comes from the folks at Demerara Distillers, using their El Dorado range of rums.

0.75 ounce El Dorado 3 Year Old rum
0.75 ounce El Dorado 12 Year Old rum
0.75 ounce fresh lime juice
0.5 ounce orgeat
0.5 ounce Velvet falernum
0.5 ounce orange Curaçao
Dash bitters

Shake ingredients with ice and strain into glass over ice. Garnish with a mint sprig and orange slice.

CHAPTER 3

Jamaican Funk

Before the spit of land that connects Jamaica's Norman Manley International Airport with Kingston proper was a highway and storm surge barrier it was something far more sinister: a linkage to Port Royal, a place that once suffered one of the world's strongest arguments for the existence of God.

While Jamaica would eventually become one of Britain's most lucrative sugar islands in the West Indies—by the 1720s it was outproducing Barbados—for the first decades of its existence, when Barbados was establishing the sugar, rum, and slaves plantation model, Jamaica's plunderous gaze was cast in another direction: outward, to the ocean.

The island, wrote Englishman Edward Ward, was "As Sickly as a Hospital, as Dangerous as the Plague, as Hot as *Hell*, and as a wicked as the *Devil*." It was "Subject to *Tornado's, Hurricans* and *Earthquakes*, as if the Island, like the People, were troubled with *Dry-Belly-Ach*," he added.

In the introduction to his report, Ward writes that his intention is nothing more than entertainment and humor, and at the time of his visit there, in 1697, he was well on his way to becoming a distinguished satirist of contemporary, and significantly colonial, British life.

Nonetheless, few would have disagreed with his assessment by anything more than a slight degree.

Seized by England from Spain in 1655, Jamaica quickly became the crossroads of the Western Hemisphere, serving as a transshipment point and grand bazaar for goods destined for and departing from ports throughout the Atlantic world. Traders from the Netherlands and corsairs from England sailed through her harbor and, like the best of the world's entrepôts, she seethed with a seedy, opportunistic cosmopolitanism.

Among Jamaica's most famous residents were those men and a smattering of women who sailed under the black flag—the pirates and privateers (the distinction was usually technical and often mutable) who menaced the settlers and shippers who'd come to the Caribbean to make their fortune.

From the beginning of Jamaica's history as an English territory, its governors were a source of the legal writs that allowed privateers to plunder enemy ships, and its ports served as a place to dispose of the loot and piss away the profit. In fact, as sugarcane rapidly became, by a vast margin, the primary economic activity on an island like Barbados, on Jamaica privateering seized that distinction. During the first few years of the eighteenth century, something like one-half to three-fourths of the island's white residents had signed on as buccaneers. One of the most famous among them was Captain Henry Morgan, the privateer who *Forbes* magazine estimated in 2008 was the seventh-highest-earning pirate of all time, pilfering the modern-day equivalent of $13 million during his piracy career. His take was a fraction of what those at the top of his field, like "Black Sam" Bellamy and his $120 million and Thomas Tew and his $103 million, raked in. But he nonetheless pleased King Charles II enough to get himself knighted and appointed as the lieutenant governor of Jamaica.

All the wealth that flowed through what would come to be known as Kingston Harbour made the island yet another jewel of the fabulous *nuevo riche* of the New World. By 1680 Port Royal had more people than any other city in the English New World, save Boston, even though the space was tiny, just 53 acres. To fit, they crowded into 800 buildings, some of which rose a then vertiginous four stories. Some one hundred of them, Matthew Parker estimates in *The Sugar Barons*, contained drinking establishments, many of which were also, of course, brothels.

You could, in other words, say that the fast and loose life of the early Caribbean was present in Port Royal then, down to its very substrate. Unfortunately, that happened to be an unsteady bed of sand.

In the late morning of June 7, 1692, divine retribution, or that inevitably infernal intersection of periodic natural phenomena and slipshod frenetic real-estate development, arrived when a temblor and a series of aftershocks hit the town. The accounts that survive—remarkably among them one from a minister (albeit one shaken from a pre-prandial tipple)—contain the usual horrors of such disasters, of tall blocks along narrow streets collapsing like the Red Sea after Moses, of entire neighborhoods sliding into the ocean, and of people sucked down into the earth and crushed when it closed back upon them. Eventually, over half of Port Royal sank below the water.

Perhaps it worked. By the time the earth stopped shaking, the reverend reported, those who remained of what he initially described as a "most Ungodly Debauched People" "cry'd out to me to come and Pray with them . . . every one laid hold on my Cloathes and embraced me, that with their fear and kindness I was almosted stifled."

Undeterred by a smattering of aftershocks, once the sun set, he reported, the town's remaining privateers set upon the "Warehouses, and Houses deserted, to Rob and Rifle their Neighbours," adding: "Multitude of Rich Men are utterly ruin'd, whilst many that were poor, by watching opportunities, and searching the wrack'd and sunk Houses, even almost while the Earthquake lasted, and terror and amazement were upon all the considerable People, have gotten great Riches."

For the Jamaicans that remained, the more solid ground of nearby Kingston beckoned.

I hadn't come to Jamaica for the pirates, however. They may be strongly associated with rum, including in the visage of Captain Morgan, the mascot of a rum brand that is one of the most popular in the world, with yearly sales of just over ten million cases. But the buccaneers, as rum scholar Ian Williams has pointed out, were later-comers to the spirit—until it shed its kill-devil image, they preferred to spend their loot on cognac instead. Later, they were little more than exceptionally avid consumers and, it would seem, rather poor candidates for future brand ambassadorship: as Frederick H. Smith points out in *Caribbean Rum*, their drinking tended to skew to the pathological. Blackbeard was reputed to throw back a half gallon of rum a day, while Morgan died of what seems to have been alcoholic liver cirrhosis.

Anyway, though the pirates certainly helped make Jamaica famous, their reign was relatively short lived—the so-called Golden Age of Piracy had largely come to a close after the first few decades of the eighteenth century, when the sugar planters finally usurped the buccaneers in the long-simmering struggle over which would be the dominant force on the island.

What I had come to Jamaica looking for, if you're up for a little poetics, is the pirate ethos of rum—in particular a visit to the rum factory at Hampden Estate, one of the most hallowed sites in the rum world, especially for aficionados of what is known casually as "Jamaican funk."

I had arrived in Jamaica several days before I had any real business there, so I decided to head up to the town of Port Antonio, in the remote parish of Portland on the northeast coast—a place nearly every Jamaican I talked to told me was their favorite place on the island.

Port Antonio was once a bustling banana port and then, having caught the eye of Golden Age Hollywood actor and playboy Errol Flynn, who may have even gone so far as to say of the area that it was "more beautiful than any woman I have ever known," it became a bustling banana port and a playground for the midcentury glitterati. Today it is neither and is instead frequently described as a place of architecture in "various states of disrepair" and the cool kids' retreat away from lousey tourist ports farther to the west.

Regardless, it was one of the lushest places I've ever been, dripping with a deep chlorophyll green. And mostly just dripping. Amid the downpours that would pass over every few hours, I sat around a guest house, and wary of repeating Morgan's fate, drank Red Stripe beer instead of rum while playing the card game Mau Mau with a spattering of German tourists passing through. Among them were a couple visiting their daughter, who was an education volunteer in Trench Town, the birthplace of Bob Marley and one of Kingston's notorious "garrison" communities that occasionally burst into politically fueled violence. As we sat around they fretted over an almost omnipresent juxtaposition in Jamaica of extreme beauty and extreme poverty cheek by jowl in a nation struggling to make something in a place that should seemingly have everything. Shortly before I left, a piece of safety equipment left in place by maintenance workers repairing part of the island's electrical grid threw the entire system off-line and the whole island went dark, with some places staying without power for nearly six hours. It was the second major power failure that year.

To get to Hampden I took an early-morning bus from the still-regal Errol Flynn Marina in Port Antonio to Falmouth, home of one of the ports in Jamaica capable of receiving some of the world's largest cruise ships since it opened in 2011. As the bus drove along the north coast, we passed by the Ian Fleming International Airport, named after the James Bond novelist, who had owned a home nearby. Today it is a resort known as GoldenEye, which was purchased in 1976 by Chris Blackwell, the founder of Island Records and proprietor of his very own Blackwell Rum. There guests can choose to stay in the Fleming Villa, complete with three bedrooms, two guest villas, a private beach, and full staff, for an advertised price of not less than $5,830 a night—or just about $1,000 more than the country's per capita GDP.

It was, however, away from the ocean that I was headed when I arrived at the bus stop in Falmouth. There I was met by Pepe Grant, the aptly named tour manager for Hampden Estate, who swung by to pick me up.

Hampden specializes in what are known as high-ester rums—rums that are brimming with flavor right off the still. They are perhaps the peaty scotches of the rum world. Instead of smoke, however, their characteristic flavors are of rich tropical fruits and an organoleptic quality known as "hogo." The descriptor, cocktail historian David Wondrich chronicles in his book, *Punch*, traces its lineage back in the rum trade more than three hundred years to a less than appetizing origin, at least at first glance.

"Derived from the term for the 'high taste' [*haut goût* in the French, where such things tend to originate] of rotting meat, it could certainly be used pejoratively," Wondrich writes. "But just as one cultivated the *haut goût* of pheasants and other game birds by hanging them for days before cooking them, so the hogo in rum came to be appreciated and even, to a degree, encouraged."

As we drove away from town, the roads, in true Jamaican fashion, became increasingly narrow, windy, unmarked, and pocked with massive potholes. Hampden had only recently started giving public tours, and Grant was enthusiastic about drawing some of the cruise ship tourists out for a distillery tour and a glimpse of the local culture, for which he was equally enthusiastic. (Part of his mission for my visit was to pick up what he thought of as some of the best jerk on the island and take it to eat in an authentic rum shop, which, being like certain VFW outposts in the States, weren't always friendly to solo travelers who wandered in from afar. When the jerk stand happened to be out, we had to settle for a patty and coco bread at the local Tastee, an experience as quintessentially Jamaican as a burger and fries at McDonald's is American). When he told me about the visitors, I didn't doubt they'd come, especially after I'd seen the facility, but as I commented in my notebook after being jostled around the whole day, I wasn't certain they all would make it either.

Hampden Estate is in Trelawny Parish, the birthplace of the world's fastest and most appropriately named runner, Usain Bolt. It's also home to part of what is known as "Cockpit Country," an extremely rugged region that attracted escaped slaves as far back as the period of Spanish rule. Under the English these communities harbored thousands of maroons, as they came to be known, and proved so much a menace to the planters that in 1730 they organized several expeditions to eradicate them. However, they fought back so fiercely, the British Empire was forced to grant them their autonomy instead, albeit on terms that were a devil's wager: thereafter, the maroons were compelled to defend free whites against future slave uprisings. Some of the autonomy these communities gained they still hold today.

For the most part, though, Jamaica's sugar industry flourished like it did elsewhere in the West Indies, and with it the rum industry. Like Barbados and Guyana, Jamaica had a constellation of sugar plantations and the requisite rum-production facilities to go with them. In fact, Jamaican rum increasingly became favored by the British, who soaked up more than a million gallons of it in the mid- and late eighteenth century. Barbadian rum, meanwhile, primarily went to North America or was re-exported from England to elsewhere in Europe and Africa. Part of what made Jamaican

A pot still, no longer used, on display at the Hampden Estate distillery in Jamaica. Though seemingly durable, the copper in pot stills slowly erodes away during distillation as it reacts with sulphur in the distillation vapor—a process that increases the palatability of the resulting product.

A gate at the Hampden Estate distillery in Jamaica. Hampden produces the exceptionally flavorful Rum Fire brand, which derives all its flavor from compounds produced in the wash, rather than during aging.

rum so popular was an enticement that has appealed to a certain subset of drinkers for as long as there have been drinkers to appeal to: raw strength.

As Smith demonstrates in *Caribbean Rum,* for the century following the beginning of the Jamaican rum industry in the late eighteenth century, the potency of the island's rum steadily increased.

"In 1832, [Jamaican Planter Thomas] Roughly described the production of concentrated Jamaican rum above 61 percent absolute alcohol, or 122 proof. In the 1840s, [fellow planter Leonard] Wray observed that the standard Jamaican rum contained 60 to 65 percent absolute alcohol, at 120 to 130 proof. By the end of the nineteenth century, Jamaican rum was generally exported at 78 percent alcohol," or 156 proof, well beyond the point at which the spirit could substitute for lamp oil, he wrote. (Proof in the United

A view of the still house at Hampden Estate distillery in Jamaica. Over two hundred years old, Hampden has changed ownership multiple times, but its unique rum is the product of an archaic process that looks extremely antiquated in comparison to many of today's modern rum distilleries.

States has always been simply double the alcohol percentage by volume. A 100-proof spirit—a spirit "at proof"—was a spirit that had enough alcohol in it that, when gunpowder was sprinkled on top, the gunpowder would ignite. If you don't believe me on this, please don't try to be a discerning rum-buying swashbuckler and try it yourself; instead, check the literature and save the rum for sipping as you do. It'll be a lot less embarrassing.) For that reason, rather than any particular measure of quality, it seemed, Jamaican rum reliably commanded the highest price. After all, the flip side to alcohol concentration is water content, and it'd take another century yet before someone would figure out how to convince affluent consumers to pay to have that commodity shipped thousands of miles from a tiny island in the middle of the ocean somewhere.

If today 156-proof rum sounds throat-searingly absurd, that means at least two things: you were neither weaned on Everclear, which on the balance is probably good, nor did you come of drinking age in Jamaica. Over the past century or so, most of the drinking world, or at least most of the drinking world with a well-regulated alcohol market, has generally settled on a standard proof for spirits of somewhere around 40 percent alcohol by volume, or 80 proof.

In Jamaica, well, try to sell a local on such a feeble rum and they are going to run you off the island, as Grant explained to me once we'd reached the distillery and started looking over some of its products, including its Rum Fire white rum, which comes in at 126 proof.

"They'd say what is this, this not rum!" he said, of something closer to the standard proof.

Of course that last objection isn't true. It's perfectly legal to sell a bottle of 80 proof rum in Jamaica, but the vast majority of the rum sold on the island is just like Rum Fire: white and 63 percent alcohol.

"It's a tradition. From the beginning of time we've been doing it. It's our Jamaican roots, as a safe haven for pirates," Grant added, laughing.

Outside, the rain from Port Antonio had followed me down the coast, and occasionally a torrential downpour would break out—at one point it started raining so hard that the distillery workers, on their lunch break, found themselves trapped in the break room, forced to wait for the rain to subside before they could start the distillery up again.

At the distillery, Grant and I were joined by Vivian Wisdom, who runs the distillery. Wisdom has spent most of his career working in the various aspects of rum production at most of the distilleries in Jamaica. Like many master distillers, he can certainly play up the romantic visage of how such a role is portrayed in rum-making literature—that pensive gaze of contemplation over a snifter of golden rum, held just so, probably set in a dusty rickhouse with improbably flattering light—but when he talks about his craft, he typically does so in terms of his background in chemistry. For example, when Grant brings up a myth that apparently circulates among his country's high-proof rum swillers that adding a bit of water to a potent Hampden rum actually makes it stronger, Wisdom interjects not only to say of course that's not true—adding water would dilute the rum, making it weaker—but then gives a quick chemistry lesson behind why drinkers might think otherwise.

"The thing is, based on the strength there is an extra thermal reaction between the water and alcohol, so it will feel warm in your hand," he said. Mixing ethanol and water, it turns out, is an exothermic process—it gives off heat.

"But the strength is not going to go up," he added. "It's just a reaction that you will start to feel."

Fair enough, if that's your thing. Grant told me that the most typical way for a Jamaican to drink his rum was to mix it with whatever juice or soda, or even milk, was nearby.

Like the rest of the Caribbean, Jamaica lacks a cocktail culture, and the closest thing to it is a Jamaican rum punch. But by the time I arrived at Hampden, I had already had plenty of Jamaican overproof rum, including in the form of what supposedly was a traditional Jamaican rum punch. To me it tasted like Robitussin, albeit Robitussin spiked heavily with Jamaican overproof rum. (When I mentioned this to Grant he quickly set about righting the experience, mixing up his own much lighter version with a fruit punch juice and some papaya and pineapple juice—the key, he said, is to not overdo the rum.)

What I'd really come to Hampden to talk about, however, was something else that made Jamaica's rums famous at their height, and is still today why they command among the highest prices in the bulk rum market: their fermentation style.

If Port Royal was to some suggestive of the existence of a retributive higher power, fermentation, for many others, is proof of a benevolent one.

In fact, the always aphoristic Benjamin Franklin himself even said as much when he said that the fermentation of grapes into wine was "constant proof that God loves us and loves to see us happy."

But fermentation is for far more than just wine. Without it not only would there be no wine, but there would be no rum, or whiskey, or vodka, or beer either. In essence, it is the alpha to the omega of every alcoholic drink and it has been tantalizing humanity for, as far as anyone knows, as long as there has been humanity worth tantalizing.

Whereas distillation is an industrial process, one that came of age during an era when the convergence of capital, technology, and far-flung trade routes spun together ever faster the world's raw materials into increasingly cheap mass-produced goods, wine and the other direct products of fermentation—beer, from grain; mead, from honey—are the primordial precursors, the hallmark beverages of the previous agrarian age.

But, in fact, fermentation doesn't need any help from people at all. All alcoholic beverages are the product of two things: some kind of sugar, be it from sugarcane, fruit, honey, or malted grain, and yeast, that powerhouse organism of the microscopic world. *Saccharomyces cerevisiae*, or brewer's yeast, has been converting sugar to ethanol for millions and millions of years—well before humans were around, even well before there was fruit. They appear to have started out consuming tree sap. What they do is find a molecule of sugar—their food, in other words—and in the process of converting it to energy spit out ethanol and carbon dioxide. You could, then, call ethanol and carbon dioxide yeast's "waste products," but just like calling molasses a waste product of sugar processing, you're really just back to that one-person's-waste-is-another-person's-treasure paradox.

The answer to when humans started treasuring this alcohol, however, isn't clear. The best evidence discovered suggests deliberate fermentation was occurring at least as far back as 10,000 years ago in China, which coincides with the general trajectory of the origins of agriculture—when humans started lassoing animals and crops like grain and sugarcane and domesticating them for their own use, just as they would eventually do with *Saccharomyces cerevisiae*. (And a useful captive it's been: Today yeast does far more for us than just make booze. It of course also rises bread, an application that harnesses its CO_2 production rather than that of ethanol, which evaporates off. Yeast has also been genetically modified and pressed into apparel production, spitting out spider silk minus the spiders by the California-based company Bolt Threads, though they declined to say specifically what yeast species they use.)

But bar-crawling behavior among us and our evolutionary ancestors seems to go back much further. Fermenting yeasts are everywhere and, especially in hot climates, eagerly begin to ferment concentrated sugar sources wherever they are—which is why sugarcane has to be processed so quickly, otherwise it'll turn to sugarcane wine. Ripe fruits do the same, especially those that have fallen to the ground. Around ten million years ago, our human ancestors started following this fruit down to the forest floor, and the five-second rule be damned, recent research suggests that it was then that they developed the ability to efficiently process ethanol—the more alcohol they could handle the more food they could eat off the forest floor without getting drunk. Alcohol, in other words, meant food, and that may be why we have developed a pleasure response to its presence today. (OK, now you're wondering if our early ancestors got drunk. Probably not, or at least probably not regularly—fermented fruit is a lot more filling way to consume alcohol than to drink an 80-proof or 126-proof shot of it. But other primates *can* get drunk. If you're somehow not already looking it up on YouTube, drunk monkeys, for the record, look just like you imagine they'd look: like furry drunk humans with all of the flirting and fighting but none of the epithets.)

But fermentation and the fermentation *process* do far more than just produce alcohol.

When Andrew Hassell of the West Indies Rum Distillery described distillation as a process of filtration, one that can be used in the skilled hands of a distiller making a series of cuts on a pot still or fine-tuning a column still to target a range of flavors he or she finds most desirable, the logical question is, where does that range of flavors come from in the first place? The fermentation process is the answer there, too.

"The molecular route from glucose to ethanol is studded with side roads and turnoffs," Rogers writes in *Proof.* And, indeed, it's the Jamaicans' enthusiasm for fermentary off-road adventures and out-of-the-way detours that has made their rum so unique.

Once the rain had let up sufficiently that we could walk outside without being instantly drenched, Grant took me on a tour of the rum-making facilities at Hampden.

Hampden has been around since its founding as a sugar estate sometime during the middle of the eighteenth century and is one of those great regal wrecks found in places where stupendous wealth has slowly withered. It's a tranquil setting—as Grant and I dodged the puddles that had filled the deeper ruts of the unpaved driveway, the estate's peacocks strutted in the passive aggressive way of a creature with something to show off. Around us greenery dripped everywhere, from cinder block walls with muffin tops of ivy to the trailing flowers in red and yellow that jumped off the railing running along the great house's deck. The deck was elevated off the ground by about a story, and Grant explained that at one time there had been barrel storage under the house.

A lot of work had clearly gone into the grounds, but the site still showed its age—the manor house's shingles were worn, the corrugated tin that sided many of the buildings was dented and rust-streaked, and buildings all over were covered with what looked like *Baudoinia compniacensis*, the sooty-black, alcohol-feasting fungus that thrives at distilleries all over the world. (No one's posted a video on YouTube of what antics it gets up to when intoxicated, unfortunately.)

Part of the reason for the state of the facility was likely the result of Hampden's history. As elsewhere in the Caribbean, Jamaica has experienced a significant decline in its sugar industry, with a number of sugar estates, including Hampden, struggling with profitability and coming in and out of government receivership.

Its current owners are the Hussey family, which runs a diversified conglomerate in Jamaica, including a boutique hotel and horse-racing and pharmacy businesses. But they also have a background in agriculture, and in 2009 they purchased Hampden from the government.

"The sugar factory was just Band-Aids all the time and eventually, if you have enough Band-Aids on a piece of material, whatever that material is, whether it's a crop, a person, or a piece of machinery, eventually the Band-Aids aren't going to be enough to hold it together, and I feel we acquired it at a time when the Band-Aids were not enough to hold it together anymore," said Christelle Harris, the family member who has taken charge of Hampden's rum marketing, of the sugar factory, which is known as Long Pond. The sugar factory sat out the 2016–2017 crop year and the government paid to have farmers' cane taken elsewhere; meanwhile, the Husseys' hope is that by upgrading the factory to produce energy alongside sugar from the sugarcane waste, the facility can be profitable.

"However, the rum distillery, thank God, has always been a financially lucrative entity," she said.

In fact, the distillery likely benefited from what could be called benevolent neglect. Like the wooden stills at Demerara Distillers, antiquated inefficiency is part of the point.

Nowhere is this truer than in Hampden's fermentation house, which like the great house dates back to the estate's founding. On the outside, it looks like a lot of the other buildings on Hampden's property—metal roof, white-washed stone walls, and in places where the whitewash has fallen away, the stones prove to be aggregate, of a jumble of shapes and sizes—something Harris said when she first saw reminded her of something that "came out of one of those old Sherlock Holmes novels."

When Grant and I walked up the short set of cement stairs and onto the fermentation floor, gripping a yellow-painted handrail that was clearly a more recent addition, I could see what she meant. As my eyes adjusted to the dimness, what stretched before me looked not only truly medieval, but also occult—less a place where rum was made, and perhaps more a factory where witches cooked up their wickedest abracadabras.

Ancient rough-hewn wood beams pressed down from the ceiling above, creating T-joints perfect for a spider to string a web, and almost closing the space between the tops of dozens of large cedar vats, the oldest of which dated back more than a century, Grant said. Between the sections of the building, squat and tight entryways had been pulled out of more stone walls, and pipes and gutters ran everywhere. Grant explained to me that when the sugar factory and distillery were originally built on the site, they were designed so that all the liquid could flow down by gravity from one section to the next.

"We've added PVC so we don't have to send anything through those channels," he said. "But, yeah man, the ingenuity of everything back then was amazing."

Inside those vats, however, was where the real wackiness was going on. There the molasses was fermenting—the yeast colonies chowing down on sugar and kicking out ethanol. But so much more was going on in there as well.

At Hampden the fermentation process can last for up to two and a half weeks, an absurdly long time when compared to the many rum distilleries that finish theirs up in two or three days, and especially to that of some of the most advanced facilities, where fermentations started by the morning shift can be just about finished by the time the afternoon shift breaks for lunch.

That meant that as we walked around, Grant and I came upon vats in all different stages of fermentation. In some, near the beginning of their fermentation cycle, the wash was caramel colored and fizzing furiously from all the carbon dioxide the yeast was producing, as if it were a giant tank of cream soda. In others it looked like plague had set in, the wash capped with a thick off-white coating pocked with large bubbles that was reminiscent of festering boils.

All of the tanks were uncovered, and it's worth noting that some distillers work strenuously to keep their fermentations as sterile and isolated from the outside environment as possible. I even saw one distillery in Brazil where the fermentation tanks were sealed off in a locked room that only a few employees were allowed to enter, as if what was really going on in there was live Ebola research. In the production philosophy of others, however, such antiseptic fermentation practices are seen as unnecessary or even disadvantageous, and it is not uncommon for distillers to ferment out in the open, with tanks exposed to all the things flittering and crawling in the fecund Caribbean environment. Needless to say, things get in that some people would probably rather not think about being in something they're eventually going to consume, which is another reason why it's reassuring to think of a still as a grand, heat-powered filter.

To someone unfamiliar with what was going on, the fermentation house at Hampden, then, looked like a place ripe for modernization—slap a museum sticker on it and build a new one, taking advantage in the meantime of all the human innovation, since, well, the harnessing of electricity. In fact, when Harris's family first saw it, that's what they figured they had to do.

"One of the first things my grandmother said was we've got to change this entire place. We have to clean it up," Harris said. But when they shared this idea with Vivian Wisdom, he implored them not to, arguing that to do so could potentially ruin the signature rum of Hampden.

"Once we understood that, we were like, OK, we're going to change out the floor boards so that people aren't going to fall through, because we have staff that we care about, but we did as little as we could," Harris said.

To understand what was so important about those century-old tanks and tumbledown ceilings, I followed Wisdom into his lab, one of the places at the estate that has entered the modern era: above us electric light burned, on a nearby counter sat a gas chromatography–mass spectrometry machine, and a marker board hung on the wall full of scribbles of weight measurements, the structural formula of an aldehyde, and the phone number of somebody or something named Sinclair.

Once we were in there, he unscrewed the cap on a bottle of Rum Fire, poured a bit into a snifter and swirled it around. The aromas in Rum Fire are potent, as I found out when I moved a bottle in my apartment one morning. As I did, a bit leaked out of the cap onto my fingers and for the next several hours I emanated the aroma of rum. It smells delicious, but it's not particularly an odor you want to give off as you go about your morning. At the tasting lab, I was hit by the rum's familiar redolence of tropical fruits, even before the glass was passed toward my nose.

Much of what I was smelling was a class of volatile compounds called esters. Simply put, an ester is what's created from the interaction of an acid and an alcohol molecule. In distilling they are among the substances called congeners—those assorted balls of Andrew Hassell's metaphor— that extend the organoleptic range of a spirit, contributing to the aroma, taste, and mouthfeel of the finished product.

Many of these esters that are formed are instantly recognizable as the aroma and flavor of fruits and are often used in confectionary to give candy its flavor. Moreover, their qualities can be radically different from those of the acids and alcohols they come from—which themselves can also contribute their own aromas and flavors to the resulting rum.

Take acetic acid, for example. It's the acid that makes household vinegar what it is. It's not one that seems destined for the pantheon of crowd-pleasing flavorings. Don't write it off, though. There's still a bit of charisma trapped in its pungency. If you take it out and introduce it to some isoamyl alcohol, what you'll have eventually is—and if only my ten-year-old self were here, he'd be so excited—banana Runts!

Well, not exactly. What'll you'll have is isoamyl acetate, a.k.a. banana flavoring, a.k.a. mixed together with some sugar, molded into the shape of a parenthesis, and coated with yellow food coloring: banana Runts. But isoamyl acetate is also a pretty common congener in high-ester rums, so my ten-year-old self would probably still be pretty excited, at least until he was told he had so many more years before he could drink.

In a wash like that at Hampden, all sorts of flavorful esters like isoamyl acetate are floating around, just ready to be filtered through a still along with ethanol and the other congeners.

The origin of that eau de Runts is at the heart of why Wisdom insisted on the continued use of Hampden's centuries-old fermentation house. What makes one rum different from another is its particular organoleptic profile—in other words, how it smells and tastes. For Hampden's rums, those aromas and flavors come from the fermentation and distillation process—very little of Hampden's rum is aged, though in the future more might be.

Stimulating the production of those esters and other congeners is an esoteric process. For esters it is basically about two things: getting acids in the wash and convincing the yeasts to convert them into esters.

Like other life-forms, within the species of *saccharomyces cerevisiae* there are all sorts of yeast strains that behave differently from one another. Some can tolerate a higher level of alcohol; others perish at lower concentrations (the eventual fate of most yeast in most booze production); some require abundant nutrients, which are lacking in rum washes and must be added; others are only suitable for fermentations within a certain temperature range, and they can vary in how long they take to convert a batch's sugar to alcohol.

Perhaps most importantly, however, is that they all produce a different constellation of congeners in the rum. For this reason, distillers—like beer brewers and winemakers—often take their yeast very seriously. Finding the right yeast is often a critical step in starting a new distillery, and today prospective spirits makers have entire catalogs of commercial yeast strains to browse. Moreover, some, particularly those who develop a proprietary yeast all their own, even consider their particular strain a significant business asset and will store samples off-site as a backup, in case a disaster wipes out all the yeast at their production facility.

However, it's not just the yeast strain that determines what a yeast will do during fermentation. Just like me and probably like you, yeasts will react differently depending on how they are treated. Put them in a nice, comfortable environment with the temperature just right, the fridge well-stocked, and the door locked tight against outside annoyances, and they go right along producing their energy, ethanol, CO_2, and little else. But rile them up a bit, make them uncomfortable, stress them out, and put them in the show ring to fight for their survival, and they are liable to throw a tantrum of other chemicals.

At Hampden, rather than relying on their own carefully cultivated yeast or picking one out of a catalog, they get theirs from the environment, which means they have their own characteristics. Once they've got them feasting on their wash, instead of coddling them they keep them exposed to the elements. In a wash at Hampden, sitting in those open-air vats, in a building with hundreds of years of biological buildup, bacteria from the environment will start to infect the wash. Some of those bacteria will begin feeding on the sugar in the wash and producing their own effluents, including acids, those crucial building blocks of esters.

To push the ester content up even higher, Wisdom will also take fresh sugarcane juice and allow naturally occurring acetic acid bacteria to convert it into a vinegar, which he'll then add to the wash in amounts of about 10 percent for the rum that goes into Rum Fire. To slow down fermentation, further antagonizing the yeast and giving the bacteria more time to produce acids, he can also adjust the nutrient levels. In pique, the yeast will also start grabbing acids and alcohols and spitting out esters, not as punishment for annoying them so—though that seems like a nice metaphor—but in attempt to make their environment a little less toxic by neutralizing the alcohols surrounding them.

Perhaps the most mythologized addition traditionally used in heavy, high-ester Jamaican rum is a substance known as dunder. Google around a bit for dunder and you'll run into descriptions of a putrescence so seemingly vile that you'll be forgiven for swearing sobriety. The dunder pits of legend are often cast as unburied graves full of all sorts of rot—severed goat heads and dead bats being the two most popular shocking additions reputedly tossed in. Reality, thankfully, is less stomach churning. At Hampden, dunder is what is left in the still after a distilling run. Called "stillage" or "vinyasse" elsewhere (and by producers of other spirits, such as whiskey), it is alcohol-free but nutrient-rich and can serve as another stress factor on the yeast.

More closely related to the mythological descriptions of dunder is a substance known as muck, which is distinctly unpleasant—its purpose is to add a dollop of acids and acid-producing bacteria to the wash, and many of those acids, like acetic acid, are pungent and generally offensive until they are converted to sweet-smelling and delicious esters. One American craft rum distiller showed me his experimental muck pit, which was stored in an old barrel. It was chocolate-brown and acrid—a cesspool that had already claimed the lives of a dozen flies and maggots.

Muck is made from dunder and other sugar estate trash and is designed to encourage bacteria and the production of acids. But its usage in rum production today is rare and seems most popular not in commercial rum production, but in the experiments of some of the more adventurous, or reckless, home distillers who have replicated muck pits in their backyards, documenting their results on enthusiast forums online. Depending on your tolerance for grotesque photos of moldy, bacteria-laden goop, it's a fascinating corner of the web to take off to.

Whether knowing the science behind distilling is enough to get over the disgust factor of seeing what some people will run through a still and then wash down their throats, it's worth remembering that as ill-advised as it would seem to be encouraging ambient bacteria to flourish in something that's going to be consumed, distilling only pulls out the volatile compounds in a solution. Therefore, a whole, live bacterium is no more distillable than you are, which is to say: partially and with disastrous effects on the organism.

As Demerara Distillers in Guyana created a range of different marks from different distillation processes, at Hampden, which only runs their wash through pot stills, Wisdom creates a number of different marks by varying the fermentation process, manipulating the amount of cane-juice vinegar and dunder and the length of fermentation, which can be distinguished by the concentration of esters they contain.

"Let's say we want a rum with 500 parts per million of esters. To set that fermentation, we are going to have to adjust the amount of cane juice we add to it, so that we don't have a large amount of acids," Wisdom said.

The result is a range of flavorful, fruity, funky rums with ester concentrations ranging from a few hundred parts per million to well over one thousand. At about 570 parts per million, Rum Fire is far from the most ester-laden rum Hampden can produce. The highest-ester rums, however, are typically reserved for other applications such as blending to add fruity notes to lower-ester rums or to use in confectionary or for aromas in non-beverage applications. They also find their way into what is known as *rum verschnitt*, a German product that is made from a small percentage of very flavorful rum mixed with a neutral spirit in the way that blended American whiskey can be made from a little bit of real whiskey and a lot of neutral spirit. Because Jamaican rum was typically used to give character to what could otherwise be a lackluster product, a long-standing law in the country prevents distilleries from exporting any rum over 1,600 esters as a way to preserve volumes.

Ester concentration alone doesn't tell you how a rum will taste, however. It is just a measure, like proof, albeit one that's correlated to intensity of flavor rather than intensity of alcohol.

At Hampden, no matter how many esters any given rum mark has, to be a good rum it also must have the distillery's signature combination of flavors, Wisdom told me.

"What are those qualities that are specific to Hampden?" I asked. Instead of turning to the adjectival, he pivoted and grabbed a bottle of an even higher-ester mark, pouring it into a snifter and telling me to take a whiff.

As soon as I did my eyes popped with the intensity and Grant grabbed my camera eager to capture the face in case I made it again.

"It almost smells like . . .," I said, trying to conjure a few aroma descriptors, but Wisdom cut me off.

"I don't want you to try to differentiate the different smells," he told me. "I just want you to get that . . ."

"That Hampdenness!" Grant interjected. Indeed it's a quality that, once you've let it lodge in your scent memory, becomes as distinctively recognizable as the aroma of, say, fresh-cut pineapple.

That Hampdenness is why all that accreted character at Hampden was worth preserving. Hampden was basically a habitat, part of which was attributable to its particular place on a particular island, and part of which had developed with the distillery over the centuries. Together those qualities made for something that, at least in the lore of rum (and it's lore that has echoed in many other spirits stories), is irreplicable.

"We've found that even at different distilleries where they might know each other's processes, the rums that they make are not going to be the same thing," Wisdom said. "I used to work at Monymusk and I used to work at New Yarmouth, two distilleries within five miles of each other, and while at Yarmouth I was trying to duplicate one of the marks from Monymusk. I worked there. I used to make that rum. At Yarmouth, I couldn't."

"I think the locations tend to have some amount of influence on the outcome of the rum," he added.

What Wisdom was talking about, in essence, was terroir, that concept frequently applied to wine and occasionally to other food and drink that links a product's particular characteristics to its particular place. Often terroir is discussed in terms of physical environment—how a certain marginal soil stresses grapes to result in a wine of a particular intensity, for example. But there's more to the idea than just that.

Chemist Rafael Arroyo, in his summary of the rum research he conducted from January 1936 to October 1942 at the Agricultural Experiment Station in what was then Rio Piedras and is today part of San Juan, Puerto Rico, wrote that he had also heard those claims that certain rums, like Jamaica's flavorful ones, couldn't be reproduced anywhere else. But he set about to see if he could do it and to figure out whether there was any truth to the assertions some of the Jamaicans' competitors were making that their rums were illegitimate and could only be the product of added flavors. One of Arroyo's research focuses was on identifying the specific bacteria that produced the most distinctive flavors of that rum and introducing them to his fermentation elsewhere.

"Previous to our investigations the idea prevailed that the types of export rums produced by the Island of Jamaica could not be duplicated elsewhere. The writer thought otherwise. . . . He started his own experiments on the fermentation and distillation of such rums. As the work developed we have been able to produce every one of the heavy rum types manufactured in Jamaica, and the samples of such rums have been declared equal excellence to the best Jamaican products by European experts," he wrote.

But Arroyo doesn't report that he precisely matched a Jamaican mark; instead, he seems to be talking about stylistic replication. Nonetheless, what's most useful about his claim is that the Puerto Rican rum industry didn't adopt the Jamaican high-ester style. In fact, the style of rum produced in Puerto Rico—most famously by Bacardí, but also in a similar style by the Serrallés distillery—is about as far from the Hampden style as you can get in molasses-based rums. The Puerto Ricans' rum is exceedingly light and dry, with the premium aged rums deriving significant flavors from the barrel rather than from fermentation and distillation.

Terroir, in other words, is a social and historical phenomenon as well.

There's certainly no reason Hampden has to produce the funky, high-ester rums that they do—there are plenty of producers of delicious, lighter rums out there who are much less concerned with fruity ester content and all the ways to boost it. There's nothing preventing Hampden from doing that out on their estate in Trelawny. Nor do they have to go to such extremes to get a good, flavorful rum. One of the most surprising things Shaun Caleb at Demerara Distillers told me was that the wash that goes into all but one of their stills is exactly the same, and it's made with commercial brewer's yeast. Yet Demerara rums are nothing if not rich and full-flavored. But that Hampden does all of these things is what makes it unique, just as all of those different stills at Demerara Distillers make it unique. If this sounds too obvious to mention, it is nonetheless something that seems to be lost in an overly acute focus on technical minutiae.

We tend to forget, I suspect, in a world of gas chromeographs and mass spectrometers and complex devices of entirely human design (i.e., the iPhone) that you can do a lot without actually knowing what it is, exactly, you are doing. We do this to ourselves, in fact, every time we take a drink. We know that ethanol, depending on the quantity, is a stimulant, a depressant, an inhibitor of coordination, a toxin, a stress-reliever, and much more, yet we have no idea why alcohol affects us the way it does or why taking a drink feels like it does. The biochemistry of alcohol is still largely a mystery. Nonetheless, we pour some rum into a glass, take a drink, and generally get the expected results—we know how to carry out the process, even if we don't understand the why behind that process. The why behind the process can in some cases be seen as merely adjunctive, interesting certainly and useful diagnostically, but ultimately beside the point, as Caleb told me when we discussed how having access to all that new equipment changed the rum.

"Over the last decade or so we have really put a lot of effort into understanding at a more chemical, fundamental level how those marks have to be maintained to preserve the quality. I'd say that's been really the only change. Everything else is pretty much as it was decades or centuries ago," he said.

What Hampden represents is not a case study of how to produce acids and alcohols and link them together into esters to give your rum delicious flavor, though it certainly does represent that. What it really represents is a process or a custom—a way of doing things—in a particular place that is bound up in a particular identity—that Hampdenness, which is something that transcends chemistry. And in fact, it must: much of the science behind what is happening during fermentation was only being worked out coincidentally with the rise of the rum industry. It was only in the middle of the nineteenth century that scientists, with reservation, began to agree that it was a microorganism known as yeast that was doing the thing. In other words, the researchers came at it long after it had already been harnessed in a plethora of exotic permutations by distillers the world over.

It was a point driven home to me when I asked Wisdom why Hampden's signature was what it was and not something different.

"Whatever it was, either it was that they just liked a fruity rum, or they discovered it by chance in their fermentation, I don't know. But over time, that is the tradition or the process that has been developed, and that is what Hampden is noted for, this type of rum," he said.

Like drinking, it exists and we like it, so why not? It was an important lesson as I made my way back to Kingston en route to my next rum distillery, where I'd encounter an aspect of rum making that was even more about producing something just so.

RUM NEGRONI

Hampden's rums are incredibly big, bold, and more than just a bit racy—even when aged in oak as they are to produce the excellent cocktail rum Smith & Cross. High ester and high proof—57% abv, to be exact—Smith & Cross isn't for the tame at heart. But just because this rum's got a bit of wildness, doesn't mean it requires a wild cocktail. In fact, one of my favorite ways to drink Smith & Cross rum is in a variation on the classic gin cocktail, the Negroni, an application that I first learned about in a recipe by Joaquín Simó published on the website PUNCH (www.punchdrink.com).

1 ounce Smith & Cross rum

1 ounce Campari

1 ounce sweet vermouth

Twist of orange peel

In the traditional Negroni fashion, stir with ice and strain into a glass over ice. Garnish with the orange peel.

CHAPTER 4

Rum Conditioning

If there was any advantage to being bumped and jostled and careened around Jamaica's narrow, rough rural roads yet another time, it was in providing the necessary frame of reference to instantly comprehend a comment one European-based rum industry veteran would make to me several months after my trip to Jamaica, about the difficulty rum producers have in doing business in a remote archipelago of islands with comparatively underdeveloped infrastructure.

"You drove into Worthy Park," he said of a Jamaican distillery he already knew I'd visited. "A beautiful, beautiful place."

Indeed it was, traveling up those winding roads until I thought we were going to run out of switchbacks, then suddenly breaking through the scrum of thick jungle to be met by the wide, coursing Lluidas valley, planted in a green bed of thousands of acres of sugarcane.

"Try bringing a pot still there," he said. "It has to go through the same road." Sometimes you get why development experts roll their eyes at the fetishization of the unspoilt.

The story, in fact, was a variation on a theme. One distiller in the country told me that to bring in a new still they had to close down over one hundred miles of road, lest they meet another vehicle on the route and become trapped.

To seemingly emphasize the point yet again, two days after leaving Hampden, I headed back out toward the center of Jamaica, not destined for Worthy Park this time but Appleton Estate, though the experience was the same. I left Kingston in the morning with Catherine McDonald, the brand's public relations manager, and Joy Spence, its long-serving master blender. We had started out earlier that morning on a smooth, paved toll road running on the drier, flatter landscape that surrounds the capital city, but quickly we crossed over into the lush Jamaican countryside. The roads narrowed and jogged into the truck drivers' bane that they were. Produce vendors stretched out along the shoulder, selling avocados and mangos and a delightful fruit Spence would introduce me to on our way back called sweetsop, which is perfumey and creamy and, I worry, far too delicate to ever become a staple along the global cold chain.

After we crested the ridge above the Nassau Valley in St. Elizabeth Parish and I'd snapped a few pictures of Appleton Estate's thousands of acres of cane fields below, we pulled into the distillery. My clothes and an orbit of the upholstery around me in McDonald's SUV were splotched with what I had hoped would be my morning coffee, and I was again raving about how beautiful and green Jamaica was.

Appleton Estate is just on the other side of Cockpit Country from Hampden, but in terms of spirits-world geography, it might as well be on an entirely different continent.

This was apparent as soon as I stepped out of McDonald's vehicle and was still futilely brushing at the coffee stains, hoping they'd fall out. As at Hampden, there were a few peacocks around, but here they were strutting along paved pathways that led around corporate displays and through colorfully painted equipment, some of it historic, some of it historic re-creations. It was clearly a place used to receiving guests and would, several months after my visit, begin on a multimillion-dollar renovation.

The juxtaposition between Hampden and Appleton was a bit like that between my Port Antonio guest house, with its steep, muddy driveway and mosquito net–draped beds, and one of Jamaica's resorts, with its all-inclusive everything and "authentic" on-beach bars. And, in some ways, the reasons for the contrast are similar, too.

Appleton is part of J. Wray and Nephew, Jamaica's oldest company. J. Wray, as the company is affectionately known by some, has in turn been owned since 2012 by Gruppo Campari, the large Italian liquor conglomerate that owns the eponymous aperitif along with dozens of other liquor brands, including Wild Turkey bourbon and Espolòn tequila. Appleton uses only estate-produced rum and, unlike the island's other producers, has long benefited from the much more lucrative revenues brought in by its widely distributed brand, which traces its origins back to at least 1749, rather than bulk rum, which until very recently made up the majority of the sales at the island's other distilleries.

Not only does that mean that the Appleton distillery has long drawn a portion of Jamaica's tourist hordes and has the infrastructure to take care of them—large restaurant; aggressive air-conditioning—but also that stored within J. Wray's facilities are some 250,000 barrels of rum, just slowly aging away, waiting until the time they will eventually be blended into one of Appleton's rums. The estate typically offers its rums in expressions of up to twenty-one years of age, and sometimes even older, such as when it has something to celebrate, like it did in 2012 when Appleton released 800 fifty-year-old bottles to mark Jamaica's semicentennial. They were marketed as the world's oldest barrel-aged rums and sold for $5,000 a bottle. Such ages are unusual, however. The general rule is that there is little benefit to aging more than about twelve years in the tropics.

Spence, McDonald, and I, along with a gentleman from an Italian sommelier and bartenders association who had met us once we arrived, walked down to one of the barrel houses. When we opened the doors and walked in, we found that maybe the barrels weren't aging quite so slowly after all.

The warehouse was dim—resting barrels need little light—and redolent of rum and wood, as you'd expect. But it was also surprisingly cool, a jarring contrast to the rising temperatures outside.

Was this the special warehouse they kept temperature controlled just for those cooler-clime visitors with a penchant for passing out, I wondered? Hardly.

"We call it rum-conditioning," Spence said. That was the way the building always was.

What was happening was that some of the alcohol stored in those barrels was evaporating and rapidly pulling heat toward the warehouse ceiling.

As I was to later learn, Appleton loses about 6 percent of its rum to evaporation per year, a phenomenon in the spirits industry that's known as the angel's share.

If you travel around the Caribbean talking to enough rum producers, one phrase you will hear repeatedly is "tropical aging." Often it is said with all the distinction and weight of a reverential proper noun—not unlike how distillers farther north love to describe their barrels as "slow aging." It's enough to think that there is something mystical happening in those barrels sitting in the warehouses ringing the equatorial latitudes. But tropical

Barrel storage at the Appleton Estate in Jamaica. Distillers the world over lose some of their product to evaporation from wooden barrels during aging, known as the "angel's share." Owing to the heat and the humidity of the tropics however, rum producers lose several times more product than produc-ers in colder climates. Barrel storehouses are also often where tax collectors do their assessing and are therefore often tightly controlled.

aging is simply what it says it is: aging that takes place in the tropics, as opposed to aging that takes place in the temperate zones.

What is a bit mystical, however, is oak-barrel aging itself.

To delve into the story of what happens when an alcoholic liquid is put into a wooden barrel and left to rest there for a while is to confront again that problem that arose when discussing funky fermentations: intentionality.

Oak barrels lend all sorts of wonderful flavors to the spirits—whiskey, tequila, cognac, as well as rum—aged in them. Oakiness is one of the big ones, of course, and often vanilla, caramel, toastiness, and those chemicals called tannins, which manifest as astringency.

The historical record is unclear as to exactly when people started putting their distillates in oak to age them as such—putting them in barrels, in other words, and just leaving them there, with the intention that they would improve with age. However, what *is* clear is that the barrels weren't originally filled with spirit to make the spirit better. Instead they were filled with spirit because it was the way to get it from point A to point B, from producer to customer.

Wooden barrels were the containers of their day, Henry H. Work writes in his history, *Wood, Whiskey and Wine*. And in one of history's happier coincidences, as it happens, their heyday coincided with the rise of alcohol distillation.

Just as the number of standardized shipping containers flowing across the world's oceans today is used as an indicator of the global economy, the burgeoning colonial-era Atlantic trade also resulted in a concomitant explosion in the number of barrels needed to haul goods between the expanding intercontinental economy of the Old World and the New. Water and food needed by the sailors and provisions for the Caribbean plantations would come sealed in barrels from Europe, and in return ships would fill them back up with sugar and, increasingly, rum to supply European markets.

So important were barrels to the era's maritime industry that British law required all ships to take on a cooper to see to the barrels onboard. (The cooper was useful for other carpentry tasks as well. As Work notes, a ship and a barrel are pretty much two sizes of the same thing, except that one's a wooden vessel designed to keep a liquid out and the other is a wooden vessel designed to keep it in.)

The rum that went into those barrels was, of course, unaged, but as it jostled around in the ship's hold it started undergoing a plethora of changes, the chemistry of which is as complicated and esoteric as what is going on in those long, open-air fermentations at Hampden. Vanillin—responsible, as you'd expect, for those vanilla notes—seeped into the rum from the degradation of the wood, which started when the barrel's wooden staves, those narrow planks that form the barrel's longitudinal run when stood on end, were first heated to be bent into shape. Joining the migration of flavors are other compounds as well, including that which gives the spirit a bit of spice and another that contributes a note reminiscent of coconut. A number of acids are also released, which help form more of those esters and their alluring flavors. Meanwhile, the charred oak of the barrel—the result of a process initially used to rid a barrel of the flavors of whatever was in it before—helps lend a caramel sweetness, while the charcoal created by the firing process also seems to reduce the presence of some offensive compounds, not unlike a countertop water filter.

Eventually spirits producers and drinkers caught on to the fact that barrel-aged rums, whiskies, and cognacs tasted better, and that those improvements usually increased the longer the spirit stayed in the barrel (unlike wine, which will evolve significantly over time just from the exposure to air, distilled spirits are fairly stable off the still and undergo significant changes only when exposed to something reactive, like wooden barrels). During the first half of the nineteenth century, the practice of barrel aging for quality became well established.

Even before then, however, correspondents in the Caribbean had taken to advocating the consumption of rum that had been allowed to sit for a while after it came off the still. Their enthusiasm, however, was not out of concern for the epicurean, but rather for drinkers' well-being. Lead contamination, leached from still parts made with the toxic metal, apparently plagued rum at the time, and letting the rum rest gave that lead a chance to precipitate out and settle on the bottom of the barrel. Kill-devil, indeed.

The reason Caribbean distillers are so eager to tout the tropical aging of their rums is that in the warmer, more humid climates of the West Indies those chemical reactions happen much more quickly than in a barrel aging in the cooler latitudes of, say, Kentucky, or at a distillery clinging to the edge of the North Sea.

"It's like dog years," Andrew Hassell of Barbados's West Indies Rum Distillery told me. "A rum year in the Caribbean is like three or four years elsewhere, so a four-year rum in the Caribbean is really like twelve to sixteen years in Scotland."

That may sound like a good thing, and it's not necessarily bad, but it comes with a significant trade-off. Just as flavor from the barrel moves more quickly into the rum than it would in someplace cooler, the rum also moves out of the barrel and into the atmosphere at much higher rates as well. And, as it turns out, the angels in the Caribbean are fonder of the hard stuff than their counterparts elsewhere.

"Humidity is probably the killer factor," explained Allen Smith, master blender at Mount Gay, on the other side of the island from Hassell's distillery.

"When your environment is humid, the net movement tends to be of alcohol from the barrel to the atmosphere. If the atmosphere is less humid, then the converse is true; you lose more water than alcohol. It is trying to reach an equilibrium inside and outside the barrel, and the one outside the barrel is not possible, it will never happen, but that's the movement," he said.

Any water a producer loses during aging can be added back in before bottling—in fact, doing so is often a key step in the production process, to bring the spirit down to proof. But the whole point of distilling is to produce alcohol to later pour into a bottle, not send off into the atmosphere. As one distiller told me, one measure of a good distiller is how efficiently he or she can do that. And aging is hardly an efficient process; it ties up capital as the distiller waits, losing a bit of potential product every second.

The problem that arises for rum producers from all of this is that for consumers weaned on scotch and bourbon, as many consumers seeking out fine, aged rums tend to be, age is paramount—and the older the product, so the thinking goes, the better it is. Especially with scotch, it's not uncommon to see whiskey aged for twenty years or longer—a supremely challenging, expensive, and perhaps not altogether worthwhile endeavor in the Caribbean.

"To get it to thirty years old, one barrel of thirty-year-old, you'd need one hundred barrels at year zero?" Raphael Grisoni, the Mount Gay managing director, asked as a point of clarification while we were standing around talking to Smith.

"It wouldn't be far off from that," Smith said.

But that doesn't stop some producers from trying to tap into that desire for decades-old spirits. Look on any liquor store rum shelf and you can see producers from all over grappling with the gulf between consumers' perception of what is a desirable age versus what they are actually able to produce.

In the United States the only legal age statements are those that say something like "four years old," or "aged four years." If that's what the bottle says, short of fraud, you can be reasonably assured that's how long the rum in it has sat in a barrel. (Time sitting outside of a barrel, say, chilling in a giant stainless steel storage tank, doesn't count, though occasionally a bottler will stick on a vintage year for various reasons; bottlers are also allowed to understate the age, calling what's really a ten-year-old rum eight years old, if they desire.) But see one that has a giant "7" or even "23" with nary a mention of the words "aged" or "years" in sight and you are probably getting something that's not quite as mature as it claims (and be wary, too, of in-store shelf tags, which on occasion repeat those numbers and erroneously claim that the product has been aged in oak that long).

But more rum producers are moving away from age statements altogether. The reason, as I learned, is that aging is not simple arithmetic— there's far more to it than just putting some rum in a barrel and letting it sit.

As Spence and I walked through the Appleton warehouse, she explained that many of the barrels were ex-bourbon, which is common practice at rum distilleries. Unique among spirits, the rules governing what can be called bourbon—in addition to requiring it to be made from 51 percent corn—stipulate that the spirit must be aged in new charred oak barrels. Once a bourbon distiller empties a barrel, it can't be refilled again with the next batch. However, a barrel's life span is considerably longer than the few years most bourbon is aged—well cared for, they can last several decades, so bourbon distilleries typically sell them on to producers of other spirits, including rum, who are then free to reuse them as many times as they want. As they do, the degree to which the barrel reacts with the spirit that's stored in it changes over the barrel's life span. New barrels are aggressive in the flavors they impart on spirits, while older barrels are less so. For that reason, barrels of different ages and characteristics give distillers yet another variable with which to manipulate the characteristics of the rums they produce.

"We have different grades: A, B, C, D, E barrels," Hassell told me. "If you put an identical rum in an A barrel, a B barrel, a C barrel, a D barrel, and an E barrel and you have them in there for a year, two years, and you take them out you will get five completely different types of rum from those barrels," he said.

At Appleton, Spence said that rums straight off the still typically go into young barrels. Once the rum has aged and they've taken it out of the barrel, say, after twelve years, they won't then turn around and put another batch of fresh rum in that same barrel. Instead they'd transfer in rums that had started off aging in a different barrel, a process that helps prevent the spirits from becoming too woody and acrid, which is a common problem with poorly managed long-aged rums. Continued aging in older barrels also contributes flavors that would not appear in a rum aged solely in a younger barrel.

Beyond time, a host of other factors influences how a barrel interacts with what's inside. Barrel size matters: smaller barrels have more surface area with which to interact with the liquid, thus speeding up aging, though as their use by American craft whiskey distillers has shown, doing so often comes with the cost of producing a spirit with a raw woody note that many find unpleasant. Each barrel itself is also different, as are different species of oak, and even the same species harvested in a different place. Where the barrel is stored in the warehouse can matter significantly, as different locations are subject to different levels of heat and humidity. Moreover, the characteristics of the rum itself affect how it interacts with the wood.

"Pot still rums age much faster than column-distilled rums in terms of transformation and flavor profile because the ester content of the pot still rums [is higher], so the aging is accelerated. It is more reactive," Spence said. Also influential is the alcohol content of the spirit when it goes into the barrels—too high and it will absorb water, drying the barrels out and causing leaks; too low and you change the flavor profile of your spirit and also need a lot more barrels for each bottle of rum you eventually bottle.

Given all that, what then is the significance of age? Does age—or rather, a label's age statement as a comparative tool—even matter?

Some distillers are unequivocal that it does not.

"It is totally uneven," Smith said of age. The philosophy is reflected on the bottles of Smith's Mount Gay rums. From the light mixing Silver expression all the way up to the brand's highest-end 1703 rum, none of the bottles gives an age statement, though on Mount Gay's website the range of ages used in some bottles is listed.

Of course, aged-rum production also lags by however many years old that rum is—what a distillery is selling of its twelve-year-old rum today, after all, is rum that was made twelve years ago, and if demand suddenly spikes above supply it will take over a decade to meet it, an unenviable position in a fashion-fickle world.

Nicaraguan rum Flor de Caña, for example, released new bottle designs several years ago that subtly dropped the bottle's age statement. What was once "slow aged seven years" became simply "7" and "slow aged," presumably meant to be legally two separate statements (the latter, rather remarkably, is also trademarked).

"Thus, today's Flor de Caña 7 may be similar in flavor profile to Flor de Caña 7 Year Old, but the rum within has no guarantee of seven years of aging," wrote Matt Pietrek, the blogger behind the excellent *Cocktail Wonk* rum blog.

Flor de Caña 7 is an enjoyable rum and at a few dollars either side of $20 is generally considered a good value, so does it matter now that it may no longer be seven years old? Aside from a label that may be possibly misleading to some—but not you, because now you've read this—probably not, at least not when it comes to deciding whether to drink the stuff. Where age statements matter, some producers have argued, is when it comes to assessing cost. (For what it's worth, Flor de Caña's website still maintains language that the rums are as old as the number on their label.)

Because producers give away product to angels, because they sequester capital, because they take effort and time to manage, barrel aging costs money. Therefore, longer-aged bottles, so the argument goes, can justifiably cost customers more, and those that are just spouting off meaningless numbers in a game of liquor-store-shelf Powerball are trying to bilk customers with marketing flash covering for a lack of real value.

It's not an invalid point. But it's also one that would seem to miss the substantial purpose of branded marketing in modern capitalism, which always comes with that one rule: *caveat emptor.*

As beautiful and aromatically pleasing as stacks upon stacks of barrels running the length of a long tropical rickhouse are, and with their staves so exquisitely and authentically weathered as to trump even the hippest specimen of Brooklyn industrial chic, and with the air thick with raw wood and rum, I hadn't come out to Appleton just to hang out and learn about barrels. Instead, what I really came to Appleton to learn was the technique that gave Spence her title of master blender.

In the rum world, production is often divided into two distinct roles, or at least two distinct areas of focus: distilling and blending. When someone is primarily focused on directing fermentation and distillation, they are often called the master distiller, while a person whose role it is to create the liquids that the customer will eventually drink is called a master blender.

Sometimes creating that final liquid is a straightforward task. In a small craft distillery, such as those popping up across America, a producer may just take whatever comes off the still, less the heads and tails, cut it down to proof, and stick it in a bottle—aging it first, if it is to be aged. They may also mix some of those aged barrels together to smooth out any inconsistency, as they may do in a tank for unaged rum, unless it is to be a "single barrel" rum. In that case, they'll fill each bottle from one barrel, letting consumers experience any inconsistencies that appear from batch to batch. Most producers will also blend in a bit of caramel color to make sure the tone of all the bottles match when they sit together on the shelf. Then it is out to consumers. Regardless of the exact process, though, the point is that there's a pretty direct path from what comes off the still to what you get in the bottle.

At Appleton and many of the traditional Caribbean rum distilleries, however, the trip from the still is, well, like those Jamaican roads, not quite so straightforward but studded with a cornucopia of flavors. Remember those organoleptic balls of Andrew Hassell's metaphor, which were whipped up in our fermentation, grabbed out in different combinations during distillation, then finally sent off for a bit of R&R for various lengths and in accommodations of various qualities? Each different set of those distillates becomes a distillery's marks, and it's the blender's job to take those marks and put them back together into something that people will want to drink, either by creating a tantalizing new rum or faithfully maintaining the consistency of a popular existing one.

While not all distilleries have a master blender—at Hassell's West Indies Rum Distillery, for example, a panel of tasters makes blending decisions—at those that do, the master blender is a bit like the rum auteur, crafting the distillery's products within the brand's identity, either following input from marketers who tell them what customers seem to want or trying to make something that they believe customers will gravitate toward because it's delicious. After the scientific reductionism of fermentation and distilling and aging, blending is a much more abstract and nebulous task. Science is going to be of little help here; instead, we're going to have to wander down the hall to the art wing. As Lloyd Forbes, the manager of a Jamaican-rum industry association called the Spirits Pool, whose job is to probably not pick favorites, told me, "There is no such thing as a bad rum and a good rum"—there's just drinkers' own cultivated tastes. But some tastes, it seems, are more cultivated than others. Few, though, are as renowned as Spence's.

Like so many on the production side of the spirits industry, Spence's background is in chemistry, which is the role she started in when she began as the chief chemist in J. Wray and Nephew's lab in 1981, after studying chemistry in Jamaica and England. There she began working closely with Appleton's previous master blender, Owen Tulloch.

Arguably more than even having good taste—in the aesthetic sense—a master blender needs to have good taste, and especially good smell, in the sensory sense, which is something that takes more than just having a working nose and a few taste buds. Just as there are some people who are "supertasters," who experience flavors to an exquisite degree, the same is true with smells.

To identify members of their staff who are particularly good at evaluating aromas in spirits, distillers will set up a battery of tests, such as placing a series of rums that are supposed to match a particular reference and seeing whether someone can identify the one with the flaw, or having them match various rums with various reference samples. What they are looking for is not whether someone can twirl a bit of rum around in their glass and spit out a tasting note to slap on the back of the bottle, but rather if they can pick up on the subtleties that make one liquid comparatively different from another, or express confidence that they are the same. Not, "This has notes of banana and lychee and sugarcane cut just this morning as the tropical sun was peaking and the warm Caribbean waves crashed in the background," but, "glass 'A' and glass 'B' are the same, while glass 'C' is fruitier."

At Brugal, a tradition-bound rum producer in the Dominican Republic, the auditioning process to become a *maestro ronero*—there are currently five—can take a year, and that's after they've already developed extensive experience in the company. (They also have to be members of the Brugal family.)

"You need to have really good taste, a really good nose, a really good sensory memory. But also it is a combination of how you manage yourself, how you get involved, and what you can offer," said Jassil Villanueva, who joined Brugal in 2011 at age 24. "We work as a team. Each one of us has particular characteristics. We have one who is really creative, really crazy, out of the box. We have some of us who are more conservative, some of us who are really good with memory and, for example, can remember that special flavor we added to that product that wasn't right and we had to change it."

For Villanueva, like Spence, it was being adept at the not altogether flatteringly named task of "nosing" a spirit that got her to the position she holds today.

"I've always been detecting various aromas that nobody else was smelling," Spence said. "But I never thought I would actually apply that to a profession."

Eventually she did, though, and in 1997 she began her nearly three-decades-and-counting tenure in the top ranks of the spirits world, which have long been dominated by men. In fact, when Spence became Appleton's master blender, she was the first woman to hold that position, not just in rum but in any category. Likewise, Villanueva was Brugal's first female *maestra ronera*. In addition to Spence and Villanueva, a slate of other women has also joined the upper echelons of spirits development, and the inequality is ever so slowly righting. Nonetheless, the gender inequality in the spririts world is a particularly ironic one because women, research suggests, have a sharper sense of taste and smell than men.

But Spence has moved on. Today she can even take on technology.

"I think my nose has become so trained that I can actually smell a rum and tell the technicians of our laboratory how many esters they are going to pick up on their machine," she said.

On our drive to the distillery, Spence was disarming, as keen to chat about Jamaica's regional cuisines and the latest scuttlebutt on the Zika virus as she was to delve into the intricacies of rum making. Nonetheless, I was a little intimidated when that Italian fellow visitor and I sat down in a small presentation building on the estate grounds. There we found four small bottles before us. Each was filled with blending rums with an increasingly darker shade of liquid labeled from A to D.

Each represented its own mark of sorts, with some delicious qualities along with obvious shortcomings that made them rums undesirable on their own. The first was a light white rum with a lot of bright tropical notes, but fairly harsh; the second was a light aged rum with a good mouthfeel but little else; the third was a heavy aged rum with abundant estery fruit notes but a poor finish; and the fourth was a longer aged rum with a wan body but a great finish of caramel and vanilla.

Our task, Spence explained, was to take these rums and mix them together to produce a final rum that would blend well with cocktails.

Now, I am certainly in no position to sign up for a contest against a laboratory's machines of analytical chemistry, like a brave Jeopardy contestant squaring off against Watson. But how hard could this be, really, I wondered? Before me were four bottles of good rum, after all, and by now I had tasted plenty of good rum. All I had to do was pour.

So I started mixing . . . and mixing.

"Flavor, mouthfeel, finish, sweetness, those are the key things" in a good rum, Spence told me.

My strategy was to start with a lot of the fourth rum, the one with the lingering notes of caramel and vanilla—quintessential oak-barrel flavors—on the theory that the rum's finish was its "base" in essence, and to build anything it's always necessary to go from the ground up. Also, my favorite rums are those with complexity, the ones that start off sauntering through the produce aisle before finding their inner Marco Polo among the spices, and finally finishing with a long, slow whiff over a cigar box. With those

Appleton master blender Joy Spence scoops up a ladleful of molasses from a pot at a tourist display at Appleton Estate in Jamaica. Because of the widespread decline of the Caribbean sugar industry, rum producers on many islands must import much of the molasses they need for rum production. Appleton is one of the few that is able to produce all of the molasses they need from estate-grown cane.

caramel and vanilla endnotes in place, I figured I could just work back, layering each flavor as if I were building an itinerary of a dream journey.

But then I would put in a splash more of the first rum, and suddenly I'd find myself lingering too long in the tropics, sun-burned and tiring of picking sand out of everywhere, so I'd throw in more fruit and suddenly it was the day after Thanksgiving bleeding into the week after Christmas and everything was leftover pie, overstewed. So I decided to throw in more of the mark with texture and found myself with something that was all touch and no taste, my rum's nose, body, and finish falling away in a trip to the seedier side of Vegas.

The goal was to take one plus one four times and make it equal something greater, yet I kept going the wrong way on the number line. And this was the introductory course—in fact, it wasn't even that. It was one being taken for participation credit only. When Spence is mixing rums, she's using far more than four marks. How many, exactly, she wouldn't reveal—the precise number was a trade secret, she said. But Appleton advertises the number of marks in some of its bottles, including stating that there are twenty used in its Reserve Blend expression, so she's working with at least five times as many as I was.

The skill required to be a good master blender goes beyond, then, having a sense of what flavors have an affinity for each other and being able to replicate those combinations of flavors with consistency. It also entails remembering the characteristics of each mark made at the distillery.

"It took quite a long time to understand the flavor profiles of the different marks, or their age, because there is a big difference in nosing and tasting a spirit when it is just distilled and the spirit after it's been aging for twelve years," Spence said. "So you have to be around for at least twelve years."

J. Wray and Nephew is the largest distiller in Jamaica and it has a lot of variables it can manipulate, including both a pot and column still and a curated range of sugarcane varieties, which they believe, in contrast to some other producers, have their own specific organoleptic characteristics that carry over when converted into molasses and on into rum.

"I know what different rums to select so that when I blend them together they will create these exceptional flavor notes, because each rum has its own distinctive flavor profile," Spence said. "In our rums, our apricot and the peach come from the sugarcane varieties; the orange peel, ginger, and nutmeg come from the pot distillation; the pineapple, banana, and lychee notes come from the column still distillation; and the coffee, cacao, hazelnut, almond, and butterscotch come from the oak aging."

In particular, Spence said, a distinctive orange peel note comes from Appleton's wide, stubby pot stills which, if some producers liken their stills to a "gooseneck," is definitely a duck, and an ashamed-looking, droopy-headed one at that.

Unlike Hampden, which skews its rum dramatically toward those fruity rum esters, Appleton's have more balance. Though Spence clearly blends in a bit of Jamaican funk, she gives the wood flavors and lighter column characteristics significant prominence, too.

The precise styling of the rum, however, depends on the type of rum that she is making. High-end sipping rums, for example, are the destination for those long-aged marks, which give them a rich base of vanilla, coffee, and cacao, while aged rums destined for classic cocktails—think (and then go ahead and make yourself one) a Rum Old Fashioned or any of the simple whiskey-cocktail stalwarts—need more young rum to give them a jolt of fruit and spice to complement the other ingredients.

"If you have too much wood and vanilla and coffee, it tends to overpower the ingredients that you use in your cocktail," she said.

Some blenders even have the ability to pull from flavors produced by different types of oak barrels. Brugal, for example, ages in both ex-bourbon barrels made from white American oak and from ex-sherry casks made from red European oak. The first rums made with liquid aged in the ex-sherry barrels came onto the market in 2010—Brugal's history dates back to 1888—and represented a cultural shift within the company from a more traditional approach to a more innovative one.

"It was when the fourth generation officially gave the fifth generation the upgrade to work by itself," Brugal's Villanueva told me.

According to Villanueva, the white American oak brings to the rum "dry" fruits like citrus and apricot, as well as vanilla, while the sherry casks are responsible for sweeter fruit flavors, like those reminiscent of plums and raisins as well as toffee. When she's concocting a blend, her palate is further expanded by the ability to either blend in marks aged exclusively in either the bourbon or sherry barrels, or to use those that have been "doubled aged," in which the rum starts out in the ex-bourbon barrels and after several years is moved over to the sherry casks to continue aging for several more.

Once a distillery settles on a particular rum expression, its goal shifts from coming up with something unique and desirable to re-creating it consistently. Like your grandma's apple pie that you promised to bring to your family reunion, the point is to maintain heritage, not get all crazy and throw in some peaches because they just looked so good. Except in this metaphor your relatives are the distillery's customers, and not only can they vow never to show up again, they can also go off and give their money to a competitor and write a scathing review online.

To do this, distillers create a formulation, a recipe of sorts, only it doesn't describe what should go into the product so much as it describes what should come out when the blender is finished crafting the product.

"Every time we are going to produce a batch we have to accomplish a certain reference sample and we have certain parameters on notes, on mouthfeel, on wood, on spice, on dryness, and it has to be approved not only by our nose and our palate, but by the lab," Villanueva said.

However, each *maestro ronero* has some freedom as to how they reach the goal—one could use a narrower range of older rums or a wider gamut

Before aging, oak barrels are burnt, a process that contributes to the mellowing and flavors of aged spirits. Historically, the tasting or charring process was used to remove the flavor of whatever the barrel had previously stored. At the Ron Barceló distillery in the Dominican Republic.

Mike Kelly, head distiller at New Orleans' Celebration Distilling, producer of Old New Orleans Rum, burns a barrel manually.

of a young and old, or blend in a barrel that's aging precociously to balance out one that's a laggard.

"It doesn't matter the age between what we use, but we have to accomplish certain characteristics that are part of each product," she said.

But finally, then rum!

Well, almost. Not quite.

Often, though certainly not exclusively, white rums, many of which are destined for mixing, will have been aged to give them a richer flavor. To take out the brown hue left by the barrel and also to mellow the sharper edges that usually accompany them, they are charcoal filtered—a process made famous by Bacardí, which has been using the process since the middle of the nineteenth century to produce its flagship white Carta Blanca rum.

Before rum is bottled it also usually needs to be blended down to the

Charred wood slats, called staves, rest on a barrel next to bottles of rum at the Brugal distillery in the Dominican Republic. Spirits makers will burn their barrels to various intensities, called char levels, depending on the characteristics they want the barrel to impart on their product.

desired proof—a number that's typically determined by whatever the lowest level is allowed by law (40 percent, or 80 proof, in the US, a few percentage points on either side of that elsewhere).

Unfortunately, bottle proof is one of life's inevitable trade-offs. The opposite of alcohol percentage by volume is water percentage by volume, and in rum making, like with other spirits, the flavor comes from the portion of the product with the alcohol in it, not from the bit with the water in it. So a higher-proof spirit has more flavor. Drank alone, it can be a more intense experience and can still be diluted to a lower proof at home if a drinker doesn't like it that way. With cocktails, a higher-proof spirit can make them richer, or less can be used. But because fewer bottles of a higher-proof spirit can be made from a given barrel, and because producers generally pay excise taxes based upon the amount of absolute alcohol in the bottle, higher-proof spirits also cost more on the shelf—an unenviable position when prices tend to be displayed in nice, big text while proof is printed in a tiny font on the label, lacking contrast. Recently, however, craft distillers have been pushing back against the eighty-proof standard and releasing less diluted rums, or even undiluted—"barrel strength"—rum. Just don't confuse them with the common, cheap 151 rums, which are a different thing altogether (they're flammable, for one).

Back at the Appleton blending room, I had taken far longer to make my blend than my Italian co-conspirator, and everyone else was impatient. I am not going to say that Spence was watching me as I poured and repoured and futilely tried to adjust my blend, making a note of each step where I went wrong, but had she, she would have seen a clumsy blender. No matter what I did, I couldn't get my blend back into balance. I'd later learn, after talking with Spence about her process, that I should have included a lot more of the mark with fruity notes.

Eventually, though, I finished my blend and Spence came over to try it. If they were going to make a formula description for the rum I created, they could have codified it with a description of Spence's reaction. When she tried it, she responded with the weak smile that anyone who has taught knows is a layered expression of "if you don't have anything nice to say, don't say anything at all" and "well, the point was to try and you tried."

On our way out, McDonald handed me a gift bag. It contained an Appleton-branded notebook, an Appleton-branded tumbler, and a bottle of Appleton rum. She also encouraged me to take my rum with me. Needless to say, when I got back to my apartment, I packed away the Appleton bottle in my luggage and left my own creation as a gift for my Airbnb host. The Appleton "Earnest Try" expression, I am only somewhat sad to report, won't be appearing on liquor store shelves near you . . . ever.

JOY

When I asked Joy Spence which Appleton rum most had her signature as a master blender, she said the Reserve Blend. Then she one-upped my question and gave me her signature cocktail to make with it. "It's simple, nice, delicious, and all of the flavors complement each other," she said. "We usually call it a Joy." How could you refuse?

1 ounce Appleton Estate Reserve Blend
3 ounces ginger ale
Orange slices
5 dashes Angostura bitters

Juice and muddle an orange slice in a rocks glass. Add ice, then the other ingredients. Garnish with orange peel.

CHAPTER 5

Chasing Brazilian ~~Rum~~ Cachaça

One cool, slightly damp South American evening, I sat on a tiny little porch in an elevated backyard oasis of the Western Hemisphere's largest city, São Paulo in Brazil. Below me was a bright yellow, molded bowl, about the size of a kiddie pool, filled with koi. A yellow slide spiraled from the bowl, as if it were a fluorescent stream flowing up into the air. At the top, the slide connected to a giant silver sphere that looked like nothing other than a midcentury fantasy space ship that had plopped down in what is inarguably one of the most beautiful countries in the world, and decided to stay awhile.

I'd plopped down myself in São Paulo after over a month of traveling through the Caribbean sipping rum—tough life, I know—and, as a resident of New York and a curious drinker, I was craving density and a change of palate. What I found I needed to change instead was my wardrobe, so I spent my first few hours in the city walking around, trying to find a jacket. "Negro?" "Negro?" I kept trying to ask the clerks in an attempt to describe in Spanish the color—*preto*, as it turned out to be in Portuguese—I was looking for. After failing in a half-dozen shops, I decided that Brazil was too colorful, even in a city known as the land of drizzle, to match my monochrome wardrobe sensibilities, so I gave up and picked up a bottle of Brazilian sparkling wine instead, which I popped open when I returned to that porch.

I was a few sips in when my host and denizen of that sphere next to me, the architect Eduardo Longo, called out a greeting. Longo built the sphere at the end of the 1970s as a proof of concept for what he imagined to be a dense development of the modernist orbs stacked in a lattice, like the game Connect Four manifest as living space. Unfortunately, the wide-scale development never happened, but Longo continued living in the sphere and now also rents out a tiny apartment on the property that's only a few feet wider than a twin bed and a bit more than twice as long, where I was staying.

Eventually Longo asked me why I was visiting. I told him I was working on a book on rum and had come to Brazil to learn about cachaça. For a moment he looked at me quixotically, unraveling what I'd just said in his mind. Then he tried:

"Rum is made from sugarcane, too?"

Brazil may share a continent with some of the world's great rum producers—Venezuela and Guyana—and lie just south of the spirit's Caribbean birthplace, but in Brazil, where sugarcane production first really took hold in the New World and where the country's cachaça producers say the first plantation stills did as well, the last five hundred years of drinking culture have differed radically, as I was to learn.

In fact, even before I arrived in Brazil, I'd realized that I wasn't perhaps on solid ground lassoing rum and cachaça together. Shortly after I began reaching out to cachaça distillers and experts, I started to notice how my book's description would be subtly changed from "a book on rum" to "a book on cane spirits" as my emails got passed up the interview chain. When I finally spoke to those cachaça makers and experts, they'd bristle every time I linked their spirit to rum. On the other side of the Amazon rainforest, and across the Caribbean Sea, the partisanship went the other way.

"I think cachaça is a terrible drink and I don't like the taste of it at all," Frank Ward, of the West Indies Rum and Spirits Producers Association had told me in Barbados a few weeks before, when I mentioned the spirit in conversation. Many other rum producers I talked to professed a similar distaste or effected a vaguely dismissive unfamiliarity with the intricacies of cachaça.

Some of this was rivalry and tribalism, no doubt (and rightfully so, as the best spirit out there is generally the one you make) but the thing is, up until about a decade ago, many drinkers throughout the world, if they even knew what cachaça was, would have agreed with Ward and the other rum producers. Many Brazilians would have as well.

Like so much in Brazil—rivers, biodiversity, urban conglomeration, political machinations—the story of cachaça is outsized and a little dramatic.

Like rum, cachaça is indeed made from sugarcane. But the similarities stop there for the most part. The spirit cachaça is most like is the rhum agricole produced in the French West Indies—the island of Martinique, primarily, and also Guadeloupe—as both cachaça and rhum agricole are made from fresh sugarcane juice, rather than molasses or some intermediate product, and both exhibit wild grassy notes and bright acidity. But even that comparison is a bit of a stretch. Good cachaças, especially good white cachaças, tend to be lighter and more delicate than their rhum agricole counterparts. But what really sets cachaça apart from rum is its sheer volume and diversity.

According to the IWSR, a global alcoholic beverage research firm, cachaça is the ninth-most consumed spirit in the world, a not-insignificant distinction considering that cachaça, unlike whiskey, vodka, and rum, is consumed almost exclusively in Brazil. Across the country there are something like 40,000 cachaça producers which issue something like 800 million liters of cachaça a year. Unfortunately, however, "something like" is the best anyone can do; both numbers are rough estimates. The problem is, the vast majority of those cachaça distilleries—something like all but 2,000—are what are known as "informal" producers—i.e., they are illegal.

While the distinction between informal and formal cachaça distilleries is important, the real divide in the cachaça market is between what is known as *cachaça artesanal* and *cachaça industrial*—that is, as you might expect, between "artisanal cachaça" and "industrial cachaça."

Brazil is by far the world's largest grower of sugarcane, producing some 750 million metric tons in recent years. (Guyana, meanwhile, produces just two million metric tons). The sugarcane fields in Brazil are vast—they can easily be well over a hundred thousand acres—and depending on market conditions, their yield can either go to producing table sugar or transportation fuel ethanol, the latter for the domestic market, which is dominated by flex-fuel vehicles that can run on ethanol or gasoline.

The ethanol that can fuel a car and the ethanol that can fuel a party are exactly the same—the former is just purer or more concentrated than the latter and lacks the congeners that can give a spirit the desired flavor and aroma, if such things are desired. What this means is that in Brazil, where massive, highly efficient sugarcane ethanol distilleries are common, highly refined sugarcane ethanol is widely available—a bit of which can easily be diverted to produce cheap drinking alcohol. Hence: *cachaça industrial*. *Cachaça artesanal*, on the other hand, is made (or is at least supposed to be made; Brazillian law bans the use of the word "artesanal" on cachaça labels, but doesn't currently have any laws governing the terms meaning) on a much smaller scale in a pot still. It's also sometimes called *cachaça alambique*, or alembic (i.e., pot still) cachaça.

Most of Brazil's distilleries fall into the *artesanal* category, but because the efficiencies are so much greater, most of the cachaça produced is of the industrial variety, which sells for just a few reis a liter—a greenback per bottle, basically. For years this cheap, massive column-distilled cachaça gave the overall category a bad name. In Brazil it got entwined with the term *cachaceiro*—a cachaça drunkard—and became associated with poverty and provincialism while abroad it got tossed in with those exotic regional liquors that have a tendency to give travelers one wild night and a lot of regret. In the past decade, however, that image has been changing. While sales of industrial cachaças are on the decline, younger drinkers are increasingly choosing to drink artisanal cachaça alongside their previous avid imbibition of popular prestige spirits like imported vodka and whiskey. It's a trend that is coinciding with the global interest in local scale and one that was proceeded in Brazil by a boom in small-batch beer, specialty coffee, and craft cocktails, the last of which, when I was there, was undergoing a particularly intense *gin tônica* phase, with bar menus sporting separate *gin tônica* categories, not unlike the exotic martini phase in the United States with all sorts of flavors. (*That* trend, blissfully, seems to have ended sometime during the recession.)

"When we started the awareness was less than zero. The awareness of the category was literally negative," Steve Luttman, the founder of Leblon Cachaça told me when I met him in his office at a WeWork space in Lower Manhattan several months before I headed to South America. "Anybody that did know cachaça had a very negative opinion. They thought it was rocket fuel."

I'd asked him to remember back to what it was like when he launched Leblon in 2005. Luttman had lived in Brazil in the late '90s. There he met his wife and discovered cachaça. When he moved back to the US a few years later, he took a job managing and marketing the orange-liqueur brand Grand Marnier, owned by the luxury conglomerate LVMH Moët Hennessy Louis Vuitton, and gained experience in spirits.

One of the first problems he ran into when he set out to launch Leblon was that, in the US, there was no such thing as cachaça. Sure, there had been cachaças on the market previously, including Pirassununga Cachaça 51 and Pitú, two of the largest cachaça brands, which together sell globally nearly thirty million cases a year. But they included such descriptions on their labels as "made from sugarcane distillate," or, perhaps slightly more appealing from a consumer's point of view, "Brazilian rum." While they could also use the word "cachaça" on the label, it carried no more official definitional weight than the brand name—anybody could call anything cachaça if they wanted. The problem was, not anything was "cachaça," and to those who knew what cachaça was, it certainly wasn't "Brazilian rum."

"You tell a Brazilian that cachaça is 'Brazilian rum,' they are going to tell you, 'Get out of here, gringo.' It's such an imperialist thought," Luttman said. "If anything, rum should be called 'Caribbean cachaça.'"

The Brazilian government had tried, several years before Luttman started Leblon, to get official recognition of cachaça from the US liquor regulating authority, known today as the Alcohol and Tobacco Tax and Trade Bureau, or TTB, by arguing that it was a distinct class of spirits all its own—as different, regulation-wise, as "whisky" is from "gin." But because it was made from sugarcane, the TTB had no interest in creating a separate category for it from "rum."

When Luttman came out with Leblon, he set out to try again—this time getting it recognized as a specific type of rum, but one that could have just the name "cachaça" on the label, sans imperialist nonsense.

"When I came on, I saw right away that cachaça, as long as it is recognized as a rum, will never be able to get out of rum's shadows and be recognized for what it is, a cultural product of Brazil," he said. "The overall taste experience that's set up when you tell people it is rum is misleading. I do a lot of blind taste tests and nobody will ever drink cachaça and tell you that it is rum. They'll usually tell you it is tequila."

To rally support for cachaça, Leblon launched a "Legalize Cachaça" publicity campaign, complete with a "Cachaça Declaration of Independence" from rum. It read, in part: "We the People, in order to form a more perfect bar, seek to establish Cachaça as 'Cachaça,' Brazil's Noble Spirit . . . endowed by its creator with certain unalienable characteristics, that among these are a fruity nose, fresh taste, and a long, clean finish." Who knew international tradecraft could be so fun?

To move their efforts along, Leblon and cachaça's supporters, including the Brazilian government, turned also to more traditional techniques of government persuasion: they hired a lobbyist and pulled out the trade agreements. The work paid off. In the spring of 2013, just in time for the 2014 World Cup, which Brazil was hosting, the TTB issued a ruling recognizing cachaça as any sugarcane-based spirit "manufactured in Brazil in compliance with the laws of Brazil regulating the manufacture of Cachaça for consumption in that country." In return, two of America's own noble spirits, bourbon whiskey and Tennessee whiskey, received similar protection in Brazil.

The conformity wasn't perfect. Even though cachaça didn't have to be labeled as "rum," it still had to follow America's rules for "rum," which, though paltry, do include the requirement that the cachaça be bottled at no less than 40 percent ABV and be made exclusively from sugarcane. Brazil, in contrast, permits cachaças to have an alcoholic strength from 38 to 48 percent by volume, which means cachaças at the lower end of that proof that are legal in Brazil aren't allowed into the US as "cachaça." Some cachaça producers also add a little bit of cornmeal, or flour from another source such as rice, to help along the fermentation, a practice which is banned by US rules, though one that seems to still be practiced.

Nonetheless, cachaça had an identity. And with that the cachaça . . . trickled in.

In 2016 Brazil exported about eight million liters of cachaça to the world, right at about 1 percent of its legal production. Of that, about eight hundred thousand liters—10 percent—went to the US and was worth just over $1.5 million. Whiskey exports from the US to Brazil, on the other hand, are worth nearly $8 million. But the availability of cachaça is growing, with excellent bottles of artisanal cachaças arriving from, in addition to Leblon, the brands Novo Fogo, Yaguara, and Avua.

What makes cachaça so unique is a confluence of factors. It is not just the fact that it is made from sugarcane. To understand it, I headed out into the cane fields.

Leblon's distillery is located in the state of Minas Gerais—"General Mines," if we are translating, and yes, it was once an appropriate moniker. Today it is the Iowa of Brazil, Luttman told me, when he found out what American state I grew up in. Indeed, I felt at home as I stared from my bus window on the way in: field, field, field, grain silo painted with the logo of some international commodity company, field, field, field, grain silo painted . . . Well, almost at home. There were palm trees and sugarcane as well, and though I didn't ask, I doubt it was tradition to pass down to whiney children tales of walking to school through the snow uphill both ways.

Instead it was hot, nearly 90 degrees, as it is for a lot of the year, when I arrived at Leblon's distillery near Patos de Minas, though not nearly as dripping as the Caribbean. I'd come with Carlos Oliveira, who runs Leblon's production and who had picked me up earlier at my hotel.

Unlike the rum producers that use molasses, cachaça distilleries, because they use cane juice, must be close to the sugarcane fields so that they can press newly cut sugarcane and ferment the juice before it spoils. In fact, at Leblon, as at many cachaça distilleries, they grow their own sugarcane, creating in essence a cane-to-cup cachaça. As we walked out to the cane field nearest the distillery, Oliveira pointed out that Leblon's production loop is even more closed than that. Gesturing to a geyser of steam pouring out from the distillery—they had recently installed a new boiler, which apparently wasn't working perfectly—Oliveira told me they power their distillery with the stalks of sugarcane that are left over after pressing, called bagasse. The technique is common at cachaça distilleries across the country. In the rum production cycle, that bagasse usually fires boilers at the sugarcane mill where the sugar is crystalized and the molasses is produced.

A short distance from the distillery we came up on the sugarcane fields. Because of its high iron content, the soil around Patos de Minas is a striking deep burnt red—scrape all the vegetation away and you could shoot a film that is set on Mars here. Nearby, a team of cane harvesters was at work, with one guy cutting and a group of several more sheering the cane of dry leaves and stacking it in what I'd refer to as a windrow if this were Iowa and we were standing in a hayfield. Above Oliveira and me the cane soared. It was several feet taller than us and some of the tallest I'd seen on my travels. When I mentioned this to Oliveira he said that was because it was new cane, undergoing its first cutting, but he also took the moment to brag about the terrior as well.

"This is a more than one hundred tonnes per hectare field. That's really strong," he said. "It's beautiful sugarcane, you know."

Today, many of the alembic cachaças available in the US are organic, including Novo Fogo, which is entirely organic, and Yaguara, which has one bottle, its flagship "blue" cachaça, that is. Oliveira told me that Leblon was moving that way—they'd long avoided chemical pesticides, turning instead to biological controls, but they had had trouble with organic fertilizers because they could introduce bacteria to the cane, which would then interfere with the fermentation process.

On a whole, alembic cachaça producers seemed to me much fussier about their sugarcane than producers of rum from molasses, likely because they felt the qualities of their cane contributed significantly to the taste of the individual product—something few rum producers, aside from Appleton's Joy Spence, felt about their molasses, perhaps because it came in more heavily processed and homogenized.

Cane cutting is a laborious process often performed under the sun in hot climates. It also requires skill, as the methodical work of this cutter at the Leblon cachaça distillery in Brazil shows.

While Brazil has extensive machine harvesting of sugarcane in the fields that are destined for sugar and fuel, I noticed cachaça producers usually hand cut their cane, though they didn't usually burn their fields prior to harvesting. In part they did so because their fields were often small and on uneven terrain, where bringing in a harvester would make little sense. But they also did it because they said it made the resulting cachaça taste better. A skilled cane cutter, they said, is able to precisely identify the best part of each cane, chopping off the cane's top at the point where the sugar content drops and the remaining fibrous stalk, if crushed, can contribute off flavors to the resulting cachaça.

Watching the cane cutter in Leblon's fields was mesmerizing in the way watching any skilled laborer perform a well-practiced repetitive task is mesmerizing. First, he grabbed a sheaf of sugarcane, then he raised his machete and brought it down at the bottom of the stalks, cutting them so smoothly the motion seemed effortless. He then turned the cane horizontal and chopped off its tops before tossing it behind him.

"They can cut seven tonnes a day or more," Oliveira told me.

It was grueling work under hot sun and unlikely to be the most desired of jobs, but Leblon and the other cachaça producers seemed to value their workers and walked me out to their fields without hesitation. Though I wasn't able to get deep enough into the story of the sugarcane cutters working in Brazil's cachaça industry to really assess how well they're treated, distillers presumably had at least one incentive to treat their field workers better than workers have traditionally been treated in sugarcane agriculture: multiple industry members told me that among the challenges facing alembic cachaça producers was finding cane cutters. But overall in the rum industry the working conditions of cane workers is a touchy subject, particularly after worker advocacy organizations linked the deadly epidemic of chronic kidney disease in Nicaraguan sugarcane workers to the rum brand Flor de Cana, though the exact origin of the disease is uncertain. As a result, some bar owners and rum drinkers dumped their stocks of the otherwise well-respected rum. Unfortunately, CKDu or CKDnT, as the condition is known in its evolving international nomenclature—the u standing for "of unknown causes," the nT for "of non-traditional"—is not an isolated occurrence. It has afflicted agriculture workers in poor, tropical areas around the world, including Mexico, India, and Egypt, and current theories link it to dehydration, long work hours over the hottest part of the day, and the presence of agricultural chemicals and their toxic residues in the water. Ultimately, I suspect, as the global spirits industry popularizes more spirits from poor nations—rum and the agave spirits have recently been two of the most popular categories garnering connoisseurs' attention—after relying on beverages primarily produced in first world countries, such as whiskey and American and European wine, they will face a reckoning over supplier working conditions like those that have confronted the global fashion and electronics industries. I hope their response will be better.

At Leblon, following harvest, the sugarcane went from the field to the nearby still house, where it started out by undergoing a process that looked a lot like what I had seen at the Uitvlugt Sugar Factory in Guyana, though on a much smaller scale. First it was loaded onto a conveyor, then it was crushed under rollers, with a bit of water added to extract the juice. As we walked past a stream of sugarcane juice, Oliveira explained that they don't work as aggressively to extract sugarcane juice as a factory producing sugar and molasses would because they don't want too many stalk components, which carry vegetal flavors, to seep into the juice.

"We don't have the same yield that we could, but we can make sure that we have the highest possible quality," he said.

To further keep out undesirable flavors, once they press the juice they mechanically filter it, trying to remove as many solids as possible. When that's done, the juice is diluted down to the proper sugar concentration and is ready for fermentation.

Sugarcane juice, in contrast to molasses, is much lighter and seems more acidic. When it ferments it produces something more like wine than fermented molasses, which more closely resembles beer. At Leblon, they start with dry yeast for the first fermentation, which takes about three days. During that time, the yeast both produces alcohol and grows itself. When the first batch is done fermenting, Leblon lets the yeast settle to the bottom, then removes the wash and adds in more fresh sugarcane juice. Because the yeast has now already been built up from the first fermentation, each subsequent fermentation with new sugarcane juice only takes about twenty-four hours.

Oliveira says he also suspects that some wild yeasts begin contributing to the fermentation over the course of a batch of yeast.

"We have never made research about what yeast do you start with and what yeast will be working in a week, because probably the wild yeast can be smarter than the yeast you start with," he said before handing me a small sample of the fermented sugarcane juice.

When I took a sip, it reminded me of a dry white, though certainly not as complex and balanced as, say, a bottle of pinot blanc from Alsace.

"The first fermentation is never the best one. Tomorrow it will be better than this one," Oliveira said. Those quality differences are smoothed out by blending before the cachaça is complete.

On the day I visited Leblon, by far the busiest area of the distillery was the still house, though here it could hardly be called a house. Instead, it was a concrete pad covered with a high terra-cotta roof open on the sides, with copper pot stills crowded in and pipes running all over connecting everything from above. One of the stills was opened for repair, with a worker crouching inside, welding. At one point he popped up and asked me, I believe, if I could grab something for him. Despite hand gestures and a search for Spanish cognates, I could never figure out what it was that he wanted.

"Desculpe-me não falo" (I'm sorry, I don't speak Portuguese), I finally said with resignation about the time, I imagine, he was realizing that his quest for a bit of help was turning into a burden.

Leblon wasn't the first cachaça distillery I had visited in Brazil. However, before I arrived, I had expected that since the brand was so prominent in the US and had been, since the summer of 2015, owned by Bacardí, the massive spirits company that produces rum in Puerto Rico at quantities unrivaled by most other Caribbean rum producers, the stills at Leblon would be of a significantly larger scale than what I had seen elsewhere. Instead theirs looked exactly the same as the cachaça stills that I had seen

While most of the cachaça produced in Brazil is made using massive multi-column stills and is considered low quality, connoisseur-worthy cachaça artesanal is produced in alambiques, or copper pot stills. Across the country, many cachaça alambiques look like these at the Novo Fogo (also known as Porto Morettes) cachaça distillery. The similarity is due to the fact that many of the stills are made by one of two companies in the country.

at distilleries near Morretes, six hundred miles away in the state of Paraná, and in Porto Alegre, an additional five hundred miles down the coast in the state of Rio Grande do Sul.

The common pot still used to make cachaça looks radically different from that used to produce rum. In fact, it most resembles the type of brandy still often used to make cognac. All of the ones I saw were separated into three parts. The pot, where the fermented sugarcane wash was heated, was round, squat, and broad, like an alien saucer or a filled doughnut. Protruding from the center, where the alien's lookout dome would be, or the hole if it was a doughnut that wasn't laden with jelly, was a neck in the shape of a column, instead of the onion dome typical of cognac stills. From the top of that column a long, thin copper pipe shot out toward another copper pot of similar design to the first, but without a column.

This was a heat exchanger, I soon learned, the same as what is often found on cognac stills but usually absent from pot stills used for rum. Its purpose is to move some of the heat from the alcohol vapor coming out of the pot still and return it to the wash in the pot still—recovering, in essence, some of the energy needed to keep the distillation process going, rather than letting it dissipate.

From there, the vapor continued to a condenser, which could either be yet another pot-shaped apparatus or one that looked like a column. Cleverly, in all the cachaça stills I saw, the end of the coil, where the distillate comes out, was a pipe that smoothly turned back and forth in its

Fresh cachaça coming straight off the still at the Novo Fogo (also known a Porto Morettes) cachaça distillery in Brazil. Owing to differences in its production, unaged cachaça is often much more pleasant to sip than unaged rum; however, cachaça producers also age some of their product in oak as well as a wide range of barrels made from Brazilian hardwoods.

fitting. Directly below was a bowl with a divider across the middle that was attached to a large, boxy, storage tank. Each side of the bowl drained into a different compartment in the tank, meaning that to make the head, heart, and tail cuts, all the distiller had to do was turn the pipe a few inches from one side of the bowl to the other. Many distilleries then take these heads and tails, further purify them, and use them for fuel for their vehicles or as solvents for cleaning.

But what was most remarkable about all the stills was not that they were made entirely from copper—in and of itself not a particularly unique feature, but all of that copper was hammered, which Oliveira told me was done for tradition.

When I asked Oliveira why all of the stills I had seen looked the same, he said that hasn't always been the case.

In the past in Brazil there would have been a lot more variety, reflecting an itinerant still-making traditional that had been carried out by the country's sizable gypsy population.

"In Brazil copper is a gypsy business. Equipment is a gypsy business," Oliveira explained.

Today, however, pot still manufacturing has consolidated, and two companies have 85 to 90 percent of the market, Oliveira estimated. The company that was at Leblon repairing stills that day was, in fact, the smaller of the country's two main still makers. Oliveira, acting as an interpreter between me and one of the still maker's employees, explained that their company has been making pot stills for twenty-five years and also has a gypsy heritage, though the people who run it no longer identify primarily as gypsy. Nor is theirs an itinerant operation. Instead they employ approximately twenty people and can build a cachaça alembic with a capacity of 3,000 liters in about three days. For the past decade demand has been steady, the still maker said, though because copper pot stills are durable goods, designed to last for decades, his company is trying to diversify their business in preparation for what they see as an inevitable drop in alembic demand.

"He is telling me that the stills are really artisanal and must be artisanal because if you develop a machine to make one hundred alembics a month, you will not sell one hundred alembics," Oliveira, conveying an answer to one of my questions, said. The stills are "still made by hand, and it will be this way for a long time," he added.

After walking around the distillery all morning, Oliveira and I stopped at Leblon's rickhouse, where he mixed me up a custom blend of cachaça. We then headed to the canteen for a lunch of traditional Minas Gerais fare, including slices of "Minas" cheese, a sort of raw-milk farmers' cheese, and *rapadura*, a brick of sugar made by cooking down sugarcane juice, mixing it with other ingredients like green papaya, roasted pine nuts, coconut pieces, and milk, and letting it harden in a square mold.

"Preserved food in a tropical country is hard. Forty years ago in Brazil, on the farms, there was no electricity at all," Oliveira said. "You can hold well-matured cheese and *rapadura* for a month, and for a trip in a horse trailer you could have this as the source of protein and carbohydrates."

With their six alembics and a production capacity of 4,000 liters of cachaça a day, Oliveira estimated that they were one of the ten largest alembic cachaça producers in Brazil. Moreover, given the financial advantage that being a part of Bacardí must surely bring, along with the fact that Leblon is sold under the moniker of Rio de Janeiro's trendiest neighborhood and beach and marketed to an international customer base, the cachaça, as interesting a story as it is for the role the brand has played in bringing artisanal cachaça to the rest of the world, is without doubt an outlier in the Brazilian cachaça scene.

The informal cachaça market Oliveira explained to me is the heart of the cachaça industry. Go thirty kilometers in any direction, he said, and there will be a small producer with an alembic selling unregistered cachaça.

It was a scene that had, at one time, been common throughout the sugarcane-producing world, where every farm in places like Barbados and Jamaica and of course Guyana had a still. Today I know of only two other places besides Brazil where that heritage continues. The first is in Haiti, where cane farm smallholders produce a conceptually similar product to cachaça known as *clairin*, which is made under much more challenging political and economic conditions. The other is in the cane-growing countries of Latin America, where bootleg *aguardiente* is popular. Interest in *clairin* only really began in 2016, when the brand Boukman and the Italian spirits house Velier started sending a a few bottles into the American market. *Aguardiente*, meanwhile, seems to have become associated beyond its home market with periodic reports of mass poisonings and deaths from methanol-tainted spirits, a contaminate that indicates that the spirit was either made with ingredients other than sugarcane or that the methanol had been added, because it does not occur naturally when pure sugarcane is fermented and distilled.

Though cachaça may be, by a wide margin, the farthest along in terms of spirits-industry interest, the availability of cachaça in the international market is still a shame compared to the variety and diversity available in Brazil.

In every Brazilian town there is a cachaça distillery, Oliveira told me when I arrived and first started asking about the product. As it were, though, I didn't even have go that far.

After leaving Leblon, I traveled several kilometers through the area's rural countryside. During my visit, Minas Gerais was at the end of a dry season that had been particularly so. As a result, a couple of small fires had kicked up and were spreading in the early afternoon, an otherwise unusual occurrence that had impacted Leblon as well. Oliveira told me the distillery had lost a couple dozen hectares of cane in a wildfire earlier in the year.

Eventually I arrived at the beginning of a long driveway. To one side was a field where green vines were strung on a trellis high above the characteristically red soil. Initially I took them for grapes, but they, were, in fact, passion fruit, I would later learn. When I reached the end of the driveway I saw a small farmstead of a few buildings surrounded by twenty-five hectares—about sixty acres—of passion fruit, sugarcane, and mango trees and a small pond—a pool, really—for aquaculture. In one of the buildings was a little copper pot still producing cachaça. Unregistered, of course.

This was another side of Brazil's cachaça industry—not the trendy artisanal producers like Leblon or the massive sugarcane distilleries producing Cachaça 51, but the legions of small-scale producers distilling primarily for their neighbors. I will call the farmer who ran this operation B.

Though B's farm provided a significant portion of the food his family ate on a daily basis—he and his wife had at least one teenage son—for cash, its main marketable crops were the passion fruit and some honey. But like small family farmers throughout the world, the revenue from such products was hardly sufficient. So, for a long time, to earn extra cash, he had worked as a hired hand, operating a tractor for neighbors. In 2012, however, he decided that he wanted to find something on his own land that he could do to earn the extra money he needed. Cachaça, he decided, seemed like the answer, even if it wasn't, perhaps, the most natural choice.

When B got into cachaça, he hadn't grown sugarcane for years, and the last time he did it was just to make brown sugar and *rapadura* for the local market. Fermentation and distilling were new to him and, when I asked him how he learned about it, he told me through a translator that he was still learning. Nonetheless, he was confident enough in his product to eagerly show it off to a visiting writer.

All around B's operation it was clear that it was a bootstrap affair. His cane crusher, in particular, looked like something straight off a colonial-era sugarcane plantation. The trough down which cane stalks were fed was made from wood, and on one side was a large, exposed belt pulley attached to exposed metal gears that turned the crushers. From there, the sugar-cane juice went into a plastic tank of the type known to shippers as an IBC, or intermediate bulk container. Sometimes called "IBC totes," these are simply square plastic tanks that can hold several hundred gallons of liquid and are surrounded by metal framing that allows them to be moved by forklifts on pallets. I saw them at distilleries everywhere I went and came to think of them as the cardboard box of bulk rum.

B's fermentation starts off with 150 grams—a third of a pound—of corn, soybean, and rice flour. He relies on wild yeast for the fermentation, which takes three days.

When B first set up his distillery, he used a tiny, rough-hewn still of pounded copper that looked to me to have been hand riveted. When I asked about it, I was told that it was at least fifty years old and had been made originally by—who else?—a gypsy.

Shortly before my visit, however, B had upgraded to a new still. It was a copper alien saucer with a column sticking up from the porthole, and if I needed any more indication that it shared an origin with all the stills at the legal distilleries I had seen, I spotted, affixed to the telltale pounded copper, a label from one of the country's two major still makers.

However, instead of firing the still by steam, as is customary for stills nearly everywhere, B had swaddled almost all of the pot in bricks, which he built with a little portal where he could load in firewood. Wood, I learned, let him build a steady, long-lasting fire that could keep the still running with little attention while he worked elsewhere on the farm. From the still, the cachaça vapor rose through an exposed copper coil cooled by water pooling in a large blue plastic bin. Once the cachaça was collected, it was practically ready to be sold. While B ages a bit of his cachaça, most of what he sells isn't aged. We tasted a bit from various barrels, and I remember that all of it was pleasing—certainly not the type of hooch that is sometimes associated with bootleg

Brazil has tens of thousands of unlicensed cachaça producers. Though illegal, their products can be revered for their craftsmanship (though plenty of bad unlicensed cachaça exists as well). Here a large barrel holds the water used to cool and condense the cachaça coming off the still at an unlicensed producer in the state of Minas Gerais.

Cachaça holding tanks at an unlicensed cachaça producer in the state of Minas Gerais in Brazil. Often customers will fill up their own container of cachaça at their local bootlegger's distillery, though sometimes bottles of cachaça are on offer as well.

producers. As we left, he gave me a bottle to take with me, which I hoped to use for more extensive and detailed comparisons against other cachaças. I toted it over several thousand miles and through the customs of two more nations. Unfortunately, before I had a chance to remove the cork, the bottled shattered in a New Year's Day liquor shelf collapse.

In the previous year B told me the operation had netted about 6,000 liters, which he sold for ten reis a liter—about US$3, a figure that could put his family in some segment of the middle class, though he was still

A cane crusher at an unlicensed cachaça producer in the state of Minas Gerais in Brazil. Because cachaça is made from fresh sugarcane juice, which perishes quickly, rather than molasses, which is stable, cachaça producers often grow their own sugarcane.

reinvesting some of his earnings to continue modernizing his distillery. He needed, for example, to tackle those fermentation vats, which should be stainless steel and have better coverings, I was told. His goal was to eventually get the distillery to the point where it could pass the regulations required for official certification, though whether he wanted to go all the way and actually register with the government seemed, at that point at least, an open question.

Many small unregistered producers "have a local market, so they ask themselves, 'Why? Why do I have to formalize? I have a good product, I think I have a good product, I have people that are buying it and if I formalize, then the government will want me to change everything, to change my structure, and then I have to pay more taxes,'" cachaça expert Felipe Jannuzzi told me a few days later as we sat drinking cachaça in a São Paulo bar. "So their product costs 16 reis, and it'd cost 60. And the government, they will not help. The taxes that the big guys pay are the same measure as the little guy."

"But that's for everything. It's for milk and cheese," he said. In fact, though, a lot of the black-market cachaça does eventually wind up on the formal market, he added, as there are registered producers who will go around and buy up cachaça from small unlicensed distilleries, blend it together, redistill it, and sell the result.

"That's how these informal guys get paid," Jannuzzi said. "But then there are specialists here that are saying, 'Ah, this is very good cachaça and I don't like the informal guys,' but then I say, 'You are drinking the informal guys!'"

Before that cachaça goes on the market, Jannuzzi said, the producers will often give it significant wood flavor, perhaps by speeding up the wood-extraction process by letting the cachaça rest in a vat with wood chips or creating a tea bag of sorts with sawdust and steeping it, techniques that are employed in cheap or knock-off versions of other spirits as well, to what are considered substandard ends.

Jannuzzi is one of Brazil's cachaça heritage's biggest advocates, and getting information like this out about cachaça is one of his goals. He became interested in artisanal cachaça as part of the wider trend toward exploring and celebrating craft and a curiosity of what Brazil's equivalent was. Caught by the spirit, he started traveling around and visiting cachaça producers, documenting what he learned along the way and eventually co-founding Mapa da Cachaça, an amalgam of sociological study, drinking guide, and advocacy organization for high-quality cachaça.

Jannuzzi explained to me that even though appreciation of artisanal cachaça in Brazil has been growing, the characteristics of connoisseurship, such as an intense focus on how each bottle is made and a celebration of uniqueness in each brand, are only just emerging. In the past few years, though, a few producers have started to highlight various points of reference around which different bottles of cachaça can be discussed. Some producers, for example, are exploring the effects of different varieties of cane on the taste and aroma of the cachaças, and a truly small handful—Jannuzzi could really only think of three—are even putting that information on the label. Others are focusing on vintage, explicitly drawing a connection between the qualities of the cane—mutable from year to year, depending on growing conditions—and the final product, just as vintners do with wine.

The bar we were sitting at was called Empório Sagarana. Styled as a traditional *boteco* from Minas Gerais—think family-friendly neighborhood pub—Empório Sagarana is a casual temple to cachaça. It has one of the city's longest cachaça lists, and the cachaça menu even starts out with a manifesto praising terroir and variety, that Jannuzzi helped write.

To really understand how great artisanal cachaça can be, Jannuzzi told me I needed to try a few white cachaças rather than the aged versions. White spirits, as sippers, tend to get a bad rap. Normally they're considered at best flavorless, like a good vodka; at worst they put the "fire" in the expression "firewater," as is often the case with the generally terrible category of white whiskeys. But some booze-making traditions can produce excellent white sipping spirits. In the past few years this fact has been especially shown with mezcal, the Mexican spirit made from the agave plant, many examples of which are incredibly rich and complex and really at their most interesting without wood. Cachaça is similar.

The cachaças that we ordered at Empório Sagarana arrived by the ounce in shot glasses, though they were meant to be sipped. One was called Serra Limpia. It was one of the first certified organic cachaças and came from the state of Paraíba in Brazil's northeast. It was a hard cachaça to describe. Dry and light and slightly vegetal, it became more tantalizing with each sip and quickly turned into one of my favorite things to drink. Meanwhile, a glass of Fascinaçâo Cana Caiana—the first word translates to "fascination"—from the cachaça hotbed of Salinas in Minas Gerais was bold and spicy, equally enjoyable but significantly different.

"When you taste white cachaças, then you understand the production process, then you can understand if the guy really cut his own sugarcane or he bought the cachaça from other places," Jannuzzi said. "You can really understand the sugarcane variety and what kind of fermentation process was going on."

But that doesn't mean white cachaças—many of which are rested for several months in large stainless-steel tanks, ostensibly to homogenize—are the only way to drink the spirit (frequently cachaça producers marketing to Anglophone customers will describe the period in stainless steel as being rested in "inox," not quite hitting the proper translation). Instead, the already remarkable variety of cachaça production styles in Brazil is further extended by the tradition of using local Brazilian woods other than just oak to age them. Among the couple dozen or so different woods used, some of the most common are Amburana, which lends some nutty notes, and Balsámo, which produces cachaças with a distinctly anise flavor. Many of these are Brazilian hardwoods that are now threatened because of widespread logging. Given these environmental concerns, many of Brazil's prominent craft cachaças producers are hesitant to encourage the continued exploitation of the resource, so some are careful to not buy barrels that could have been made from improperly harvested wood. The producer Novo Fogo, for example, sought out an alternative source of wood for the zebrawood barrels it uses, which were made from planks reclaimed from an old house.

If interest in nontraditional wood-aged cachaças continues to grow, the variability in cachaça seems to be almost endless. After Jannuzzi and I left Empório Sagarana we stopped by his apartment, where he showed me a little lab experiment: dozens of jars filled with white cachaça with chips of dozens of different types of wood floating in them. He was trying to figure out which other woods might produce desirable characteristics that could be used in future cachaças.

Right now, though, diversity in cachaça—once the distinction between alembic and industrial cachaças is covered—tends to be discussed mostly in terms of regional differences linked to custom. For example, cachaças from Brazil's south tend to be lower in proof than those from elsewhere, while those from around the town of Salinas typically take a lot of flavor from balsam wood and therefore have a strong anise characteristic.

On my last day in São Paulo I visited the city's *mercado*, the municipal market, with Marcello Gaya, Leblon's brand ambassador. Ostensibly the trip was to see the range of fruits Brazil's leading mixologists had at their disposal to use in endless variations of the caipirinha (if you knew of the varieties of pineapple you are missing out on you'd be reading this book on a plane). But toward the end we stopped by a booth selling liquor. There, dozens and dozens of different bottles of cachaça were stacked on a shelf that rose to the ceiling. For a moment I thought about dashing out to the street hagglers nearby and finding one who could sell me a suitcase to stuff full of every bottle that wasn't available in the States. Unfortunately, I had too many more miles to travel to weigh myself down with a couple cases of booze, so instead I had to resign myself to the hope that the nascent cachaça market in the US will continue to expand. Thankfully signs so far suggest it will.

RABO DE GALO

The caipirinha is the classic Brazilian cachaça cocktail and the local variant on the holy rum/sugar/lime trinity that's found throughout the Caribbean. Beyond the caipirinha, Brazil, like much of the rum-producing Americas, has little else for a traditional cocktail culture. But there's one exception: the Rabo de Galo, literally "tail of the rooster," or a "cocktail." Variants on it are endless, but most include vermouth. Recently the drink, along with cachaça itself, has experienced a bit of a resurgence among São Paulo's craft cocktail bartenders. This version comes from Yaguara, a new cachaça brand and Rabo de Galo champion.

1 ounce Yaguara Ouro
1 ounce Yaguara Organica (the blue bottle)
1 ounce sweet vermouth (preferably Carpano Classico)
Twist of lime

Pour the first three ingredients into a mixing glass with ice. Stir until chilled and strain into a cocktail class. Spritz and garnish with lime twist.

CHAPTER 6

Whose Rum Is the Real Rum?

On one of those too cold, forever-too-close-to-nightfall New York January days, I arrived at Newark Liberty International Airport destined for another berth in the rum archipelago. Instead of turning toward the equator following takeoff, however, we veered sharply north and then headed east over the Atlantic. After clearing European Union customs in Reykjavík, Iceland, I boarded another plane for a quick skip over Scotland and the North Sea and arrived in Amsterdam, bleary-eyed and discombobulated. I can say this much about the relatively poor, relatively fragile nations of the Caribbean: it's simpler to get out of their airports, where the only option is a taxi and gallant bonhomie, than a place with trains and buses and cars and a public transportation system that requires more than just handing the operator a roughly accurate fistful of coins and smiling.

In fact, about the only things Amsterdam has in common with much of the rest of the rum world is that it's watery and that sometime in the middle of my first night in the city a component of some sort failed at a key power station, throwing the center of the Dutch capital into darkness. The trains stopped, the police took to the streets to replace roadway illumination with their car headlights, and at least one Dutchman called the police emergency line to report that his iPad wouldn't charge. When I made it down to breakfast, shortly after the power had come back on, the hotel manager told me it was only the second time in his five years of working at the hotel that such a thing had happened. It was a fluke, in other words, a little valentine from this book's narrative angels. It is that wateriness, it turns out, that is Amsterdam's primary connection to the rest of the rum world. It's a point that was emphasized as I walked across the city's charming bridges to my destination in the thawing city.

Amsterdam is, of course, famous for its connection to one psychoactive substance in particular, but I was reminded that it does well in the more widely legal one of alcohol as well. After leaving my hotel, I passed the House of Bols, a temple—or rather a "a cocktail and genever experience"—for that difficult Dutch precursor to gin. Within a few blocks I found myself in front of yet another "experience," this one for Heineken, the beer that has done more to spread the color green around the world than anything else, save chlorophyll. Yet I pressed on, crossing into the Canal Zone. Eventually

I arrived at my destination's address, a traditional Amsterdam canal house, and took in a deep breath—no rum.

It's easy, I think, to take a look at all the bottles on a store's shelf—each fancifully designed (for the most part), each with a back label telling an enticing story (for the most part), and imagine the journey of the rum inside back to the tropical country it came from and the aging barrels, the still, the fermentation tanks, and the cane field where it was all made. In fact, triggering that fantasy is usually a significant point of that label. Conversely, it's easy to take a look at a distillery and imagine that story forward: From here at Appleton comes the rum that's in Appleton Estate Rare. Here's a cane field, there, on the other side of the world somewhere, is a rum bottle. Just draw a straight line and you'll connect the two. In some instances that story is exactly right. However, often it is much more complicated.

I'd arrived in Amsterdam after talking to producers throughout the Caribbean. Many of them, I realized, had centuries of history in rum production, but the brands under which they would sell their rum were often relatively young, which left me wondering how, exactly, they had been selling their rum all of those years. A distillery without a brand, seemed to me when I first started thinking about it, as wrong as a distillery without a still—something missing a key component.

The answer for many of them is that much of what they do and much of what they have done is produce rum for the bulk market. Back in the time of rum's origins, the era when pirates would call into port and reluctantly load up on several barrels of rum when no cognac was available—"yo, ho, ho, and this bottle is empty," being prelude to mutiny in my mental mirage—and shipfuls of Royal Navy sailors would chase behind them provisioned lock, stock, and, well, to extend a metaphor, barrel, most rum was sold in bulk. But that was three hundred years ago. To understand the market for bulk rum—and therefore the market for a significant portion of the rum we drink today—it's important to understand what happens behind the doors I was standing in front of. So I rang the bell.

"We change intangible ideas into tangible liquids," said Carsten Vlierboom, the man who greeted me, once we'd been talking for a while in his conference room at the back of the canal house.

Vlierboom is the managing director for E&A Scheer. As I sat there energetically drinking a cup of coffee his assistant had given me in an attempt to fight the lingering chill left from a heater still trying to catch up from the night before, he explained what he meant.

It requires going back to E&A Scheer's origin which, as it happens, goes back to the age of the pirates and their navy pursuers, though exactly how far back the company goes is a bit of a mystery.

"Our logo says 1712," Vlierboom told me. "In 2012 we thought we were going to be a 300-year-old company. We had a historian come in. He was going to write up the whole story, and the oldest document he could find was 1763, so he just chopped fifty years off."

Regardless—1712 or 1763—E&A Scheer stretches back to a time when most of the Western world was still European soil and a significant going concern was linking the colonies in the new hemisphere with their colonizers in the old.

According to the account written by that historian, celebrating the company's now 250th anniversary, the brothers Scheer, Evert, and Anthonie founded the company after they arrived in Amsterdam from Germany, joining extended family who had previously made the same move and who had already established themselves in the wine and spirits trade. For a while the brothers worked in the booze trade, presumably for their family, but not long after their arrival they went into independent business together as traders. In the late eighteenth century they frequently sent wine and spirits to the Dutch Caribbean and shipped tropical products, including sugar, back. In the nineteenth century, however, the company

E&A Scheer—the brothers deceased at this point—began expanding in the trade of distilled spirits from the colonies, including the sugarcane-based spirit arrack, produced in what was then known as Batavia, which today is Jakarta, the Indonesian capital located on the island of Java. By 1830 rum from the British West Indies joined arrack as a frequent import.

For the next century and a half the company focused on consolidating its business in the spirits trade, first in arrack, which was an ingredient in what was then the popular Swedish *punsch*, and later, when that specialty market became saturated, in rum from the Caribbean. Today they import a variety of rum marks from sugarcane distilleries located in more than twenty countries and also own the Liverpool, UK-based Main Rum Company, which specializes in rare and well-aged rums and one-offs. Between the two firms they hold enough rum in Europe to fill many millions of rum bottles—though that last step is not their job.

"People will refer to us as traders, but this is not true," Vlierboom told me. "A trader is nothing else than a Rolodex—you know somebody who produces something, you know somebody who wants something, and you tell the producer 'Okay, send the tank there.' We never do that, because if you do that you are not adding value."

What E&A Scheer is, in reality, is a special type of master blender—one that works for people without distilleries rather than with them.

While some of Scheer's business is with retailers selling own-branded products, a supermarket's house brand of rum, for example, their most interesting work happens when someone comes to them with one of those "intangible ideas" and wants a tangible rum.

Say you want to create a rich, complex rum layered with flavor. You don't want it to taste strictly like the rums they make on Barbados, or as distinctly estery and funky as they make them at Hampden, and maybe it should be something a little lighter than what is coming out of Guyana. The idea that new and deicious rums can be created from a mash-up of rums from around the world is not a particularly radical idea. In fact, you could find inspiration for the above blend by flipping through a book of recipes for drinks from the era of tiki—that golden age of American rum cocktailing. The high priest of the style, Don the Beachcomber, created some of his best cocktails by mixing together several distinct rums in each, such as an ounce or two of rums from Puerto Rico, Jamaica, and Guyana.

"I've never actually seen the quote, but he is reputed to have said, 'What one rum can't give you, three rums can,'" Jeff "Beachbum" Berry, tiki scholar and the cocktail mastermind at New Orleans's Latitude 29 bar, told me. "I think somebody might have made that up."

But rums that are blended as part of the tiki tradition are rums that are blended one cocktail at a time. If you want to create cases of the rum, perhaps because you've got a market in mind that you think is willing to pay, say, $30, $35 a bottle and have a story to weave the whole thing together, you can come to E&A Scheer to get your liquid. In other words, you bring the brand, including the idea of what you want to sell, and E&A Scheer will get you the rum.

Vlierboom is adamant about the fact that his company is not in the retail business, that it creates bespoke blends for people with brands but is very much in the background.

"Some of my clients would object to us having too much publicity or being too much in the spotlight because it is their brand," he said, eyeing me and my notebook.

"You came in here because we had a conversation and you said something about how you want to see how all this blending works. That's what we do. That's why I agreed to meet you. I don't agree to meet a lot of people," he added.

I wasn't sure how serious he was being, as E&A Scheer has a very detailed website at the not inconspicuous address of www.rum.nl. Perhaps it was just dry Dutch humor. Regardless, among the things on the website is a "blending tool." It's a rubric of sorts that potential customers can use to describe a rum they want to create based on various dimensions, including body, age, application, and market, which is then sent to E&A Scheer's blenders.

I submitted a few before I visited and Vlierboom sketched some notes. But before he told me what he would put in them, he had some questions.

"Part of what we do very much is listening to people," he said. "The most challenging thing is to get exactly the idea of somebody, not only on paper but into a liquid. If I am not completely clear, I'll send three samples of what I think somebody means, and if they clearly have a preference for one direction, then I can move from there and make a second set based on those."

In particular, Vlierboom can run up against that ever-present problem in wine and spirits of trying to translate flavors and aromas into words. Among Vlierboom's employees it's not much of a problem, as they can use their own internal E&A Scheer "rum language"—"I think you should put 10 percent of 1-5 in there," he offered as an example of the lingo they might use. But E&A Scheer exports to more than forty-five countries, and talking to people with so many different linguistic and cultural backgrounds can be challenging. For example, if someone says they want a note of pineapple in their rum, the question becomes what kind of pineapple are they really looking for: fresh cut or tinned? Or someone says they want their rum "stronger." That means they want their rum to have more flavor, right? Possibly. Or maybe what they really mean is they want it darker, Vlierboom said.

Once Vlierboom and I were communicating well, we got down to actually making some rums—or imagining how they would be made, anyway, because as cool as it would be to have my own rum, I'm certain I'd drink all the bottles long before I'd mange to get a business plan together to sell them.

One of the rums I'd proposed was a heavy-bodied aged rum, small batch, priced from $40 to $60 on the shelf and aimed at "spirit pioneers"—"drinkers who haven't touched a bottle of bourbon in years and whose bar is already filled with obscure mezcal," I wrote as I filled out the blending tool. I was thinking, perhaps, of you, reader, in other words.

Bottles of rum from around the world at E&A Scheer in Amsterdam. E&A Scheer buys rum from many of the world's best distilleries and blends it to the specifications of its customers, serving as the supplier to brands without their own distilleries.

"With complexity, the best thing to do is use different aging techniques with different producers," Vlierboom explained, holding my proposal. "Then you'll have the bourboney notes from this producer, you'll have the French oak notes from that producer, you'll have the sort of creamy notes from another producer, and you can put that together and somebody will think, 'Oh, shit, that's really good!' The trick is that you need to find recognizable points, lots of little peaks, but not to have one peak predominate the blend."

"I think these are the nicest things to put together," he added.

Some of the most common rums to make it into E&A Scheer's blends are those from Jamaica because there is so much flavorful rum produced on the island, Vlierboom said.

"We have several intermediate Jamaican blends which are very different in style—one is very fruity, one is leathery, one is sort of rum-and-raisin style," he said.

But Vlierboom can also pull from more obscure places outside the traditional Caribbean rum islands, such Fiji or Thailand, or that Batavia arrack from Indonesia, where bulk rum tends to be cheaper.

Beyond just creating layers of flavor, one of the reasons Vlierboom suggested that my "oh, shit!" rum have components from multiple producers was to build flexibility into the blend. One of the value propositions he offers to customers is that E&A Scheer, with its vast supplier network and large stocks, can navigate around the problems inherent in working in the places where rum comes from.

"You've been to the Caribbean. Have you ever tried to buy a cask?" he asked.

The answer, unfortunately, was no.

"Can you imagine it's difficult?"

Indeed, I can't imagine exactly how I'd scribble down on my customs form a description of one vague enough to slip it through border control

"Imagine you want to create a rum brand. You could go to one of the islands and find a distiller, but you never know who you are talking to, how dependable they are, if they are going to be there next year, if there is going to be a hurricane next year—there are a lot of uncertainties," he said. "They produce in a very difficult environment."

The antidote to that, Vlierboom said, is, as it is in so much of life, diversity.

"We create what we call intermediate blends. An intermediate blend will be like eight or ten components, because if one of the components is no longer available, you still have the other nine to balance out that quality," he said.

Another reason a nascent brand may want to work with E&A Scheer, Vlierboom said, is that his company will make and sell rum in small quantities—say 1,000 liters, an order size a distillery might be loath to fulfill. (If you want *really* small qualities, a different Dutch company, operating at www.rumblender.nl, will even make you your own custom rum blend, though the shipping fee from Europe is hefty).

At the other end of the market, the advantage E&A Scheer offers distillers is access to a larger market, one that also provides immediate cash flow—something lacking when rum is left to sit in barrels. Angels, woefully, do not settle bar tabs.

While E&A Scheer fills a particular storied and interesting space in the rum world, they are not the only company that works in the bulk rum business nor are they the only one to make blends for third-party brands—a point Vlierboom doesn't try to hide. "Don't make it too simple or just come out with a statement like 'all of the rums in the world are being produced in Amsterdam,'" Vlierboom cautioned as I was getting ready to leave. In fact, distilleries will make custom blends for brands and even buy a bit of rum from another distillery if their customer wants a flavor profile they don't produce. Moreover, other companies will work with brands to produce bespoke rums—though perhaps in a less ecumenical style than E&A Scheer.

One of the most prominent is a company called Oliver y Oliver which operates in a strange part of the Dominican Republic rum world. To get there I had to drive to the far edge of greater Santo Domingo, passing through a gate into what is called a *zona franca*. These are Dominican Free Economic Zones, set up to encourage commerce and exempt businesses located therein from certain taxes and government regulations.

Oliver y Oliver is an independent bottler. They sell rum under their own brands—Opthimus, Cubaney, Presidente, and a slate of others—as well as make rum for other people. Their origin story predictably goes back to nineteenth-century Cuba—common roots for several rum producers in the Spanish Caribbean, including Brugal and Bacardí.

To make their rums, Oliver y Oliver buys column-distilled rum, mostly from producers in Panama and Guatemala, at two different strengths: 75

percent alcohol by volume and 95.5 percent alcohol by volume. Their aim is to produce a heavier rum than many of the other light Spanish-style rum producers, but not one so heavy that it resembles those made in Jamaica or Guyana.

They then age this rum in what they call a "solera" system. It's a method of aging that's common among producers in Latin America—Venezuela, Guatemala, and Columbia all have distillers who claim to use a solera system. However, the technique traces back to Spanish sherry production, where it has been used for over two hundred years.

A traditional sherry solera is made up of multiple levels of barrels. At the bottom are barrels that contain the oldest sherry in the solera; at the top are barrels that contain the youngest. When a sherry maker is ready to bottle the product, the wine is taken from the bottom solera, but not all of it is removed. Then the bottom barrel is refilled with sherry from one level above it, which is then refilled from the barrel above that one, and so on.

Many in the rum world who don't favor solera-aged rums complain that the term is exploited for marketing purposes by producers who don't actually use a solera, at least not in the way it is used in Spain. Instead it's used to simply refer to any type of fractional blending method. Again, the extent to which this matters is determined by the extext to which you care about authenticity and the accuracy of what's on the label versus what is in the bottle.

To make their rum, the producers at Oliver y Oliver first take their 75 percent rum and age it about ten years. They then mix it with some 95.5 percent rum which has been aged for a considerably shorter period of time, as few as six months. That blend is called the *carta solera* and is left to rest for about eighteen months, after which it's checked by one of Oliver y Oliver's master blenders and adjusted with the addition of more lower-proof or higher-proof rum until it conforms to their standards.

From there, the *carta solera* becomes *ron madre* and is moved into casks where it is aged for five years. When it is bottled, about 30 percent of the

Rum aging in former wine barrels at Oliver y Oliver in the Dominican Republic. While rum has traditionally been aged in ex-bourbon barrels, for reasons of both scarcity and experimentation, rum producers—like makers of other distilled spirits—are increasingly using barrels that previous held other alcoholic beverages.

rum is left behind, and the barrel is then refilled with rum to be used the next year and so on.

When Oliver y Oliver started out and for many years thereafter, they aged their rums in ex-bourbon barrels like most of the rum industry, but as demand and prices for those barrels have tightened, the company has switched to wine casks instead—a forced change that's turned out to be better than expected, Pedro Ramon Lopez-Oliver, the company's director general, told me.

"We are doing much, much better with the wine barrels than we were with the bourbon," he said. "It's younger barrels, much better quality, and the wood has a better effect on the rum—faster, stronger, at the same time more delicate and the flavors are different."

Producers of solera rums say the fractional aging method helps them achieve consistency just as it does with sherry, but it also makes determining an age difficult. United States regulations, like those in many of the Caribbean islands, require age statements to indicate the youngest rum in the bottle, but many solera producers label their bottles with numbers that, while not official age statements, seem intended to suggest an age. Sometimes these can represent how long the rum has been in the solera, while other times they are average ages of the rums that are blended. But sometimes they seem to have been plucked from some marketer's mind, with no actual connection to the rum in the barrel. Not all of the rums Oliver y Oliver produces have age statements, but on at least one that does, Presidente, "23 años solera" describes the age statement as one that's qualitative rather than chronological, an explanation that seems unlikely to assuage solera's critics, but it is nonetheless a welcome disclosure.

While many rums on the shelf today, including premium brands, are made by companies like E&A Scheer and Oliver y Oliver, over the past several years Caribbean rum distillers have been increasingly creating and promoting their own brands. In Jamaica, Lloyd Forbes, the manager of that country's rum producers association, the Spirits Pool, told me that until recently bulk rum made up about 75 percent of the country's production and J. Wray and Nephew was the only company that had its own prominent brand. Now every producer on the island has its own brand, though none has as much prominence off the island as Appleton, while the percentage of market share held by rum sold in bulk has fallen to 35 percent. Barbados's distillers have also made a similar though less dramatic shift.

The reason for the shift comes down to, of course, dollars. In rum, as in pretty much anything, branding is where the money is.

"Commodity rum will sell for a couple of dollars a liter, while aged and blended rum will sell for four or five times that, and by the time it's reached a bottle it is substantially more," Forbes said. Traditionally, though, it was foreign companies that controlled the more profitable segments of the market.

"The rum industry in Jamaica was born out of colonial times and provided raw material for developed countries to establish strong brands," he said. "There was no comparison to that, of the earnings of the Jamaican industry."

Owners and marketers of the small brands, however, say developing a brand is difficult in a world where the biggest multinational spirits conglomerates—such as Diageo, which owns such brands as Captain Morgan rum, Johnnie Walker whisky, and Tanqueray gin, or Pernod Ricard, which owns Malibu rum, Jameson whiskey, and Absolut vodka, among others—individually have annual sales that exceed the GDPs of Barbados or Guyana and would make up a significant proportion of Jamaica's.

"That is for me the biggest challenge, getting a commercial presence in markets to make it worth your while," said Frank Ward, who until recently was chairman of the Barbados-based West Indies Rum and Spirits Producer's Association. Many Caribbean producers, he said, are too small and lack the capital to effectively market themselves outside the islands where they are located.

"They produce fantastic products, but they don't have the wherewithal to maintain access in these key markets, especially if they have to go up against multinationals who can basically spend their way and buy all of the shelf space in the bars and in the supermarkets," he said.

Ward, whose family used to own Mount Gay, experienced that problem firsthand when he worked on his own brand, Mount Gilboa, named after a previous name for the site of the Mount Gay distillery. Though the rum is no longer available, Ward gave me a bottle of it when we met in Barbados. A hundred percent pot still, it was wonderful, funky, and complex, clearly meant to appeal to people who considered themselves connoisseurs of rum and have drunk around the category for a while. If anything, it should have been a rum poised to take off amid the rum renaissance—and, in fact, the last of his stocks were bought and released by the Italian independent bottler Velier, whose attention is one of the highest accolades in the rum world. Unfortunately, it didn't.

While the end of the rum had more to do with the sale of the Mount Gay distillery, Ward still struggled to get it out on the market.

"At Mount Gilboa I had a distributor drop me simply because it was a small brand and it wasn't bringing in the volume and cash that was expected," he said. "You have to have a distributor, and your distributor is not in it to be charitable. Your distributor is in it to make money."

The result is that the successful Caribbean rum distilleries and brands are increasingly owned wholly or partially by European spirits conglomerates. Among them are the Italian Gruppo Campari with Appleton, the French companies Rémy Cointreau with Mount Gay and Maison Ferrand with the West Indies Rum Distillery, and the Scottish company Edrington with Brugal. While those companies have infused marketing knowledge and capital into the distilleries, helping bring some of the West Indies' flagship brands to a wider market, it's hard not to hear the echoes of colonialism in the purchases.

But what rum producers are more likely to point to in terms of difficulty in gaining market share is a rather obscure American tax policy known as "cover-over."

To understand cover-over, we need to start with a basic piece of information: all distilled spirits in the US, for human consumption anyway, and excluding a few arcane and relatively inconsequential exceptions, are assessed an excise tax by the federal government of $13.50 per proof gallon, a proof gallon being one gallon of spirits at 100 proof, or 50 percent alcohol by volume. The government, in essence, is taxing absolute alcohol here—the point being that your 190 proof bottle of Everclear carries more tax than your 80 proof bottle of rum. For the latter, in a standard 750 ml bottle, $2.14 of the price is federal excise tax.

What the cover-over policy does is take the vast majority of tax from every single bottle of rum imported into the US and has it—get this curiosity of bureaucratic linguistics—"covered over" (meaning "transferred") to the Puerto Rican and US Virgin Islands governments, which, don't forget, represent Americans. In other words, every time you and anybody else in the US buys a bottle of Bajan or Jamaican or Venezuelan rum, those two governments get about two bucks. Altogether it adds up to some serious cash: about a half-billion dollars annually.

Even more inscrutable than the policy's name is the method by which it allocates tax between the two islands, but the important part is that it is based on the relative amount of rum production in each.

The law is an old policy that started in 1917 for Puerto Rico and 1954 for the Virgin Islands, and though the law doesn't specify what the two territories must use the money for, it has generally been seen as an important revenue stream into the general fund of each, with the idea that it would help the two islands with development. A small portion would also be used to help market the islands' rum.

But a significant feature is that if you're the government of Puerto Rico or the USVI and you want more cover-over money—and why wouldn't you?—you just need to gin up a little bit more rum production within your jurisdiction, and bingo, your treasury gets a spike.

In fact, that's exactly what the Virgin Islands did in 2008, when it agreed to grant Diageo a slate of subsidies widely reported to be worth $2.7 billion in exchange for an agreement by the UK-based spirits conglomerate to produce American-bound rum for its Captain Morgan brand—the world's fourth-largest rum brand—for the next thirty years in the territory. The deal came with a $165 million distillery built by the government on the USVI island of St. Croix for Diageo's use.

For the Virgin Islands the appeal was clear: it was estimated to shift $6 billion in cover-over subsidies to the government's coffers from Puerto Rico over the course of the agreement. Because Puerto Rico has legislation limiting to 10 percent the amount of cover-over money it can spend on rum promotion, the deal in effect shifted money "that's now being used to build schools and restore tropical forests in a US territory . . . into what is essentially a $3 billion tax break for London-based Diageo," a reporter for the investigative journalism nonprofit ProPublica wrote. Cruzan, a fast-growing rum brand owned by Beam Suntory, is also produced in St. Croix with similar subsidies.

"We had estimated when we first started working on this problem that some of these companies, the amount of subsidies that they were getting was greater than their cost of production," Ward told me, echoing a position held by others opposed to the policy. "They basically could distill the rum, give it away, and they would make money. You cannot compete with a situation like that." (Diageo, for its part, has disputed that characterization in the past.)

Buoyed by particularly strong imports of Dominican Republic rum, the value and quantity of rum exported from WIRSPA member countries to the US have remained relatively unchanged over the past several years, and just off from historical highs, United Nations trade data show. However, both Barbados and Jamaica, the former of which in particular relies on the US market for the largest percentage of its rum exports, have seen several-million-dollar declines in the amount of rum they've sold the US over the past half-decade.

Nonetheless, the Caribbean nations have been reluctant to bring the issue to the World Trade Organization for fear of US retaliation and uncertainty over what leverage they would have to push the issue anyway.

As fun as abstruse international trade policy may be, for our purposes here, the real question is not whose lobbyist is most worth his weight in tax dollars, but what this has to do with the rum in our glasses. After all, few people who buy a car or the gasoline that goes into it fret over the fact that auto manufacturing and the petrochemical industry are two of the most heavily subsidized industries in the US, and if they do fret over that fact,

I imagine they do so more as taxpayers than connoisseurs of vehicles and fuel. In rum, however, the problem goes back to those funky Hampden fermentations and those ancient Demerara stills and even the master blending of Joy Spence at Appleton and Jassil Villanueva at Brugal. Though all are done in the process of producing the same product—rum—they are all incredibly unique processes. You're not going to take a sip of Hampden's rum and confuse it with the style they make in the Dominican Republic.

What is harder not to confuse are the rums produced in Puerto Rico and the Virgin Islands. The four most prominent brands in the territories—Captain Morgan, Cruzan, Bacardí, and Don Q—all for the most part use large multicolumn stills to produce an extremely light rum, much of which becomes the base for rums destined to be finished with a confection of tropical flavors added after it's produced. Don Q produces a few great sipping rums and Bacardí is trying, but really these are rums meant to be mixed with cola or into fruity cocktails.

Beyond the tax subsidies, light multicolumn-distilled rum also happens to be where the economies of scale really kick in, giving those distillers an edge over producers clinging to old stills and arcane fermentation techniques. None of this is to say that such operations inherently produce rum unworthy of connoisseurship—Don Q disproves that, as does Brugal, which also uses a large multicolumn still. The latter spits out 75,000 liters of rum a day, which the *maestros roneros* at Brugal are proud to note is very low in congeners because they believe flavor should come from the barrel. Bacteria need not apply.

The problem with the cover-over policy is that rum is not petrochemicals, nor even midmarket sedans. Instead it is a product of craft, rather than mass homogenization, and one where variety is prized above much else. If those rums produced in Puerto Rico and the Virgin Islands were the only rum available—if the rum retail environment becomes too inhospitable to the distillers doing something unique and

Stacks of barrels at the Brugal distillery in the Dominican Republic. Because of the cooling effect from all the evaporation, rum barrel storehouses are often comfortable respites in a hot climate.

traditional and essentially anti-modern for them to keep their rums on the shelves—all that flavor and heritage that drives the appreciation of the spirit would be lost. A second problem arises if people come to see rum—as too many already seem to see rum—as merely the drink it is mostly promoted as by the Puerto Rico and Virgin Islands producers, something cheap and mixable to blend into the saccharin image of lazy beach days and sunsets behind palm trees and to be forgotten as soon as reality returns. Under a view like that, no one would be compelled to take it seriously in the first place.

But weak brands and problematic government subsidies aren't the only problems rum has, unfortunately. Even more frustrating, especially on the global level, is the question of what, exactly, is rum. This may seem like an odd question to come up three-fourths of the way through a book on the topic of rum. But there's a reason I've been avoiding it: take a half-dozen different bottles labeled "rum" from a half-dozen different producers in a half-dozen different countries and, well, you could get a half-dozen different answers. And even those might not tell you what you are actually getting.

Dotsero, Colorado in the Rocky Mountains—yes, we're at the temperate latitudes again—I am sad to report is most likely named just as you might guess: it's a corruption of the phrase "dot zero," which is what some surveyor apparently wrote on his map as the starting point for a new rail line he was drawing a century ago. Today it has a population of seven hundred, no post office, and clings to either side of Interstate 70. The number you want is 133, for the exit. Perhaps that's progress. But when I mentioned I was going there, my aunt, who has lived in this part of Colorado for several decades, told me that, despite driving past it countless times, she was never sure if it was anything other than a pull-off.

Nonetheless, among Caribbean rum makers in the summer of 2016, Dotsero, two thousand miles away, was one of the most infamous spots on the rum archipelago. That's because Dotsero is a pull-off with a distillery, and for several years that distillery was making rum.

For the past two decades, as the American craft-distilling movement has exploded, injecting innovation into what was for a long time the sclerotic business of liquor making in the US, it has transformed the categories of whiskey and gin. Beginning around 2010, the trend hit rum. Within a few years there were well over one hundred new American-made rums on the market from distilleries stretching from coast to coast and even up into Alaska. While most of the sugarcane grown commercially in the US comes from Florida and Louisiana, with a comparative sliver of production in Texas and Hawaii and a truly tiny smattering elsewhere, the country's rum-producing distilleries are more likely to be surrounded by snow than sugarcane fields.

It may seem strange that so much rum would be produced so far from its natural habitat—while craft distillers by definition produce far less liquor than mainstream producers, there are certainly more individual rum producers in the US now than all the legal distilleries in all the Caribbean islands combined. However, to students of American drinking history, the recent boom in rum production is really just a return to the country's distilling roots.

Long before the US was a whiskey-drinking country—long before, in fact, it was even a country, it's European and European-descended residents were swillers of rum. Millions of gallons of it flowed in from the Caribbean each year and flowed into the large punch bowls common in the nation's taverns of the time, lubricating early colonial society before, eventually, lubricating the revolutionaries who would eventually break the country free from the British Empire.

Alongside the rum flowing up from the Caribbean, however, were millions of gallons of molasses, and early American settlers were no ignoramuses about the transformative potential that could be had by mixing in a little yeast and running the whole thing through a still. By the middle of the eighteenth century there were about 150 distilleries on the Eastern Seaboard producing several million gallons of rum a year. In New York City, around the same time, more than fifteen distilleries annually issued a half-million gallons, meaning there was enough local rum alone for every man, woman, and child in the city at the time to toss back nearly a gallon a month.

While America in the few decades up to the revolution and for a few decades thereafter was a particularly bibulous place, drinking at least twice the per capita average than has become the norm today, those drinkers didn't particularly care for the rum produced in North America—if you wanted a good drink in the thirteen colonies, you asked for rum from the West Indies. Some locally produced rum fueled the fur trade with the Native Americans, but increasingly the rum produced here had a foreign destination, particularly the African coast, where it was exchanged for slaves destined for the Caribbean sugar plantations. Tellingly, Newport, Rhode Island, one of America's most important colonial-era ports, boasted strong industries in both rum production and slaving expeditions.

But rum's key role in the American colonial experience didn't survive independence, though it did help spark it. Among Britain's many affronts to the North American colonists were the 1733 Molasses Act and the subsequent 1764 Sugar Act, leveling duties on those products, which had become key to the colonial economy.

"Molasses," John Adams wrote, "was an essential ingredient to American Independence."

Despite, or rather because of that, rum, tainted as a product of European imperial control, quickly lost market share following the end of the Revolutionary War to the nascent nation's homegrown spirit, whiskey, which was first made from rye and then from the even more American grain of corn.

American rum production eventually ceased and, with a few exceptions, the spirit itself became an afterthought in the country's collective bar for the next two and a half centuries.

What had everyone talking about Dotsero, however, was not the fact that the distillery there was making rum in North America—by then the rum-distillery renaissance was old news and Caribbean producers were (rightfully, for the most part) confident that their centuries of experience, terroir, and price point would produce rums that could hold their own against the newcomers. Instead, they were appalled because the distillery was making its rum—or, if I am going to accurately reflect the distillers' opinions I should say *so-called rum*—out of sugar beets. In the world of rum, where consensus is rare, the universal condemnation of the practice was striking. I had to go to see this sacrilege for myself.

It's hard not to like Stoneyard Distillery when you see the place, even if you arrive in the middle of a snowstorm and are worried that your roads home are on the brink of closing, as I was when I arrived shortly after New Year's in 2017. The distillery is located in a low-slung, metal-roofed building surrounded by a few others in the style of what I think of as historic western slapdash—thin walled, thrown up in a fever to join the latest boom, and intended to last only until it was time to move on to the next. There was various industrial equipment and debris around the distillery. The whole place looked like a depot, which in essence it was. As the distillery's name suggests, the location is a stone yard owned by master distiller Max Vogelman's uncle, who let him a bit of space when he wanted to get into the booze business.

Before craft distilling was big in Colorado—and it is big: I once had a distiller in the nearby Arkansas Valley tell me that area had more distilleries per capita than anywhere else in the country, though that's a hard statistic to evaluate—craft brewing was the thing and Vogelman followed the not unusual path from one to the other.

"I was probably twenty-two or twenty-three and a friend was making beer—a bunch of friends were making beer—and one in particular I was kind of talking with, we just thought it would be cool to build a still and run some beer through it," he told me when I arrived.

The more Vogelman learned about distilling, however, the more he realized that if his goal was a drinkable liquor, distilling beer wasn't the best way to go about it. While producing beer is essentially the first fermentation step in spirits making, the goals, and therefore the process, are generally different if you are making a craft beer to bottle versus one to run through a still.

In many ways Stoneyard Distillery embodies the core ethos of American craft distilling. It's not a slick operation built with loads of investor capital and a turnkey idea plugged into turnkey equipment. Instead the owners are Vogelman and his business partner, Jim Benson, who used to

The hand-built distillery set-up—one of the hallmarks of innovation at American craft distilleries— at Stoneyard Distillery in Dotsero, Colorado.

be Vogelman's boss when Vogelman was working in construction. Most of the equipment is custom made or repurposed.

As we walked around the distillery, Vogelman pointed out what were milk-cooling tanks from the 1960s and 1970s that they now used for fermentation. The pot the wash boils in was once used by a bakery to mix batter, and the boiler that produces the hot water to heat it was originally installed in someone's mountain-home driveway to melt off the snow. The still, meanwhile, is a tall, skinny, shiny, stainless-steel thing that looks ever so slightly like an old round gas pump. Vogelman built it himself.

"I remember a month before we actually fired this up, [Benson] was asking me, 'OK: percentage, what do you think the odds are that this is actually going to work the way you want it to?' And I was like, 'I honestly can't sit here and tell you that it is going to work, because then all that is going to happen is you are going to be really pissed when it doesn't,'" he said. In the end, it worked. The distillery was soon producing booze, and Vogelman said he felt he was in a better position than many other distillers because his intimate knowledge of the setup put him in a good position to fix or change any small thing that might not be working as it should. Now he just had to face the next challenge to be overcome by any new distiller: selling the stuff.

In the US, distilled spirits are regulated by the federal Alcohol and Tobacco Tax and Trade Bureau, or TTB, within the Department of the Treasury. Among the items the TTB is supposed to check before approving the label that allows a product to go on sale is whether it actually conforms to the category in which it is being sold. For each, it looks at the rules that lay out the requirements for a spirit to be included in that particular category—or "class"—of spirits, which are known as the standards of identity. The standards of identity for "bourbon," a type of "whisky," for example, require that the booze in a bottle labeled "bourbon" be made from at least 51 percent corn. If it isn't, a spirit maker has to go searching for another section of the standards to put the product in. Within "whisky" there are many, including "rye," "scotch," and "blended."

Rum is far simpler. Indeed, its regulations simply state that it must be made from the juice, molasses, syrup, or other byproducts of sugarcane—not beets—and that it must not be distilled to such a high proof or otherwise altered to the point that it no longer has "the taste, aroma, and characteristics generally attributed to rum." The latter is a requirement across most spirit classes, but seems to have little applicable meaning—gin, for example, is supposed to be principally of juniper, but there are plenty of gins out there in which connections to the berry seem to stop at the lexical.

Vogelman told me he was hardly trying to pull a fast one when he decided to make sugar beet rum, nor was he trying to skirt the laws. He said when he initially looked up the rules, he thought they merely said "sugar" and were agnostic to the source. This seems unlikely, as the rules have clearly indicated "sugarcane" for decades, but the best memories are fickle things. Regardless, the initial labels submitted by Stoneyard for approval by the TTB clearly state—twice, in fact—that the spirit is made from sugar beets. Despite that fact, in the summer of 2014 the TTB approved Stoneyard's Colorado Rum.

While there are rums made from sugarcane in Colorado, including the well-regarded rums from Montanya in Crested Butte, which uses Louisiana sugarcane, in many ways Vogelman's sugar beet rum made sense. In local-obsessed Colorado, where the state Department of Agriculture administers a label for local products called "Colorado Proud" and NATIVE bumper stickers adhere to Subarus and rusted-out Fords and bikes alike, the state produces nearly one million tons of sugar beets a year. From those sugar beets, Vogelman uses highly refined granulated white sugar—just like you'd buy in the grocery store. Unlike molasses or sugarcane juice, white sugar, regardless of its source, is nearly pure sucrose—99.95 percent is the common purity given—so Vogelman figured from an organoleptic standpoint it wouldn't even matter. When he tried a batch from white cane sugar, which would have been permissible to call rum, he said it was indistinguishable from what he was making from beets.

For about two years he kept busy tearing open bags of beet sugar, fermenting it, running the wash through his still, nicknamed "Twinkie" because the bakery that the boiler kettle came from was a former Hostess bakery, and getting his Colorado Rum behind bars and in liquor stores in the area. A few local news outlets covered the story of his local take on "rum," but aside from a few comments on those articles, little attention seemed to be paid to the discrepancy between federal code and Vogelman's process. In the meantime, the TTB continued to approve labels for Stoneyard and also approved at least one additional label for the Kentucky-based Wilderness Trail Distillery's Harvest Rum, which is made from sorghum, another plant that is definitely not sugarcane but that can be pressed to exude a sugar-laden, molasses-like syrup. Wilderness Trail, which launched its sorghum "rum" in 2014, when the distillery was known as Wilderness Trace, reportedly was upfront with the TTB when it sought its label approvals as well, and even had to lobby the agency to get the designation approved.

For Stoneyard, the turning point—or at least the article that many people I talked to referenced—came in June 2016, when spirits writer Kara Newman published a piece on Liquor.com titled, "You'll Never Guess What This Rum Is Made From," pointing out the peculiarity.

In the comments, however, rum fans were not up for a game. Instead they bluntly criticized Stoneyard and Liquor.com for promoting a rum that wasn't, despite TTB approval. One particularly incensed interlocutor—screen name "thekkannuck"—even tried to pin the whole thing on American hegemony, writing: "I don't give a hoot what yankee regulations are because rum is made with SUGARCANE! nothing else. guess what, you wont be able to peddle your junk outside the Empire because there are regulations out there!"

Max Vogelman, distiller and founder of Stoneyard Distillery in Dotsero, Coloardo. For a while, Stoneyard was one of the many new American rum producers to come to market in the early 2010s. However, because their spirit was made from Colorado beet sugar, rather than sugar from sugarcane, regulators eventually decided their product couldn't be called rum. The two sugars are virtually chemically identical.

Vogelman's spirit wasn't the first time sugar beets and sugarcane clashed. At the beginning of the nineteenth century, when the Royal Navy cut off shipments of tropical products to France during a conflict between Britain and France, the French, spurred by Napoleon, set about developing a soon-flourishing sugar beet industry. Perhaps unsurprisingly, it was followed in short order by a soon-flourishing sugar beet spirit industry as well. While the resumption of trade eventually quashed France's early forays into sugar beet sugar, further improvements in sugar beet processing eventually saw a resurgence in the industry, one that contributed to the downfall of Caribbean sugar production, which in turn spurred planters in the French West Indies to leave the sugar market altogether and make rum directly from the fresh-pressed sugarcane juice, creating rhum agricole in the process.

Several months after the international uproar in response to his rum, Vogelman says, the distillery got a call from the TTB. He was given the choice of either switching to cane sugar and keeping the "rum" designation or keeping the beet sugar and calling the product something like "spirit distilled from Colorado beet sugar." It was a tricky trade-off, forcing Stoneyard to either compromise on its local identity or label its product with, well, "spirit distilled from Colorado beet sugar," which doesn't exactly strike confidence in a neophobic customer standing in front of the liquor-store shelf. In the end, though, they stayed local and went with the awkward designation.

"I completely understand where they are coming from. They are trying to preserve rum as this is what rum is, they are trying to define it and keep it as a thing," Vogelman said, but "if the rum guys really wanted to preserve the state of their industry, it shouldn't be that it is made just from sugarcane. It should be that it's made from something with actual characteristics of the actual organics of the sugarcane."

Part of the problem goes back to the TTB, which, even in an era of hostility toward public institutions, is widely regarded as being particularly overburdened. For the first seventy or so years following Prohibition, federal alcohol regulators on the permitting side of the business had a sleepy job—booze making was a heavily consolidated and conservative industry, with just a few predictable players producing a steady amount of predictable paperwork. The craft spirits boom changed all that, with so many new distilleries needing permits that had scarcely been issued in decades and asking questions, such as about whether rum can be made from sugar beet or sorghum, that no one had ever asked before.

"We actually went to Congress to lobby for more money for the TTB," Roberto Serrallés, whose family has been making rum in Puerto Rico for over 150 years, said at an industry conference during the Stoneyard controversy. "It's the only time an industry actually goes and tells the government, 'You know what? We need more money for our regulator.' It is crazy."

One of the reasons that the reaction against Stoneyard was so strong was because it tapped into an even bigger frustration of rum producers and rum aficionados worldwide: that the category was full of deception, its boundaries were hazy, and many of what were seen as the most egregious practices were not only perfectly legal, but perfectly opaque as well. Maybe "thekkannuck" was right to dismiss Yankee regulations, but as it turns out, the world beyond is just as dark and uncharted.

For months, in interviews with residents of the global rum world, a particular locutionary quirk kept popping into conversations whenever we approached the topic of rum regulations and what one could permissibly do when making rum and still call it "rum." "Well, when you talk to Richard Seale . . ." they'd inevitably trail off.

The day I finally got to talk to Seale at his distillery in Barbados, C. J., the Barbados-born, Brooklyn-raised cabbie who'd become my de facto driver on the island, picked me up at the guest house where I was staying along the island's south coast to take me ten miles to Seale's Foursquare distillery in St. Philip Parish. As we drove away from the coast, we passed through a series of subdivisions and C. J. eagerly pointed out oil derricks.

"Few people know Barbados has oil," he said. Certainly I didn't. As it is, there is little anyway—Barbados's crude oil exports bring in less than a third as much revenue as its distilled spirits exports.

It's almost too narratively neat to say that the distillery, which is part of a complex called the Foursquare Rum Factory and Heritage Park, seemed from the beginning an endeavor in radical transparency. However, unlike nearly every other distillery I toured, where my visit was so well organized that a distillery employee often came to pick me up, when I arrived at Seale's I wasn't greeted by anyone, nor was I immediately confronted with a gatehouse or a glistening retail room. Instead, just beyond the parking lot was a shaded path and a sign in English and Spanish pointing the way to the distillery, which was open for self-guided tours. Had I wanted to, I could have wandered around at will, peaking in on various parts of the rum-making process, maybe even jumping over the occasional EMPLOYEES ONLY placard that separated important equipment from the self-guided tour path and seemed about as persuasive as a KEEP OFF THE GRASS sign does on a perfect spring day. Instead I tracked down an employee who called Seale and sent me to wait on the distillery's veranda. As I did, one of those little green lizards endemic to the tropics tiptoed across the railing, hidden just enough to foil my lazy attempts to snap a good photo of it.

When Seale came down, he ushered me into a tour. We stopped by the fermentation tanks. I scribbled a few notes about Foursquare's fermentation, then we rushed off to see the stills and Seale explained how, in the Barbados style, he blends his rums from a combination of pot- and column-distilled rum. By the time we'd made it to the bottling line, the tour had become almost awkwardly perfunctory. "Is this the largest bottling line in Barbados?" I asked at one point. "I think it just looks that way because we have a lot of different products," he responded. Clearly we had other topics we wanted to talk about and as a result I ended up having to email him several months later to get the specifics of what actually goes on in his distillery.

The oversight had nothing to do with the quality of Seale's rum. Foursquare's are cult products. Released under the labels Doorly's, R. L. Seale, and Foursquare Rum Distillery, they aren't all distributed in every state in the US and often don't appear behind generic bars or in top rum roundups. But among rum fans they are cherished finds, particularly those under the Foursquare label that are sometimes bottled at cask strength and finished in barrels that were previously used to age port or Zinfandel. I consider his best products nearly unmatched by anyone else making rum.

Yet what Seale is at least as well known for is leading the campaign against rum's biggest controversy: that there's sugar in it.

Taking the meaning one way, there is, of course, sugar in rum. In fact, there is sugar in all spirits. That's what yeast converts to alcohol. In rum, that's simply sugar found in the sugarcane. In other spirits, that's sugar that comes from the breakdown of more complex compounds— for whiskey, the starch in grain, traditionally broken down by enzymes from sprouted grains called malt; for tequila, the inulin in agave, which is broken down by the roasting of the piña. But the sugar in mash doesn't last long. A good distiller will turn all of it to alcohol—or rather ensure that the conditions are correct for the yeast to turn all of it to alcohol— during the fermentation process. But even if a distiller doesn't quite get it right—even if there is still a bit of sugar left over in the wash, none of it should make it to the final product. Distilling, as you'll remember, can only condense volatile compounds, and sugar, as you have had plenty of time to contemplate if you've ever had to scrape out the charred black mess of sugar spilled on a baking sheet and stuck in a hot oven, is not volatile. Rum, then: naturally sugar-free. Curious for a product of sugar-cane, perhaps, but true.

That said, it is not uncommon to see references scattered around the Internet, and sometimes even in publications that ought to know how to do a better job writing about these things, that state rum is sweet because it comes from sugarcane. Before labeling these statements nonsense—and in what many of them intend to imply they are pure nonsense—for clarity's sake it's worth taking a moment to split this statement nearly to death.

Taken one way—the way in which, I am afraid, many who use it do not mean it—it's right to say that a rum or any other thing tastes the way it does because of what went into it. Making something, after all, is to follow a causal relationship. Therefore, if you detect "sweetness" in a rum that has been made purely from molasses and yeast nutrients fermented with yeast, distilled, aged in oak barrels, and blended with limestone water, it'd be accurate to say that that "sweetness" came from those particular ingredients combined and modified in that particular process. What you'd be more accurately talking about in that case though, it seems to me, is the "sensation of sweetness"—the same "sensation of sweetness" we reference when we talk about some bourbon whiskeys or certain bottles of spring water being "sweet." But in rum, it's a sensation of sweetness that really doesn't have anything to do with the sensation of sweetness in sugarcane itself, which comes from sugarcane's unusually high sucrose content.

To imply, then, that rum is sweet in the same way that sugarcane is sweet because it is made from sugarcane and therefore contains sugar is wrong for the very reasons of distillation science I outlined above.

So is rum "sweet"? It can be. It can contain a "sensation of sweetness" that comes from talented fermentation, distillation, and aging of rum made just from yeast and molasses. Try a glass of Appleton 21 and you'll see exactly what I mean—round, rich, and with a bit of "sweetness" even though there is nary a fugitive sucrose molecule from sugarcane to be found. (Though I feel I must, at the risk of being pedantic, add that charred oak can give off compounds that are sugars, but in quantities so minute that for our purposes here it's best to think of them as the equivalent of all those other organoleptic components that go into forming rum, such as banana-like isoamyl acetate.)

More often, though, bottles of rum are sweet because they contain sugar. Full stop. This fact is what Richard Seale likes to publicize to shock rum drinkers.

The modern rum renaissance is less than a decade old. From a market perspective, spirits are classified by price and labeled with a semantic dance around the word "premium," which has no absolute relation to quality. So-called super-premium rums begin somewhere around $25 a bottle on the shelf, ultra-premium rums around $50; below that are the just premium rums or your cheap basics, which are known as "value" products. For the past few years rum has seen middling growth worldwide and declines in the US in terms of volume, but the losses have mostly been at the bottom of the market—high-end rum has been growing strongly.

As it has, many of the rums that have come to make up the top segments of the market have been aged rums, often dark, deeply flavorful, and praised for their sweetness and smoothness, the latter a term virtually devoid of accepted meaning that generally refers to some quality between doesn't-taste-like-gasoline and tastes-like-Coca-Cola. In 2013, Seale revealed that in many of those rums, that sweetness and therefore some of their lushness came not from the distillers' skill at fermentation, distilling, and aging, but from their skill at blending in a bit of sugar before the rum reached the bottle.

While the addition of small amounts of sugar to cognac is a fairly well-known practice, the other popular hard spirits—whiskey, rum, vodka, gin, and tequila—are frequently touted as being sugar-free drinking choices for people on low-carbohydrate diets. However, in some cases this advice is wrong, at times wildly so. In the US, federal regulations allow a certain amount of undisclosed sugar in certain types of distilled spirits. Vodka, for example, is allowed to have up to two grams of sugar per liter, a slight amount to be sure, but enough to render that supposedly flavorless product slightly more palatable. In what is a shock for many spirits aficionados, certain types of rum and whiskey—but not scotch, bourbon, or any labeled "straight"—can have added colorings, flavorings, and "blending materials" (i.e., wine or sugar) of up to 2.5 percent of the product by volume without having to disclose them on the label.

Aside from the coloring bit, which everyone pretty much knew about, in the spirits world the fact that whiskey and rum could have sugar and flavor added to them has been a tightly held piece of information, if not exactly a secret, given that it exists in US code and has been laid out in TTB publications. The reason is that it seems nonsensical: if sugar and flavoring can be added to products labeled "whiskey" and "rum," then it raises the question of what, exactly, is the point of those entire other categories of "flavored whiskey" and "flavored rum." As it is, the difference is that flavored rum can be bottled at a lower proof—60 proof, as opposed to the "rum" category's minimum of 80—and can contain more than 2.5 percent of flavoring, coloring, and blending materials by volume. "Flavored rum" also has to be labeled with the dominant flavoring. To cop the example the TTB uses in the outline of its regulations, if you make a "flavored rum" with a bunch of butterscotch flavoring in it, you have to call it "butterscotch-flavored rum." You can't call it "marzipan-flavored rum." (Actually, the government says you have to call it "butterscotch-*favored* rum," but I think that's a typo.) However, if you add flavor to your regular rum, you can call it just "rum."

In 2016, in an effort to "streamline and modernize" their permitting process, the TTB even issued a ruling, saying that rum to which the only material added was "sugar, brown sugar, molasses, or caramel" need not undergo a formula approval, which had previously been required when stuff was added to a bottle of rum other than the stuff normally needed to make a bottle of rum.

Meanwhile, other flavors can still be added to rum if you tell the TTB about them and the TTB decides that such things are "customarily employed therein in accordance with established trade usage." Such approvals are considered trade secrets and exempt from federal records disclosures. However, many have suggested that, at the bare minimum, vanilla flavoring has been added to rum not labeled flavored rum.

The revelation that rum may have added sugar in it set rum aficionados to scouring their liquor cabinets for offenders. To figure out which bottles were slipping in sweetener, they turned to the websites of Systembolaget, the Swedish government's liquor monopoly, or its Finnish counterpart, Alko, both of which publish information about sugar content in the products they sell (they are at www.systembolaget.se and www.alko.fi; only Alko has an English-language option, but on Systembolaget's site the number you are looking for is the one listed under "Sockerhalt").

However, neither of those sites comes close to capturing the full range of rums on the market around the world—Alko in particular is limited. So, to investigate rums further, they turned to a bit of amateur chemistry, breaking out hydrometers. Hydrometers—thin glass tubes with a glass bulb and weight at one end—are almost as ubiquitous in spirits making as stills. Their purpose is to measure the percentage of alcohol in a mixture; they do so by measuring the comparative density of liquids. The addition of sugar increases the density of the rum to which it has been added. Given that all bottles of booze have their alcohol content listed on them and alcohol is lighter than water, before you stick your hydrometer in you can figure out what the expected density would be if there has been nothing else added to the rum. Any difference between the expected density and that reported by your hydrometer can then be compared to a nifty little chart developed by the rum blogger who pioneered the technique, Johnny Drejer, on his website, www.drecon.dk. Ever since Drejer popularized the hydrometer method for assessing sugar, many rum bloggers have taken to publicizing the amount of sugar in any bottle of rum they get, data which has been collected and published on the forum at www.rumproject.com, a site run by the particularly vocal blogger Capn Jimbo (the pseudonymous impulses of rum bloggers, like those of rum marketers, seem to trend toward the nautical).

None of these sources, unfortunately, can say definitively how much sugar is in your rum, nor can they be used as an absolute judge of the comparative sweetness between two bottles of rum. For one, Systembolaget and Alko reflect the sugar content of bottles available in their respective markets, while the numbers on Capn Jimbo's Rum Project Forum are crowd-sourced from various places around the world. Producers sometimes release different liquid in different markets, in part to comply with various local laws, such as variances in lowest allowable alcoholic proof, and it's possible for them to change how they make a rum over time.

Secondly, the hydrometer method is subject to the skill and honesty of the testers—though fortunately in many cases it is cross-referenced with other testers and other publicly available information. It also makes the assumption that the proof on the bottle is accurate, which it should be, and that whatever is in the liquid that is causing the apparent discrepancy in density is sugar, which, given the list of allowable additives, it may not be. Finally, it doesn't reveal what type of sugar is used. Fructose, for example, is sweeter than sucrose, while white table sugar is going to create a different flavor range than molasses, which carries with it a bit of bitterness, among other qualities.

Maddening, yes. But a start nonetheless.

What's much clearer is why distillers add sugar: consumers want it, even when they say they don't once they figure out that it's in there.

"Humans generally have a sweet tooth," said Frank Ward, the former Barbadian rum producer. "I myself don't like rums that have had sugar added to them. I really don't like them. But I have recognized, and a lot of people have recognized, you add sugar to rum and the consumer is going to prefer that to an unsugared rum."

Ward and I were sitting in the sprawling patio garden of an off-beach bar along Barbados's south coast. As Ward sipped on a glass of rum from the adamantly unsugared Doorly's range made by Seale, he explained a taste test he conducted with a few friends in Trinidad and Miami.

"I said, 'Turn around, don't look,' and I added a few drops of cane syrup to rum and said, 'Now tell me which one you prefer,'" he recounted. You know where this is going.

"These are rum drinkers and they all preferred the one that had sugar in it."

Same rum. A bit of sweetness. And the winner is: sugar. It's a story that rum producers tell over and over.

"The addition of sugar and also glycerin"—oh yeah, there's likely that in some rums, too—"what it does is it tends to mask a lot of imperfections," Ward said.

Sugar can also balance out the bitterness in rum that can come from extended aging, Andrew Hassell of the West Indies Rum Distillery told me. Hassell doesn't use sugar in the Cockspur line of rums his distillery produces, and overall says he prefers to create flavor just with what he is able to produce off the still and through barrel aging, but sometimes his distillery's customers—those selling a brand with rum made by the West Indies Rum Distillery—are interested in the technique.

"I am making generalizations, but in general, if I give you a twenty-year-old rum it's going to be pretty bitter," he said. "Sugar for alcohol is like salt for food; it is flavor enhancer. The reality is, yes, that rum does have a lot of flavor in it, but it is overpowered by the bitterness. If you can neutralize that bitterness, what is in there is actually really good."

Like Ward, Hassell told me that he thinks the average rum consumer—not connoisseurs, but those casual drinkers who make up the mass of most any market—don't particularly care about what goes into rum, provided it tastes good. As I was talking to both men, I couldn't quite discern the degree to which that opinion was genuinely held rather than just good diplomacy. WIRSPA, where Ward was chairman, holds an umbrella over more than a dozen rum producers, some of whom use sugar, while Hassell was responsible for maintaining and cultivating customer relationships in a competitive market, and neither seemed particularly keen to court controversy. But to many of the rum aficionados who sidle up to the bar with their hydrometers at the ready, as well as to producers who don't use sugar and aren't particularly worried about offending those who do, sugar and other additives can be seen as heresy. They consider them at best little more than cheats, a cheap way to skill-lessly make a tasty product, and at worst outright deception.

When I asked Seale how good a very old rum would be, given that years in a barrel can lend bitterness, he jumped in.

"Well if it's not any good, don't blame the rum, blame yourself. If you screwed it up, you screwed it up. The only reason to age something is not to ruin it," he said, before catching himself and adding: "or to market it."

Ultimately that last comment gets to the heart of the debate about sugar and other additives and whether it's right— regardless of legality—to sell a rum marked simply as "rum" to which additional sugars and flavorings have been blended in.

As blunt as Seale likes to be and as much as he has a reputation for being a bit cantankerous, he's also careful to not outright condemn a bit of added sugar, provided whoever is doing it is honest about it. But he also tends to see the use of additives as an affront to rum's heritage and is quick to note that in Barbados and Jamaica, two islands firmly at the center of rum's history, the practice is banned for rums that are sold locally.

Most of the companies adding sugar "are modern companies and their style of spirits making is alcohol plus," he said, meaning they use a modern multicolumn distillery to produce an almost vodka-like sugarcane spirit and then blend back in flavors until it is tasty and reminiscent of rum, rather than trying to make a tasty rum in the first place.

That may be so. However, the addition of sweetener and flavoring to rum is hardly a modern phenomenon (nor, it's worth mentioning, one relegated to rum exclusively). In his book *Caribbean Rum*, scholar Frederick Smith writes that in the late eighteenth century many producers blended "signature" ingredients into their rums. Indeed, for something originally known as "kill-devil," doing so would seem almost advisable—though Smith also notes that oftentimes their choice of blending materials ended up just making the rum even more lethal. Nearly two hundred years later, midcentury Puerto Rican rum researcher Rafael Arroyo also identified several rums made through the addition of flavors, though he was quick to slap the labels "spurious" and "artificial" on such examples. Today many of the producers who release rum with sugar and admit to doing so put the practice in a similar historical context. Perhaps the most famous to do so is Alexandre Gabriel, a cognac maker who fell for rum and launched the line of sourced rums known as Plantation. (In 2017 the company also bought Hassell's West Indies Rum Distillery). Gabriel says his addition of sugar to rum is inspired by an equivalent technique common in cognac called *dosage* and helps smooth out the flavor. Having the latitude to do so, Gabriel has said, is part of what makes rum such an exciting category with the potential for a wide range of styles and innovation compared to other spirits, which are more tradition-bound. The argument that rum is more diverse than other spirits is oft repeated, but, for reasons that will be discussed in the next chapter, it's one that's also usually employed in a way that renders it a false equivalency.

Regardless, the arguments of tradition as a way to justify sugar addition carry varying weight for the anti-sugar camp, but many people settle on the opinion that if the practice continues, consumers should at least be made aware of it.

"The problem is people want to hide. People sometimes ask me, 'Oh, what's wrong with adding sugar?' I say, 'Well, ask the guys who are lying about it.'

They are lying about it, so they know something is wrong. If you think adding sugar is a good thing, you tell the world," Seale told me, launching into a "When you talk to Seale . . ." moment.

"You can macerate fruit in your rum"—oh yeah, some producers do that as well—"but you write on your label 'rum with macerated fruit.' But don't say 'rum,' like my rum, like Jamaican rum and your macerated fruit. You want to put vanilla in your rum, no problem, but you put 'rum with vanilla.' You like rum with vanilla, off you go. But you see the problem here is that really if you do something well, you should want to shout about it. But the reality is people want to hide what they do, so I want to put vanilla in my rum because I want to dupe you that I am so skilled and age my rum and you believe that this vanilla is from the still and my sugar, so I can't tell you about my vanilla because I am just plopping two blops of vanilla in. If you do something well, you shout it to the world. If you are making rum and you are growing vanilla and you are doing something wonderful, you will tell the world: 'I am rum with vanilla and this is what I do.'"

Substantially, I agree with him. Seale and those of his persuasion ultimately tend to distill their advice to consumers into a "drink what you like, but be careful what you pay for," message, a sentiment echoed by Joy Spence of Appleton, who told me, "If I am going to drink something premium, I want it in the same category as a good single malt, which has no carbs in it."

But rum producers like Spence and Seale also have another motivation for wanting rum generally to be produced without additives, or at least undisclosed additives: the practice is a competitive disadvantage. In the Caribbean, rum produced for the local market is not allowed to have any added sugar or flavors, though distillers can add them for rum that will be exported to a jurisdiction, like the US, where such additives are permitted. Moreover, their styles are linked to the use of pot and traditional column stills, which cost more to run than a large, modern column still that producers can use if they are just compounding their rum from highly refined, near-flavorless spirit and additives, which can also increase an end product's palatability without all the time and angel's share losses of Caribbean aging.

In the end, though, the debate isn't really over sugar and flavorings. Instead it takes us back to that slippery question of what, exactly, is rum and who gets to answer that.

PARASOL

Many rums celebrate their connection to a particular place, but a few embrace the spirit's global trappings. Among those that do is Denizen rum, a brand that showcases two multi-island blended expressions and proudly proclaims its link with the master blenders of Amsterdam—i.e., E&A Scheer. In this cocktail, brand ambassador Shannon Mustipher, a spirits educator and consultant, takes the rum's cosmopolitanism a degree farther by mixing Denizen's Aged White Rum with the elegent and not-too-overpowering Cognac-based Banane du Brésil liqueur from the French liqueur producer Giffard. She then completes it with honey syrup—the rich, complex stand-in for sugar-based simple syrup—and fresh lime juice in a clear nod to that rum classic, the daiquiri. If you're feeling a bit more adventurous, she says you can use passion fruit syrup instead of honey for a fun alternative.

2 ounces Denizen Aged White Rum

0.5 ounce Giffard Banane du Brésil

0.25 ounce honey syrup or passion fruit syrup (see below)

0.75 ounces fresh lime juice

Combine all ingredients in a cocktail shaker with ice. Shake well. Strain into a coupe and garnish with lime wheel.

To make honey syrup: Mix equal parts honey and water in a saucepan over medium heat until all honey is dissolved. Cool and store in refrigerator.

To make passion fruit syrup: Use passion fruit juice in place of the water.

CHAPTER 7

Let's Have a Drink

The debate over whether rum can be made from beet sugar, or have sugar added to it prior to bottling, or be blop-blopped with a bit of vanilla flavoring, is ultimately a debate over authenticity. Authenticity is a term that's been bandied around so much that it's begun to lose its meaning; it is, unfortunately, becoming inauthentic itself. But in its pre-fad meaning it gets at something powerful, namely the idea of what do we mean, exactly, when we call something "rum," and just as importantly, who gets to decide what that means? There are all sorts of explanations of where "rum" went wrong. You can blame the world after Prohibition, when America began to lose its drinking sensibilities. You can blame it on the fact that Bacardí became the brand synonymous with rum and sold it light and cheap. By the early 1980s it held two-thirds of the world rum market. You could blame the rise of spiced and flavored rums that followed, joining the flavored vodkas and trendy monstrosity cocktails that almost issued from the "Sex and the City" set itself. You can blame the fetishization of age statements in whiskey that translated to similar expectations for a spirit aged in a vastly different climate. You can blame marketing, like many people seem to, but that's sort of like blaming yourself.

Really, I doubt any of those things can be fully or even primarily to blame, and I am suspicious of the whole notion that rum has fallen. Few broadly marketed, brand-driven, consumer-facing consumptive categories would stand up well to significant scrutiny. Try to tear into some of the most popular yet obscure-to-western-palates spirits labels around the world (surprise: there's some, um, interesting "whiskeys" and "brandies" out there), or try to unravel one of those buck-or-three bottles of wine that seem to find particular purchase at upmarket grocery chains. As the work of Rafael Arroyo has shown, the category has been laden with suspicions of deception for a very long time.

What *is* new is that suddenly so many people—including you, I hope—care about rum. Those who champion authenticity most vociferously are the connoisseurs. When "rum" was mostly Bacardí or something in the flavor of "Blueberry Lemonade" or "Island Melon," there were few connoisseurs and few, therefore, who cared much about whether the rum they were drinking was made in a way that embodied tradition and bespoke craft. (In all fairness, it's also important to note that many rum devotees I spoke to singled out Bacardí's basic white rum, its Carta Blanca, for praise as a straightforward, no-frills product at a commensurate price. "I think it is a really good white rum . . . because it does what it says it will do," one person said.)

Richard Seale of Barbados's Foursquare rum distillery divides a spirit's transition from a low-value, mass-market product to something worthy of connoisseurship into two phases: that of the fanatical and that of the critical.

"What you tend to find is that in the fanaticism stage everything is good. Every. Thing. Is. Good. If you do a skew of the ratings, everything is skewed and a lot of the writing is regurgitating a press release," he told me. "When you are a fanatic, some overnight company you've never heard of splashes out a beautiful bottle in a beautiful box and says 'thirty years old,' and it has the most crème de la crème label on it and the story is beautifully written, and heck, when you are a fanatic you want to believe."

Rum, wallowing in the fanatical stage for a decade, is only just now starting to cross into the critical, where reviewers will call out rums with nefarious age statements, undisclosed additives, or hazy origins. Evidence can be found of this on rum's most contested digital grounds, including the r/rum subreddit on Reddit, the "Global Rum Club" page on Facebook, and Matt Pietrek's blog, *Cocktail Wonk*, at www.cocktailwonk.com. The web forum at Capn Jimbo's Rum Project at www.rumproject.com, which makes up for whatever it lacks in posting activity with a rampaging zealotry, not only publishes an extensive list of test results for added sugar compiled from the hydrometer method and the Alko and Systembolaget sites, but has also gone on to calculate the score distributions awarded by prominent online rum reviewers, finding widespread grade inflation. Throughout these venues, it is understood that those with the most serious rum palates reject rum with added sugar and flavorings.

But percolating up through those denunciations are a few retorts—after all, if those added sugars and flavors are legal, and for the most part they seem to be, and if those nefarious age statements are really just creative label design with meaningless numbers that don't fall afoul of the letter of labeling law, then are they wrong? Are such things not just like those who produce rum from cane syrup and first-press molasses panning those who make it from blackstrap molasses (i.e. a critique based on differing style preferences rather than an actual qualitative judgment)? In short, the question is, if it tastes good, why not drink it?

The answer from the advocates of "pure" rums often is: because those drinks just aren't rum. Simple, then, if it weren't for the follow-up question: what *is* rum?

In the summer of 2016 that question was put to a panel of high-profile members of the rum industry at the annual Tales of the Cocktail festival, which every year brings together bartenders, spirits producers, and the libationally enthusiastic to New Orleans for nearly a week of seminars on everything from sustainability in the booze industry, to the role played by insects in shaping drinking culture, to the economics of running a spirits brand, all of which is fueled by a seemingly endless slate of tastings.

The panel titled, "When Is a Rum Not a Rum? The Big Rum Debate," came not long after everyone started talking about Stoneyard, that Colorado "rum" with a curious ingredient list and was made up of a fascinating amalgam of people. On it was that ubiquitous crusader against added sugar, Richard Seale of Barbados's Foursquare distillery; as well as Alexandre Gabriel of Plantation Rums, one of the foremost proponents of sugar addition; Ben Jones of the rhum agricole producer Rhum Clément, which operates in Martinique under exceptionally strict regulations for rum; and Roberto Serrallés of the Puerto Rican distillery behind Don Q, which produces light rum in the Spanish style on large multicolumn stills. They were led by Ian Burrell, a man with the enviable job title of "global rum ambassador."

The question of whether rum could be made from anything other than sugarcane, the first to come up, was quickly settled: universally, of course not. The agreement didn't hold as the discussion wended into more controversial topics. However, if somebody was trying to prime the panel for fireworks, it didn't work. All of the panelists were too used to collaboration and probably too aware of just how extensive their mutual interests were. Unfortunately, if they were trying to prime it to find an answer to the question posed in the session, that didn't quite work out either.

Instead, the panel was a showcase of why it is so hard to settle on just what rum is. If "rum" were meant only to include that which is produced by the people on the panel, it would have to include the rich and nutty rums of Foursquare, made in Barbados; the lighter, funkier rhums of Clément from Martinique; and the light, oak-driven rums from Don Q in Puerto Rico, to say nothing of the wide range of rums imported and blended by Plantation, which is based in France.

But they wouldn't only have to contend with the stylistic differences of each of those companies. They'd also have to work with the regulations set out in each of the producing countries for rum, which are sometimes in direct conflict with each other.

Barbados follows the CARICOM rum standard, which mandates sugarcane products only, bars flavoring and sweetening for "rum" destined for sale in the Caribbean market but allows such things in "rum" that's going to a place where they are allowed, like the United States. It also requires age statements to reflect that of the youngest rum in the bottle.

Rhums agricoles in Martinique, meanwhile, fall under the rhum agricole AOC, or Appellation d'Origine Contrôlée, the French certification that protects the name for products produced in a certain area under a certain set of standards, such as those for Chablis or Champagne. AOC agricoles must be made in one of several regions of the island of Martinique from fresh juice from sugarcane cultivated under rules that limit irrigation and restrict harvesting to the months from January through August. Furthermore, the rules set a floor limit for the juice's sugar content and pH, limit distillation to column stills of a certain range of styles, and lay out the meanings of the terms *blanc*, which indicates rhum rested for at least six weeks; *élevé sous bois*, which indicates rhum aged at least twelve months in oak; and *vieux*, which indicates rhum aged at least six years in oak. Crucially, they must also have a minimum concentration of congeners to prevent distillers from making an extremely neutral spirit that's more reminiscent of vodka.

Puerto Rico's rum standard requires that all rums produced there must be aged a minimum of one year (white rums like Don Q Cristal and Bacardí Carta Blanca are carbon filtered to remove the color) and must be made from molasses and distilled in a continuous column still.

Plantation rum's portfolio, meanwhile, is global, sourcing rums from places like Guatemala, which has a geographic indication similar to Martinique's, but one that requires its rums to be made from "virgin sugarcane honey" (i.e., sugarcane syrup rather than blackstrap molasses, the use of which is verboten) that comes from certain varieties of sugarcane, which must be hand cut. Guatemala's rum standard further lays out several different aging categories based on the solera method. The use of sugar, meanwhile, is freely allowed.

"Rum is probably the most democratic of all spirits. It is made throughout the entire world and it has been made for a long time in a lot of ways," Serrallés said at the event. "That is the inherent confusion in the category. In the US that's the problem . . . right now it is too loose, it is just basically sugarcane—and they are not even policing that part—sugarcane molasses and then distilled below a certain proof."

But what would it take to tighten those regulations? Serrallés made a proposal.

"What about aging? Does 'rum' have to be aged?" he asked. "I am of the idea that for it to be 'rum' maybe it should spend some time in a barrel."

Almost before he could complete the sentence, the moderator, Burrell, who is from Jamaica, interjected in cheerful indignation.

"What?" he responded. "The rum I grew up drinking, Wray and Nephew Overpoof—no age! Pure rum! 100 percent."

"Which is fine. Then that would be 'unaged rum,'" Serrallés continued. "There's 'rum' and there's 'unaged rum.' That is just an idea," the tone of his voice betraying that perhaps he already realized he had lost and may not have been entirely serious in the first place.

In that easy exchange was the problem with narrowing rum's definition: with so much allowed now under the moniker of "rum," whose heritage do you decide to throw out—whose rum, in other words, do you decide can no longer be called "rum"?

Absent industry agreement, Richard Seale and Luca Gargano, the latter of the Italian cult rum bottler Velier, have started applying their own categorization that is based on the still types used to make the rum. In some aspects, it mirrors the terminology and gradation used in scotch whisky.

Their classification starts with the term "Pure Single Rum," for rums made entirely in pot stills; then it has "Single Blended Rum," for rums that are a blend of pot-distilled rums and those distilled in a "traditional" column still (i.e., not a large multicolumn still, but the smaller column stills used by Seale and others); then there is "traditional rum," which is entirely from a traditional column still, such as those made under the AOC Martinique regulations; then finally there is simply "rum," which is everything else and which Seale told me he's occasionally taken to calling "industrial rum"—"just to stir the discussion" (the French use the term as well, as *rhum industrial*, but for molasses-based rums). "Single" in this scheme is meant to refer to all the rum coming from the same distillery, and the convention is meant to be flexible enough to attach extra gradations to the classification, such as "agricole" for sugarcane-juice rhums or "aged" and "unaged" designations.

"The classification is not trying to tell you these two rums taste the same," Seale said. "It is trying to give you a common root to how they are made, and that will give you a framework for understanding why they taste different, so if you said to yourself, 'Well, why does a single blended rum from Barbados taste different from a single blended rum from Jamaica?' you now have the tools to understand it. The first thing you will understand is . . . they have different fermentation, so they have this common single blended, but they have different fermentations and traditionally Jamaica uses more pot still in their blends. This is a million miles away from 'light,' 'gold,' and 'dark.'"

Seale also believes it will help customers figure out how to value what they buy. "Pure Single Rums" made on inefficient pot stills, perhaps after long, exotic fermentations like those done at Hampden, necessarily cost more to produce than a rum distilled on a large multicolumn still and then made pleasing through the addition of sugar and other flavorings; however, on the liquor-store shelf, price often doesn't correspond accordingly.

"You see this hysterical thing where some of them, as you pay more, you get more sugar, because the tool of premiumization now is if it tastes sweet, it must be good and therefore how do I make this rum more premium than the other? I just add more sugar," Seale said. "So the big challenge for those of us in rum who are traditional producers, if we don't win this war about communication, there is no place for us."

As Seale outlined his mission, which he frames as preventing rum from following the economics of vodka, where value is concocted by master marketers rather than master distillers, I found myself nodding more vigorously with each word. Of course I want a rum market that's able to sustain centuries-old producers like Hampden, with their funky fermentations, and Demerara Distillers, with their ancient, or ancient-esque, wooden stills, rather than one dominated by giant spirits producers quick to jettison heritage in the pursuit of volume and eager to grab any shortcut available. I want that for the reasons that people want artisanal beer and straight-from-the-farm slow food, and handcrafted bookshelves, and hand-knit scarves, which is to say for reasons that are substantially intangible and that don't fully conform to the impulses of modern capitalism.

"Tradition," one rum-industry veteran told me, "is a solution for a problem that doesn't exist anymore."

While it is laudable that the categories provide the consumer with more information than the name of simply "rum," I worry that ultimately they do too little and are too broad to catch on. Even as Seale was explaining them to me, he had to stop to add how they could be further subdivided so that a rum could potentially have a name like "Unaged Pure Single Rum Agricole," a description that would fit the extremely funky and grassy rum produced by St. George Spirits in Alameda, California (though, because it is made outside of Martinique and in a pot still, it would not qualify as an AOC agricole). I imagine if Seale and Gargano's classification system was widely adopted—right now they are its primary users—such a term would eventually come close to rolling off the tongue as easily as does "single malt scotch whisky," which itself was only coined in the middle of the twentieth century. But it still wouldn't provide the information many of rum's most committed fans are demanding: primarily, whether there is any added sugar or flavorings (and if so, how much), and secondarily, a more consistent age-statement regime.

By focusing its gradation on the device used to make the rum I am, moreover, afraid that while it could discourage high-priced rum made from cheap distillate and added sugar and flavors, it would unnecessarily punish excellent rums that would fall into the generic "rum" category because they are made on modern column stills, much the way blended scotch is often seen as categorically inferior to single malt, even though many great examples can be found.

Ultimately, I want to value all exquisitely made rums, whether they are from Hampden's pot stills, a combination of Seale's pot and column stills, or the large modern stills used by producers like the Dominican Republic's Brugal and Serrallés's Don Q from Puerto Rico. I find both Brugal's 1888 and Don Q's 2005 Signature Release Single Barrel, to take two examples, to be exceptional examples of barrel-dominant rums well worth their price.

Seale and Gargano's classification system isn't the only way Caribbean rum producers are trying to wrest back control of their spirit's classification, however. In the past several years, a few rum-producing countries, including Guatemala, the Dominican Republic, Jamaica, and Venezuela, have worked to create their own geographic indication for rum, much like Martinique's rhum agricole AOC. Because each of these settles on different regulations—for example, Venezuela's requires its rums to be aged for at least two years but allows added sugar; Jamaica's, meanwhile, is perfectly fine with straight-off-the-still rum but bans any additives but a bit of caramel coloring—they don't give a universal definition for "rum." What they do, however, is let each producing country define rum how they want it, providing a floor of information. It's a system that is far more detailed

The copper pot stills at Mount Gay Distillery in Barbados. One of the aspects that makes rum unique from other spirits is that individual distilleries often use multiple types of stills. At Mount Gay, rum is made from a blend of pot- and column-distilled rum.

Column stills—which can produce a purer, but less flavorful, product than pot stills—come in a range of sizes. Some, like this large multi-column still at Ron Barceló in the Dominican Republic, tower into the sky and are highly sophisticated and precise.

than what current regulations provide and makes it possible to talk about "Jamaican rum" and "Dominican Republic rum" the way drinkers can today talk about "scotch" and "bourbon" and "cognac."

Ultimately, though, the geographic indication system covers only a fraction of rum in the world. Right now, the only way to truly know how your rum is made is to chase down information on individual bottles, a frustrating task that occasionally leads to web forums laden with rumor and far more often simply ends in an opaque miasma of marketing, where stories and claims often contradict reality. Frankly, this is unacceptable. I unwaveringly believe consumers have the right to know exactly what is in what they are drinking before they put it into their body. Just as people have come to expect ingredient lists on food, the same should be true on alcohol.

Luckily, it seems that I am not alone, and more spirits brands are catering to consumers who want more nutritional information about their products. Mezan, a new independent rum bottler, has even turned the opacity of the rum world into a marketing advantage, selling rums that explicitly state on their labels that they are "unsweetened" and "uncolored." Meanwhile, Ed Hamilton, a veteran rum figure who quit his job in the petroleum industry nearly three decades ago, bought a sailboat, and traveled around the Caribbean, filling his website, the Ministry of Rum (www.ministryofrum.com), with a wealth of information before eventually deciding to import his own rums and sell them with an exquisite level of transparency and detail. The site for his importing company may not be pretty, but on www.caribbean-spirits .com you can find photos of the distillery where the rum he bottles comes from and learn that the rum in your hand was, for example, imported as bulk rum in 1,000-liter IBC tanks, filtered with a five-micron filter, and bottled on a six-bottle gravity feed filler. The color of the spigots? Fuchsia, it seems. Try to get that information from your average spirits company.

"I say, if I ever say anything that's not true, I deserve to have my ass kicked, but on the other hand, when other people hide the truth or make up lies, they deserve to have their ass kicked. I think it's fair," he told me with a signature boisterousness that, along with his prominent mustache and penchant for boats, makes me think of him as one of the closest people in rum to a pirate.

Remarkably, greater transparency is also coming from the level of massive spirits companies as well. Diageo, for example, has started to publish breakdowns of the calorie counts of its spirits on www.drinkiq .com as well as the amount of fat, protein, and carbohydrates. The Venezuelan rum brand Diplomático provides similar information on its website (rondiplomatico.com). While both have a ways to go (at times, I found both their websites glitchy), that information can help you get a glimpse of what's in your rum. One way is to take a look at calorie contents. Because alcohol has seven calories per gram, a one-ounce pour of 40 percent pure rum contains just over nine grams of alcohol and therefore just over sixty-four calories. Since higher-proof spirits have more alcohol, they have more calories per a given volume. But any drink with a calorie count higher than what's to be expected from its alcohol content contains additives, likely sweeteners. Unfortunately, the technique doesn't reveal flavorings that might not contain calories, or significant calories, but as more companies release nutritional information on their spirits, it's one tool to help reverse engineer what's in your booze. More importantly, it is a trend that seems to conform and therefore be driven by not just connoisseurs of rum but the growing health consciousness of the general public as well.

"For spirits, it's not a mandated requirement to put on nutritional facts, but the consumers are becoming much more aware and they want to have much more information, even down to allergens," Joy Spence, the Appleton master blender, told me. "We get a lot of requests—'Do your rums have any allergens?' 'Can vegans drink your rums?'—so customers are becoming more and more sophisticated in terms of nutritional facts." When asked, Appleton provides answers to those questions, Spence said.

The more brands hear from consumers who want this information, the more likely, I suspect, they will be to provide it. So if you're not satisfied with the information you can get about a particular rum, email away.

In the drink guide that follows, I've decided to be ecumenical. It's not that I'm adverse to telling you what I think you should drink. Any rums I mention in the drink guide as being excellent or among my favorites represent drams, either neat or in a cocktail, that I'd be pleased to sit down with. Mostly these are rums from the traditional Caribbean producers and mostly these are unsugared. There are exceptions, of course. Among the emerging American rum scene, which still has quite a ways to go, there are some outstanding craft distillers, in particular Richland Rum, which is made in pot stills from sugarcane syrup in Georgia; is full of well-balanced oak, caramel, spice, and a bit of citrus; and has an exceptionally long finish. I also enjoy Diplomático Mantuano, which performed great in a blind tasting I once participated in, even though it has some added sugar, a fact that's readily available on Diplomático's website (their higher-end Reserva Exclusiva, which has five times as much sugar, is far too sweet for me). In fact, even if you're adamantly opposed to sugared rums, it's probably worth it to try a few, just so you can learn to identify them. In general, sugared rums tend to be softer and their flavors, on my palate at least, evolve less distinctly. People sometimes refer to them as "doped" rums, and it's almost like they are speaking sloppily.

Nonetheless, ounce for ounce, nothing has pleased me as much as the traditional Caribbean-island rums. Most evenings I'm reaching for a bottle from Jamaica, St. Lucia, Barbados, the Dominican Republic, or Haiti. Not only do all these islands produce unadulterated rums of amazing complexity, they also do so at remarkably accessible price points. (If you're concerned about sugar, though, you're best off going with one of the traditional producers like Brugal or Barceló for rums from the Dominican Republic; other brands labeled as being from there can be laden with sugar and additives.) A bottle of Appleton Rare, a twelve-year-old rum from one of the world's foremost distilleries, costs less than $40. You're going to be hard pressed to find such a value in any other product with alcohol in it.

But rum's breadth is one of the best things about the category and deserves to be explored. Rums from the Spanish Americas—such as those from Don Pancho in Panama and Flor de Caña in Nicaragua—tend to be refined and elegant, pulling a lot of their flavor from wood, and often make great sippers for drinkers who already enjoy high-quality whiskey. Some of them are so rich that it's almost a shame that they don't come with a cigar. For anyone familiar with Latin American culture, the place where these rums fit into it will be apparent from the first sip. If you're reading this outside of the US or in a time when vestigial trade policy has finally been cast off, you also have access to a whole world of Cuban rums, long a center of standout Spanish-style rum production and also the place that gave rum its interwar cachet (thank you, Prohibition and Hemingway).

Meanwhile, the rhums agricoles of the French West Indies—Martinique, Guadeloupe, and, if you are a jet-setter or have access to a really good spirits retailer, Marie-Galante—tend to be funkier, more vegetal, and a bit more biting. But some of the aged expressions, such as the higher-end ones from Rhum Clément in Martinique or Damoiseau in Guadeloupe, make for fantastic sippers. Generally, you'll pay more for rhum agricole—unlike most of the rest of the Caribbean powers, France, after all, held onto her islands and the rhums from there trade in the euro and are subject to E.U. regulations and French labor law.

But you can go even farther. Follow the longitudes out and stick a pin in any landmass within the cane-growing latitudes and you'll probably strike something that, in the weakest definition of the spirit at least, can be called rum. For example, Berry Bros. & Rudd, a London-based independent bottler, and Samaroli, an Italian one, bring in rums from Fiji, though both are costly and require effort to find. Also available in the US is Penny Blue from Mauritius. From Madagascar is Rhum Dzama. From Australia there's Bundaberg, and the Seychelles has Takamaka, though those are going to require international travel to get. The Philippines' Tanduay and India's Old Monk and McDowell's No. 1 Celebration are all massive best-sellers, particularly in their home markets, though they don't have wide connoisseur appeal, at least not beyond their novelty factor. Overall, while there are some gems there—the Fijian and Mauritian rums, specifically—these rums are really more for the adventure, but perhaps someday they could become mainstays.

If you really want to have an adventure in rum, however, your best bet might be to break out the cocktail shaker. It also helps if you don some curious headwear, throw on a loud shirt, and stuff your pockets full of every damn swizzle stick you can find.

One of the great things about rum's incredible diversity is its incredible versatility. Not only can it go snifter-for-snifter against any of the world's best brown spirits, it also excels on equally exceptional terms inside cocktails. Rum, in fact, is responsible for one of America's greatest cocktail movements and, like a great American mix, one of the country's great spectacle movements as well: tiki.

"For me, it started when I was about six years old," Jeff "Beachbum" Berry told me over cocktails one afternoon. "I grew up in the San Fernando Valley in Southern California and at that time, in the mid-1960s, tiki was still in the golden age, which was from 1934 to the late 1970s. At that point, there were at least two or three Polynesian-themed restaurants in any town of about any size. And my parents, who were from New York, liked Chinese food, so they would go to a place called Ah Fong's. For a suburban Chinese place it was amazing. There was an indoor lagoon, and the bar had a little miniature island scene with a hut and foot-tall fake palm trees. Even the carpeting had palm trees. Behind the bar there was dawn-to-dusk lighting changes. For me, as a six-year-old, it was—well, I wanted to live there."

Berry and I were sitting at Latitude 29, the New Orleans tiki bar that might just be the apotheosis of his childhood wonderment—sans the indoor lagoon—and I was sipping a Navy Grog. Like a true tiki master, Berry was tight lipped when I asked him for the exact specifications of his version. The standard is a mix of rum, lime and grapefruit juice, and honey, and it was Frank Sinatra's favorite drink at the bar where it originated, Don the Beachcomber's, in the 1940s.

"These were very chic, expensive places. They were not tacky," he said. "Don the Beachcomber, that was a place Orson Welles and Marlene Dietrich went to. It was sort of the Spago of its day."

Tiki, though it wasn't called that then, got its start when Donn Beach, née Ernest Raymond Beaumont Gantt, a wanderlust ex-bootlegger, opened his tropical-themed restaurant just off Hollywood Boulevard right after Prohibition. Combining his globe-trotting palate with a wave of cheap but high-quality rum the era's illegal booze peddlers had left over from that noble experiment gone awry, Donn began whipping up some of the most complex, flavor-dense cocktails the world had ever seen. Because of the abundance of rum, Donn was able to make his cocktails with affordable twelve-, fifteen-, seventeen-, and even thirty-year-old rums, Berry told me. In the process, he even managed to resurrect America's love of the spirit, saving the category from the low-life slump it had fallen into before Prohibition. Americans, having suffered through more than a decade of inconsistent, often low-quality, occasionally deadly booze, a time that saw most of the country's top bartenders head to friendlier shores or straighter occupations, were enthralled.

"He'd been open only three years in the 1930s before there were 150 copycats from coast to coast," Berry told me. To prevent the theft of his recipes, Donn began to formulate them in code—out went "cinnamon syrup" and "Angostura bitters," in went "#4" and "#8."

"It was like industrial espionage to pry them out of the bartenders who knew them," Berry said of the time when he started to try to crack the codes as an amateur tiki aficionado in the 1980s and '90s, when he was working in Hollywood. "That was their passport to employment. If they had this secret knowledge, they could basically write their own ticket during the golden age."

While tiki is most known today for its shtick of tropical extravaganza, Donn's real innovation was how to mix a litany of ingredients into amazing layers of flavor. In particular, he was adept at mixing various styles of rum into a supremely complex base spirit—something that was almost unheard of in cocktails before. The Navy Grog I was sipping, for example, was a mix of a white Puerto Rican rum, a dark Jamaican rum, and a Demerara rum—in other words, dry and floral, heavy and molassesy, and smoky, respectively, a combination that didn't exist with just one rum.

"You would never see anybody putting two bourbons in an Old Fashioned, or three gins in martini," Berry said. "I think he was kind of a genius."

Tiki drinks can be incredibly fun and, if mastered, rewarding to make. Because they often call for over-the-top garnishes and outlandish drinking vessels—think fistfuls of mint and ceramic mugs in the likeness of Polynesian deities—they make impressive party tricks. But with ingredient lists that run both long—well over a half dozen—and obscure—passion fruit purée, peach liqueur—they also require a very well-stocked bar and a bit of spirits-store sleuthing. Thankfully, though, rum takes well to much simpler concoctions.

One of the best ways to understand Caribbean drinking culture is to visit a produce market. With seemingly as many varieties of citrus as all the types of fruit in a northern supermarket in deep winter, to say nothing of a bounty of other fruits that are often unrecognizable, it's quickly clear why most mixed drinks on the islands follow a simple formula: rum + juice (and also rum + coconut water and rum + soda). While there, juice whatever's in season, throw some rum in it, a bit of ice if you prefer, and you'll often have the perfect drink to cut the tropical heat.

Pepe Grant, Hampden's tour manager, told me the typical Jamaican will mix rum with pretty much anything that's around—from aloe vera juice to milk. ("Won't that curdle?" I asked, and Grant just let out an energetic laugh, indicating I was missing the point.)

"You know, this is Jamaica, when it is hot, you see all of these hills with these trees, you are going to find someone cooling out under a tree," Grant said. "So a man who might be cooling out under a coconut tree is going to be drinking rum and coconut water."

Case in point, I was sitting next to Grant, who makes an excellent rum punch, so I was drinking my rum in punch.

Indeed punch is one of the great ways to drink rum and, as spirits historian David Wondrich shows in his exploration of the format's history, *Punch: The Delights (and Dangers) of the Flowing Bowl*, one of the earliest. It is almost essentially communal—punches are to be prepared in large batches and generously ladled out to friends and passers-by. If you're throwing a party, go for a punch, but make sure to seek out a genuine recipe lest you end up with that frightening fraternity concoction, known in my university days as jungle juice.

But rum can be mixed in an even simpler concoction or on a single-serve scale. In fact, if well made, I'm pretty sure I could be content without ever having any other cocktail. What you call the holy trinity that is rum, lime, and sugar depends on exactly what type of rum is your tradition and where you are. If you're in the French Caribbean using rhum agricole, it's the *ti'punch* (literally "small punch," making the stylistic connection between it and its bowl-filling counterpart explicit). If you are in Brazil using cachaça, it's the caipirinha, and if you are elsewhere using rum it is the daiquiri, though at one point, if you were in Cuba, it would have been the *el draque*. Of these, the daiquiri is the most refined and my favorite because if it's made properly (and we are not talking here about those slushy flavored Bourbon Street horrors) with fresh squeezed lime juice and is shaken and strained it is transcendent. A standard template is two ounces rum, one ounce lime juice, and one-half ounce simple syrup, but the daiquiri can be a tricky drink and you're going to have to adjust those based on the type of rum you are using and the qualities of your limes, which can vary to a remarkable degree throughout the year.

Recipes for the daiquiri often specify white rum, and some even seem to think they're supposed to specify the lightest possible rums available. In many cases, the latter is just someone looking for citrus-flavored vodka; the former, meanwhile, isn't wrong, just shortsighted. Great daiquiris can be made from Spanish-style white rums, but they're great vehicles to explore funky Jamaican rums, agricoles, cachaças, and aged rums as well.

The daiquiri can also be recombined into many different drinks. In fact, Berry points out that the combination of those three ingredients is really the foundational math of the more complicated rum cocktails.

"A tiki drink at rock bottom is a Caribbean drink squared or a Caribbean drink cubed," he said.

But even without having to resort to so much multiplication, people have endlessly tinkered with the daiquiri's equation. Ernest Hemingway famously had his with maraschino liqueur subbed for the simple syrup and a bit of the lime juice left out in favor of an addition of grapefruit juice. As the story goes, he ordered these as doubles—a "Papa Doble"—a practice not recommended, less for the sake of moderation than for the fact that a cocktail at that volume warms up too much during the time it takes—or *should* take—to drink it. But this isn't a book just on daiquiris. So instead I leave you with two simple variations to pursue on your rum adventure. If you're bored of the standard daiquiri, throw in a dash or so of your favorite bitters—Angostura and orange bitters have become two of my favorites—and swap out the simple syrup for a superfine sugar, which is a frequently relayed bartender trick that increases the concentration and depth of the drink.

When in doubt, though, try the rums that follow neat first to understand them. Sip them without ice, at room temperature, and try them at various intervals of time in the glass—sometimes spirits benefit from a bit of time to open up out of the bottle. You can use a brandy snifter, though a wine glass also works quite well. For many of them, the high-end aged rums in particular, this is all you'll ever need to do to enjoy them. But once you get a sense of what's going on, go wild.

NAVY GROG

(Contributed by Jeff Berry from *Beachbum Berry Remixed: A Gallery of Tiki Drinks*)

   0.75 ounce fresh lime juice

   0.75 ounce white grapefruit juice

   0.75 ounce soda water

   1 ounce honey syrup*

   1 ounce Demerara rum

   1 ounce dark Jamaican rum

   1 ounce white Puerto Rican rum

Mix all ingredients in a cocktail shaker, shake with ice, and strain into glass with an ice cone (Berry's ice cone mold is available from Cocktail Kingdom, www.cocktailkingdom.com). Since its recent return to the American bar, many bartenders also add in a bit of allspice or pimento dram, an allspice-flavored liqueur. Experiment to taste.

*Honey syrup, as seen in the recipe for the Parasol (page 200), is made from a 1:1 ratio of honey and water.

CHAPTER 8

The Rum Guide

What follows is a guide through forty-three of the most interesting, iconic, and innovative brands working today, covering everything from Mantinique rhum agricole to long-aged sippers from Barbados and the Dominican Republic.

Owing to a variety of factors, including local law and taxes, spirits prices vary considerably across the US, and between stores. The prices for bottles that follow were derived from their suggested retail prices, or the average price listed on the eminently useful website www.wine-searcher.com. The figures in this guide therefore should be considered a reasonable midpoint—you may be able to find a bottle for a few dollars less, or have to pay several dollars more, depending on where you do your shopping.

APPLETON
ESTATE

With a heritage that stretches back more than 250 years, Appleton is one of the most iconic Caribbean rums on the market and one that is fully committed to producing spirits without additives. Thankfully, it is also one of the most widely distributed. The rums that come out of the distillery, which is located in Jamaica's Nassau Valley and uses a combination of pot and column stills, aren't the funkiest of the funky Jamaican rums—for that you have to go to Hampden. But they still display the island's signature richness and complexity, and under master blender Joy Spence, one of the most accomplished in the business, they are worthy of every bit of praise they get and probably more. Every decent rum collection needs at least the twelve-year-old Appleton Rare, which is an exquisite balance of barrel flavors, spice, fruit, and citrus, and at a price point of a few dollars either side of $38 is one of the most affordable sippers out there. Meanwhile, if you're looking to splurge, the Appleton 21 Year Old, at $135, is an incredibly complex and rich sipper also well worth the price. At the other end, the Reserve Blend ($27) makes an excellent daiquiri, one that proves there is no reason to hew to the rule that the cocktail can be made from white rum only. Appleton is part of J. Wray and Nephew, which is today owned by Gruppo Campari and also makes Jamaica's standby white overproof rum, which has its application in tiki and other cocktails but otherwise is best left to the experienced.

BACARDÍ

Ubiquitous Bacardí. You may wonder what it is doing here, but at 17.23 million cases sold in 2016—that's over two hundred million standard 750 ml bottles, folks, though I suspect a good portion of Bacardí's buyers go for the 1.75-liter format—Bacardí is the world's top-selling rum and it'd be remiss to leave it out. The big boy always has haters, but I was frequently surprised to hear rum-industry veterans praise the brand's flagship Carta Blanca ($13), which is aged and then carbon filtered for clarity, for being straightforward and honest. It claims to be light, dry, and cheap, and that's exactly what it delivers. You're not going to pour some into a snifter, sit down, sip it, and contemplate life's great questions. But if you're having a party and need to whip up some cheap fruity drinks . . . well, sure. Bacardí's older products are less even. Recently Bacardí released an ultra-premium Facundo line (see page 264). Lastly, Bacardí does have an interesting story. For that check out Tom Gjelten's engaging, if occasionally hagiographic, *Bacardí and the Long Fight for Cuba: The Biography of a Cause.*

BANKS

Banks is a testament to what blending rums from multiple origins can do. Its core white 5 Island ($30) and golden 7 Island ($36) expressions bring together nearly two dozen marks each from, well, five and seven islands, including a bit of Batavia arrack from Java. (Pop quiz to see if you've been reading this book or just drinkin': what might a multi-island blended rum with some Batavia arrack in it indicate?*) The Banks website instructs you to sip these rums neat, with the cheeky line "mixing won't improve our rum, but should certainly improve your cocktail." Go ahead and do so. Each is layered and complex. But they work great for cocktails. In particular, I absolutely love the 7 Island in a Royal Bermuda Yacht Club. Use the recipe from Punch at www.punchdrink.com rather than from Banks's website. I also like swapping out the Velvet Falernum for Lucky Falernum from the Washington state–based craft mixer outfit BroVo Spirits. There's some story here about who the eponymous Banks is, but it's mostly marketing blah, blah, blah. There's no heritage here. It was started by some folks who know good booze. They didn't disappoint, and then Bacardí bought the brand in 2015. Done. Drink.

*Answer: E&A Scheer played a role in its creation.

BARBANCOURT

At the height of the colonial era, when Haiti was French and known as Saint-Domingue, its part of Hispaniola was one of the most valuable places in the world, sending more sugar and other tropical products to Europe than anywhere else. That ended following the slave revolution of 1791 to 1804 and the crushing political instability that ensued, to say nothing of the ninety million gold francs—the equivalent of tens of billions of dollars today—the new nation was forced to pay France in compensation and the long refusal by many nations to even recognize its legitimacy. While the country is not an insignificant rhum producer today, for a long time the only brand that made it out was Barbancourt. Thankfully it's a very worthy ambassador. Made from sugarcane juice instead of molasses, its flavor is nonetheless closer to, but often lighter and more tropical than the molasses-based rum made elsewhere in the Caribbean, rather than the rhums agricoles of the French West Indies. The aged rhums, in particular, are excellent sippers. Confusingly, they are often referred to by the number of stars on their label, which doesn't correspond to their age—the "three star" ($21) is a four-year-old rhum, while the "five star" ($26) is an eight-year-old. There is also a fifteen-year-old rhum ($49), which has no stars. All are very well priced for their quality and invite experimenting.

BARCELÓ

One of the Dominican Republic's two major rum producers—Brugal is the other—Barceló's rum is made in the traditional formula of Spanish producers, which is to say a large column still, fairly neutral spirit, and lots of wood aging. Barceló, however, does it with one exception: they use sugarcane juice instead of molasses. Sipping these rums, though, you wouldn't know that—disproving the idea that all sugarcane juice distillates are grassy and funky. Like their counterparts elsewhere, these are reserved sippers on one end and light cocktail mixers on the other, though I find you have to go pretty high up in the line, such as to Imperial ($33), made from ten-year-old rum, to really get much complexity and flavor.

Barceló used to be owned by a family of the same name, which, since losing control of the original brand, has developed a new brand under the Dubar Imperial moniker. Though not available in the United States at the time of this writing, it is also worth checking out if you're ever in the Dominican Republic (as is, for that matter, Ron Barceló's distillery and tasting room, which is exceptionally well appointed and organized and an easy day trip from Santo Domingo, the island's capital).

BATAVIA ARRACK VAN OOSTEN

Batavia arrack is one of those "other" cane spirits. It is made in Indonesia, the former Dutch East Indies (Batavia is now the capital city known as Jakarta), following an ancient technique practiced by Chinese ethnic minorities who use molasses, cane juice, and a bit of red rice, the last to start off the fermentation. High in esters, it is most known in the modern cocktail world for its use in punch and tiki drinks. It's oily, floral, and big with a long, slightly harsh finish, but nonetheless it clearly echoes rum. Long a staple of E&A Scheer's trade—it's used in the liqueur known as Swedish *punsch*—it was for a time unavailable in the US. Today the Batavia Arrack van Oosten brand ($30) is imported by Haus Alpenz, a specialty spirits dealer that's also responsible for Smith & Cross rum ($32) and St. Elizabeth Allspice Dram ($37), another traditional punch and tiki staple made with a base of Jamaican rum.

BERRYS' OWN SELECTION, BERRY BROS. & RUDD

The London-based wine and spirits merchant Berry Bros. & Rudd bottles a nice variety of expressions from rum-producing regions all over the world—including some you can't get away from (Panama, Barbados) and some you almost never see (Fiji, anyone?). They're often quite unique rums and, in my experience, divisive. The St. Lucian rum is one of my all-time favorites—incredibly intense, it is perfumey, funky, with oak and caramel, a bit of bitterness, and spicy finish. Frankly, it's probably something that's really cool after you've spent months and months drinking a lot more reserved rums. Once my father poured himself a glass of it. He then sat down, took a sip, and promptly made a face that, for someone who's a case study in Midwestern reservedness, was incredibly, negatively emotive. Then he got up, poured a bit of water in it, took another sip, and threw the rest into the drain. Conversely, I found the Fijian rum to be too woody and uninspiring to fall in love with. However, my uncle, who has been praising Flor de Caña since before it was available in the States, won't stop mentioning how much he likes it. But, as they say, fortune favors the bold and it's no less true in rum drinking.

BOUKMAN

Barbancourt may have long been virtually the only Haitian rhum available outside the country, but that hardly means it is the only Haitian rhum. Instead, the country is full of small-scale farm-distilleries selling a fresh-off-the-still sugarcane juice rhum known as *clairin* to the local market. Only recently, however, has anyone put it in an internationally acceptable bottle and brought it to the world market. Among the producers doing so are the Italian specialty rum bottler Velier, and Boukman ($45), a brand of *clairin trempè*, or spiced rhum, started by Adrian Keogh. Keogh likens *clairin* to mezcal before that Mexican spirit gained international renown. The approximately five hundred Haitian distilleries encompass a wide range of rich terroir. For Boukman, Keogh sources his rhum from two producers, one in Croix-des-Bouquets and the other in Cap-Haïtien, then has it infused with a range of native woods, bitter orange peel, and spices, including allspice and bitter almond extract. The result is dry—there is no added sugar—and balanced: the spices are readily apparent, especially on the finish, but the rhum's sugarcane heritage is clear. While it's good enough to sip on its own, I suspect it will do particularly well in cocktails.

BRUGAL

Long a paragon of tradition-bound Spanish-style producers, the Dominican Republic's Brugal, under Jassil Villanueva and the fifth generation of *maestros roneros* in the past few years, has gone on to release some of the most exciting Spanish-style rums. Chief among them is Brugal 1888 ($50), named after the year of the company's founding. It is a "double maturation" of rum first aged for six to eight years in white, American oak ex-bourbon barrels, then blended and aged another four to six years in red, European oak ex-sherry casks. The process adds another layer of richness and makes the 1888 a bit fuller bodied, more lush, and fruitier than your traditional Spanish-style rum, though it still retains the characteristic dry, wood-forward style of Dominican rums.

Most of the rest of the line is more traditional and all are solid rums, though I've come to be particularly fond of the white Extra Dry ($20), which is aged for two to five years and has just enough flavor to make a light but interesting daiquiri.

CAÑA BRAVA

Caña Brava ($32) is a Panamanian rum made by the revered and prolific Francisco Jose Fernandez Perez, known almost exclusively as "Don Pancho," at his Las Cabras distillery and bottled by The 86 Co. Like all of the bartender-friendly bottler's products—they are also the makers of Fords Gin—this is a rum aimed straight at bartenders, with its signature bottle design which prioritizes graspability over svelteness, and its slightly over-proof strength, at 43 percent ABV. Don Pancho is Cuban trained, and he makes this three-year-old rum in the traditional Spanish style: column distillation, wood aging, and then filtering. Flavorful and dry, it fulfills its promise as a rum for cocktails like the daiquiri or the mojito and is worth checking out. Before you serve what you've substituted it into, though, be sure to make a couple of test cocktails. I found when using it that if I didn't have my cocktail ratios finely tuned, everything would be off. It's a good general rule anyway.

CAPTAIN MORGAN

The thing about Captain Morgan is that, though they often add all sorts of flavors, at least they say as much. Why does your coconut rum taste so much like coconut? Because it says right there on the label that they add coconut flavor. (If you want to know not just if there is sugar in your rum but how much, you can go to Diageo's Drink IQ website and find out.) By measure of transparency Captain Morgan is hard to beat and that's worth something, even if it is still not destined to make the rum a connoisseur's favorite sipper. But at just over ten million annual cases, that's probably not the point.

CHAIRMAN'S RESERVE

Chairman's Reserve ($28) is the flagship brand of St. Lucia Distillers, one of the Caribbean's rum-making gems, and, with the release of their Forgotten Casks expressions ($45), increasingly regarded as one of the most innovative distilleries in the region. The distillery uses Guyanese molasses, a fermentation of about twenty-four hours, and a combination of pot and column stills to produce incredibly full-bodied rums with plenty of spice and a bit of petrol and burnt sugar. These rums show up fairly often in bottlings by other brands—this is the only distillery on St. Lucia—and it's fun to taste Chairman's Reserve alongside the others. In particular, the standard issue Chairman's Reserve is much more restrained and less perfumey than the St. Lucia from Berry Bros. & Rudd, which comes entirely from a pot still, but take a second and you can find the common hints of spice and smokiness in each.

CLÉMENT

The Martinique agricole rhums produced by Rhum Clément are all excellent examples of their type available in the US. The V.S.O.P. ($40), aged for at least four years, and the X.O. ($57), aged for at least six, are cognac-like in their quality, with clear wood notes that should please an adventurous whiskey drinker as well. But equally enticing is unaged Canne Bleue ($35), a single-variety rhum that showcases agricole's signature funkiness and sugarcane and grassy finish. It's fairly big and makes a great candidate for everything from tiki cocktails to a simple daiquiri or ti' punch. Clément also produces a couple of agricole-based liqueurs, including the Créole Shrubb ($29), a complex orange liqueur that's essentially triple sec with a graduate degree, and its refinement rubs off on cocktails if you swap it in for a more run-of-the-mill orange liqueur.

COCKSPUR

Cockspur is produced by the West Indies Rum Distillery, by far the largest distillery on Barbados but one that has primarily been focused on distilling for other brands since its founding. When the distillers benefiting from the American cover-over subsidies took most of that business, the distillery began focusing more on bespoke production and its own brands. While its two top products, Old Gold ($21) and 12 (or VSOR in some markets) ($30), are well-made, dry, flavorful rums, they both have a note of wood-oak bitterness that some may find displeasing. (Andrew Hassell, the distillery's managing director, says the Bajan locals prefer a bit of bitterness, so that when the rum is mixed with soda it won't become too saccharine.) However, the distillery's real standout expression, in my opinion, is its Fine Rum ($18). Just short of a sipper, the rum is nonetheless an impressive value. Complex and flavorful, it works well for cocktails.

DAMOISEAU

Produced on the island of Guadeloupe in the French West Indies, Damoiseau is a rhum agricole made outside the Martinique AOC regulations. Its aged expressions are some of my favorite rhums agricoles, with all of the complexity and tempered strangeness of their agricole counterparts but overall lighter than what aged English-style rum often exhibits. But what's particularly exciting about Damoiseau is that their Pure Cane Rum ($35) white agricole is available in the US at 110 proof—a strength that Dani DeLuna, a founder of New York City's rum enthusiast group Cane Club, the brand ambassador for Boukman, and an all-around rhum agricole fan, says is commonly found in many bottlings from various distilleries on the French Islands but is rare in the US. Rested six months in in ex-bourbon casks, the more concentrated spirit brings along a lot more flavor—try it in a daiquiri or a ti' punch to get a sense of what is going on, but then go wild.

DENIZEN

Denizen produces both an aged white and an aged golden rum, and while they are both well-priced cocktail rums, what's particularly interesting about them is their story. They set it on a "quiet side street in Amsterdam" that's "nothing particularly exceptional," except for the fact that it is there where "some of the last practitioners of alchemy in the world" work. While they don't mention E&A Scheer by name, you know who they are talking about. Their goal with the two blends was to "free the flavor" that's been sequestered by big rum brands in the name of efficiency. The result is a bright and tropical white rum, the Aged White Rum ($18), that's blended with rums from lighter Trinidad and high-ester Jamaican, including some Hampden. The aged golden Merchant's Reserve rum ($30), meanwhile, is a blend of several Jamaican rums and rum from the Le Galion distillery in Martinique, which, unlike its neighbors, produces rum from molasses rather than sugarcane juice. It was inspired by tiki wizard Trader Vic for a version of his Mai Tai and is ester-y, but with a good balance of barrel flavors. The white rum claims to be three years old and the Merchant's Reserve to be eight, which they say right on their back labels. These numbers are a little wily though, and not far below the "age statement" on the white rum is a description that says it contains some unaged rum. Sorry, folks. Maybe call your senator.

DIPLOMÁTICO

If I had a shot for every person who told me how much they loved Diplomático after I told them I was writing a book on rum, serious rum, I'd have a long, long hangover. If I had one for every internet commentator who denigrates the brand because of its use of added sugar, I'd be dead and still drinking. Diplomático is a polarizing rum. Partly this is because it's widely distributed and heavily marketed. But it's also because, well, in its flagship expression, the Diplomático Reserva Exclusiva ($40), there is, for a rum, quite a bit of sugar in it: four grams per hundred milliliters (by comparison, a Coke has more than twice that). I find it too sweet. But the rest of the line has quite a bit of merit, provided you don't mind a little sugar (and to Diplomático's credit, the sugar content of their rum is readily available on their own website, under nutritional information).

Diplomático is unique in that the distillery uses not only multiple types of distillation—they have a pot; a hybrid pot-column still, which they call a batch kettle; and a column—but also because they make their rums from both molasses, which is fed into the pot still and, in a Latin American rum tradition, *miel de caña de azúcar*, which many in the industry would call a sugarcane syrup but which is often translated more literally (and enticingly, I suspect) as "sugarcane honey."

The results include the Mantuano (0.75 grams of sugar per 100 ml) ($24), from rums aged up to eight years, that, in a recent blind tasting I participated in was particularly popular for being easy sipping, but with just enough funk to make it interesting. Most interesting to me, though, is their Planas (0.25 grams of sugar per 100 ml) ($29), a white sipping rum that has been aged for up to six years and filtered. It has a distinctive sugarcane note, like many cachaças, but also subtle but clear vanilla and spice flavors from the barrels.

DON Q

It's easy to see Don Q as the light, dry, Puerto Rican rum that's not Bacardí, and while you can certainly use the lighter rums as Bacardí replacements if that's your thing—both distilleries are working in a similar style—where Destilería Serrallés, the brand's producer, really excels is in its long-aged sipping rums. Both the Gran Anejo ($60), a blend of rums aged from nine to twelve years, and the 2005 Signature Release Single Barrel ($40), which is ten years old, show that a style of rum production often maligned for resulting in flavorless rum can, when used correctly, make a rich, complex spirit. Both are dry rums with clear wood-barrel flavors, including cocoa and Christmas spices that should please those whose palate also has an affinity for bourbon. Among the two, it's the 2005 Signature Release Single Barrel I prefer, not least because the closure on the otherwise elegant Gran Anejo bottle is stubborn. Bottle design aside, the 2005 Signature Release Single Barrel is a little lighter and less palate-fatiguing than the spicy caramel, cocoa finish of the Gran Anejo, which is nonetheless delicious.

EL DORADO

This is the international brand from the legendary Demerara Distillers Limited in Guyana. Their portfolio is deep, but the most common range from a white three-year ($18) to a twenty-one-year-old ($100), with particular lodestars at the three-year and eight-year ($25) expressions. Across the brand, El Dorado is able to show off the rich complexity they can achieve by blending marks from so many different stills, and many of these bottles make clear the rich, almost smoky character long associated with Demerara rums.

To the frustrations of many connoisseurs and prominent bartenders and distillers in the rum industry, however, El Dorado is one of the brands that appears to add sugar to some of its bottles, but claims otherwise. When I asked Sharon Sue-Hang Baksh, the master blender, if they did in fact add sugar during a tasting at DDL's facility, she told me straight out that they didn't. Based on my palate, the websites for the Swedish and Finland liquor authorities, and reports from the online rum community, the case seems otherwise, particularly with the longer-aged rums, which may need it. While some of these rums are overpowered by a soft sweetness, the eight-year-old and the three-year-old are well worth trying. Though pricey and not as easy to find, so too are the brand's "single barrel" releases, each of which represents one individual mark from the sugar estates that would come to make up DDL. They are excellent and a great way to compare the variability in rum.

FACUNDO NEO

Facundo is Bacardí's attempt to go after a portion of rum's expanding higher-end market, and the bottles certainly carry the price points to vault them to the top. The origins of these rums trace back to Bacardí's development of a 150th anniversary special release and a realization that the light-rum behemoth was also sitting on large stocks of long-aged rum, heretofore primarily reserved for the family. All produced in the Bahamas, where corporate Bacardí is based, Eximo retails at about $60, Exquisito at just under $100, and Paraiso at $250, plus or minus not enough that you should care if you're buying a $250 bottle of rum. Unfortunately, the rum inside doesn't quite justify the price for me. In particular, they generally seem too woody. What is interesting in the Facundo line, however, is the Neo. Just a smidge under $50, Neo falls into a category of ultra-premium white rums that I hope we start to see more of. I'm not sure I want more white rums that have seen as much oak as this one has, and I am not sure it's quite as balanced as it could be, but it's aromatic and fruity and with some caramel and vanilla presumably from that wood. If it convinces a few people that white rum can be high-end, then it has done its job. Consider it an educational addition to your bar.

FLOR DE CAÑA

One of the best known Spanish-style rums, Nicaragua's Flor de Caña produces a wide range of typical dry rums. Despite a spate of bad press in recent years, due both to the fact that Nicaragua's sugar workers were one of the first groups publicized to be stricken with chronic kidney disease, and label changes by Flor de Caña that many saw as an effort to avoid straightforward age statements, the rum has long been regarded as a well-priced standby.

Avaliable in everything from what's described on their website as a 4-year old white rum, the Extra Seco ($15), to a 25-year-old expression ($150), the lower end rums are reliable in cocktails, while the higher-end rums are worthy sippers for those who like their rum with dominant wood.

FOURSQUARE

These are the so-styled true rum lover's cult rums. Richard Seale, the fierce advocate for the traditional Caribbean rum producers and their unsugared rums, makes several lines at his Barbados distillery, including Doorly's, a well-priced line of more traditional rums, and the high-end Foursquare line. The Doorly's rums are reliable mixers and sippers, dry, not too heavy, and not too woody, made from a combination of pot and single-column distilled rums. If they are available in your market—and unfortunately, their US distribution is patchy—they are good everyday rums. But it's in the distillery's eponymous Foursquare line that Seale showcases the talent and innovation that has made him such a prominent distiller. While releases of the Foursquare rums come and go, among the best when I was tasting was the 2004 Exception Cask Selection, Mark III ($75), labeled a "single blended rum" per the classification system promoted by Seale and Velier's Luca Gargano. At 59 percent ABV, it was a rum that shows how proof can just be a number. The 2004 sips remarkably well on its own— no water, definitely no ice—its higher concentration corresponding not just to alcohol but also to the rum's complex unraveling of lush, tropical flavors. Aged for eleven years, for this bottle Seale uses ex-bourbon casks only, but he's also released expressions aged partially in ex-port ($50) and ex-Zinfandel casks ($60), the latter of which is particularly worth seeking out. At the risk of becoming too rhapsodic, this is among the few distilleries to watch for category-defining innovative releases.

HAMILTON

"I was lucky enough to have a boss years ago that told me that I wasn't a good employee and I needed to find something else to do with my life. He said, 'Well, what do you want to be doing in five years, and write it down.' So I wrote down, 'Go sailing,' and he says, 'OK, now write down five things that you are going to do to make that happen,' and I wrote down, 'I quit.' And five years and two months later I bought a sailboat, a small boat, and went to the Caribbean. I didn't really think it was going to be a twenty-year trip, but it was." This is the story Ed Hamilton told me when I asked how he set out on the path that led him to become one of rum's leading acolytes. As he tells it, over those twenty years of sailing, Hamilton dropped in on rum distilleries throughout the Americas, grilling the staff at each on their intricacies of rum production (his civilian background is in chemical engineering). The accumulated knowledge became the basis of his encyclopedic website, the Ministry of Rum (www.ministryofrum.com), and a company that imports some of the Caribbean's best rums into the US. Among them are a line that bears his name and includes bottlings from the core rum producing countries of St. Lucia ($47), Jamaica ($26), and Guyana ($26). Hamilton is an evangelical of transparency in the rum world, and he documents the path his rums take to the market in exquisite detail on his importer website (www.caribbean-spirits.com). His Demerara rums in particular are great examples of the style without added sugar.

HAMPDEN ESTATE

Inarguably the best rum with the worst branding, on the outside Rum Fire ($30) resembles a twelve-year-old boy's aesthetic refracted through a suite of '90s-era desktop publishing software and a burning curiosity to see just how saturated that new color ink jet printer can go. The rum on the inside, however, is contained as if in a time capsule—this is the rum issued from the archaic pursuit of esters carried out at Hampden Estate's creaky Jamaican distillery, with its weeks-long, bacteria-friendly fermentation and pot distillation. It's bold, at 63 percent ABV, and incredibly flavorful, with bright, intense tropical fruits on the palate and an incredible floral nose that is truly singular in the spirits world. You can do wonderful things with this in craft cocktails and tiki drinks, but it's also great to play with in a daiquiri—vary your ratios and consider, perhaps, splitting the spirit with a lighter rum, or use it for a punch, as Pepe Grant, Hampden's tour manager does.

LEBLON

When Leblon came into the market two decades ago, cachaça was hardly known, and if it was it was known as little more than vile fuel for hangovers. Leblon is far, far from that. Both its standard white release ($24) and its aged Reserva Especial ($25; 375ml) are light, well-structured, and eminently pleasing. The typical cachaça notes of grass and fresh sugarcane are obvious but not overpowering in the white, transforming into a fantastic nose and a brown-sugar palate with just a bit of spice in the Reserva Especial. Overall, they are great introductions to the category. But they also, unfortunately, undersell cachaça's potential. Both are a little like a beach read—easy, breezy, fun, but possessing too little complexity to really be memorable. Leblon has the talent and stocks to produce some really exquisite cachaças. Now that they've gotten everyone to pour it into a glass rather than a gas tank, I hope to see in future releases bottles that are able to showcase cachaça's serious side and seize a bit of the spirit's rightful shelf space alongside fine cognac, tequila, and Caribbean rum.

LEMON HART

One of the oldest brand names in rum, Lemon Hart—as much as it may sound like a cocktail moniker, it's actually a person's name—traces its heritage back more than two hundred years to a blender and supplier of Demerara rums to the British Royal Navy. But what's really given the brand its prominence is the tiki trend, where the high-proof version, Lemon Hart 151 ($33), is frequently called upon for its spicy, complex, high-proof character. Over the years the brand has roamed around a number of liquor conglomerates, landing at Pernod Ricard in 2005 and being bought in 2010 by the Quebec-based wine and spirits company Mosaiq. Though Mosaiq updated its label—which they estimated dated back to sometime in the 1980s—the rum still comes from Demerara Distillers in Guyana.

MEZAN

This rum is billed as being "untouched," which Alexandre Gabriel of Plantation Rums rightly pointed out at the "When is a Rum Not a Rum?" panel is marketing hooey masquerading as anti-marketing hooey. ("What does 'untouched' mean?" he asked. "Is it made with one's elbows?") But if we faulted a rum too much for marketing hooey, we'd be little more than a parched sourpuss, and as far as rum marketing goes, Mezan isn't too bad. In fact, it's an interesting specimen: a line of sourced rums capitalizing on all the perceived deception of the other brands by touting what it is not: in addition to being "untouched," it is also "unblended, unsweetened, uncolored, and only lightly filtered." All things I can firmly get behind, though as Mezan's own release, the blended Jamaican XO ($30), shows blending isn't necessarily a bad thing. They are often vintage labeled, which is of arguable relevance for non-sugarcane juice rums but is a nice way to track batches. The bottles here cover familiar ground so far: Jamaica, Guyana ($55), and Panama ($45), but are nice examples of their type. In particular I was pleased to try the Guyana rum from the Port Mourant wooden pot still, which showcases the spirit's bold, petrol-y flavor, unhampered by sugar.

MONTANYA

Karen and Brice Hoskin distill these well-regarded rums in the utterly charming Colorado mountain town of Crested Butte, where their distillery is right on the main drag and features a bar and tasting room directly below their copper pots. The Hoskins make their wash from a combination of molasses and cane sugar grown and processed in Louisiana and distilled under an open flame, which Karen Hoskin told me when I visited helps caramelize their wash in a way that a more traditional steam-heated still wouldn't, bringing in a richness of flavor that they wouldn't otherwise be able to achieve. They then finish their rums with the addition of a bit of Colorado honey. Of the three expressions Montanya currently produces—Platino ($28), Oro ($30), and Exclusiva ($55)—the Platino is my favorite. Aged twelve months and filtered to remove color with a coconut husk filter, it makes tremendous daiquiris and is a great American replacement for white rums from Spanish producers. Their aged rums continue in the Spanish style—though the mountain altitude and climate mean their angel's share losses are significantly less than a Caribbean producer's would be—in that they are oak-forward, especially their Exclusiva, which is aged for three years, partially in casks originally used for Colorado whiskey and then in ex-port casks from one of Colorado's wineries.

MOUNT GAY

Barbados's Mount Gay claims to be the oldest rum and continuously produced spirit in the world, and with a documented history tracing back to 1703 it might as well be. Long a favorite of the yachting class—a 1982 *New York Times* article reports that the rum gained popularity in Newport and at the New York Yacht Club by sailors who'd pick up a bottle while island hopping from Antigua to Grenada—what those three centuries of heritage mean exactly, I don't know, but thankfully the distillery, now owned by the French conglomerate Rémy Cointreau and under the direction of master blender Allen Smith, hasn't become hidebound over all that time. The Eclipse ($20) expressions, which come in gold and silver varieties, are typical pot-and-column-distilled Bajan rum and worthy mixers. But in recent years, the distillery has really been promoting its aged sipping rums, which include a Black Barrel ($30), designed to woo whiskey drinkers; an XO ($50) that's made from a blend of rums aged between eight and fifteen years; and a line of special releases called the Origin Series ($95), which showcases two rums side-by-side that have had one of their production variables changed, such as being distilled exclusively in pots or columns.

For some reason the folks at Mount Gay seem to be really fond of the Black Barrel. Frankly, I think it's just got too much wood, by a significant margin, to really showcase what the distillery is capable of. But their XO—fruity, spicy, and amazingly complex—is stellar. If I was stuck on a desert island, I'd jump into the ocean and swim to Barbados for the stuff. Meanwhile, the Origin Series is a fun—if pricey—way to enhance your rum knowledge a bit.

NOVO FOGO

Novo Fogo's cachaças are great and you should drink them. In particular, they've focused on bringing into the American market a sampling of the exotic woods that make up the cornucopia of cachaça variety in Brazil. Their Tanager ($35) with Brazilian zebrawood and oak is a particular treat, with a body of mango and spice. But here's what I really want to tell you about them: if you're ever looking to do a distillery tour in a beautiful, peaceful, far-flung location, go here. Novo Fogo is located in the Atlantic rainforest—Brazil's other rainforest, not the Amazon—that's squeezed into a narrower border of land between the ocean and the mountains. The nearest town is a place called Morretes (pronounced mo-het-es). It's tiny and colonial and gorgeous, just like the distillery itself, which used to be known as Porto Morretes before the Novo Fogo team bought it. All the cachaças Novo Fogo produces are organic.

OLD NEW ORLEANS RUM

I have to admit that I'm a little taken with the heritage of this rum, not the least because it comes from New Orleans, a city I adore, and because the distillery was founded by James Michalopoulos, an artist who indulged me for nearly an hour in a conversation about another topic I find important, the financial viability of the arts and local manufacturing-based economies—one of the key reasons, I believe, to support local craft spirits. Nonetheless, this rum is remarkable as well for being one of the first mainland American rums after the style went extinct after Prohibition's repeal. Made from Louisiana sugarcane, their range includes the standard issues, including a white Crystal ($25) and an aged Amber ($28) rum. They also make a bottled ginger cocktail called Gingeroo ($17) and recently released a 20th anniversary blend ($80). Dry, yet with a chocolate cake–like quality that lingers on the finish and Christmas spices, the Amber in particular is unique and delicious.

OLIVER Y OLIVER

Although based in the Dominican Republic, Oliver y Oliver mostly uses rum produced elsewhere in the Spanish Americas—primarily Panama and Guatemala—to produce its rich, sweet, solera-aged rums, which it sells under a constellation of brands, each aimed at its own market and in its own style. Among them are the Unhiq, Ron Cubaney, Opthimus, and Presidente, which together represent a wide range of bottles and a wide range of prices (Oliver y Oliver also contract blends and bottles for others). These aren't likely rums that will appeal to a Caribbean rum purist easily incensed by additives and age statements that don't reflect the age of the youngest rum in the barrel. But I can attest that if you leave a few bottles around in your liquor cabinet, plenty of casual drinkers will pour them into a glass and quickly begin raving. While I'm generally partisan with the rum purists, I can see why people like these—as a drink, several of them have considerable appeal. In particular, I found the Opthimus lush, well balanced, and complex, though I am still going to think of these as a category unto themselves.

PENNY BLUE

Rum from Mauritius, an island nation in the Indian Ocean thousands and thousands of miles from nearly every other rum mentioned here, is a bottle with considerable novelty appeal. Thankfully it's a worthy enough sipper that it likely won't make you wish you'd chosen something more traditional. The rum comes from estate-grown cane and is produced in column stills by the Medine distillery, which dates back to the mid-1920s, and bottled without added sugar from casks selected with the help of the London-based merchants Berry Bros. & Rudd. There are a few different expressions, but only the XO ($75), which is released in batches, makes it into the US. I tasted Batch No. 2 of the XO and found it to be enjoyably medium bodied with toffee notes and a pleasant but not overpowering amount of new oak on the finish. The distillery also produces a vanilla spiced rum called the Pink Pigeon ($40), which—go figure—comes in an all-black bottle and isn't the worst way to get your daily allotment of tropical spices.

PLANTATION

This is the brand of Frenchmen and rum aficionado Alexandre Gabriel. While Gabriel irks some advocates of traditional Caribbean rum for his enthusiastic use of added sugar in rum—a technique he says he models after the similar method of *dosage* used in cognac production—there's no doubt that Plantation has been responsible for bringing considerable attention to rum amid the recent rum renaissance. In part this is the product of wide distribution and slick marketing—Plantation is part Maison Ferrand, which produces Cognac Ferrand, Citadelle Gin, and a number of other prominent spirits—but it's also a reflection of the innovation Gabriel has brought to the category. While Plantation's line includes a number of bottles from the places that fill out the portfolios of many rum brokers, where it really stands out is in its blends. Most notable among them is the 138-proof O.F.T.D. ($30), or Old Fashioned Traditional Dark, a collaboration between spirits historian David Wondrich and tiki masters Jeff "Beachbum" Berry and Martin Cate of New Orleans's Latitude 29 and San Francisco's Smuggler's Cove bars, respectively. It is a huge rum made from a blend of Jamaican, Guyanese, and Barbadian distillates that can do some amazing things in cocktails. Even more stunning is the Stiggins' Fancy Pineapple Rum ($32), which I guess is technically a flavored rum, but deserves a class all its own. Made from rum infused with pineapple meat and blended with rum that's been infused with pineapple rinds and redistilled, the mixture is then reaged. The result is multiplication, the product of two of the world's greatest things that is amazingly better than the sum of its parts.

THE REAL MCCOY

Anybody who's spent any serious time researching something knows the endeavor is teeming with tantalizing rabbit holes just waiting to suck you away from the task at hand for long periods of time. Many fall down. Few emerge from them with a rum brand, however. But Bailey Pryor did. Pryor, the owner of Real McCoy, is not a distiller, nor is he even a spirits industry veteran. Instead, he's a documentary producer who, while working on a film about Bill McCoy, the Prohibition-era rumrunner whose safe-when-so-much-was-not bootleg liquor gave rise to the expression "the Real McCoy," wondered if anyone had trademarked the brand. Remarkably, they hadn't, so Pryor jumped on it. Trademark in hand, he just needed the rum.

Over the course of his research, Pryor had found a photo that showed McCoy with barrels of rum marked with custom stamps that showed it originated in Barbados. When he flew down to the island to figure out which distillery it came from, however, he learned that no one could tell him for sure where McCoy was buying his product, but many suggested it may have been the family of Richard Seale, who were active rum traders in the 1920s. Naturally, when he met Seale, who today runs Foursquare Rum Distillery, he fell down yet another rabbit hole, that of the quest for unadulterated rums, and he has since become a prominent voice for unadulterated rums and honest minimum-age statements. He also has adopted Seale and Luca Gargano's rum classification system.

Today, Pryor's Real McCoy brand bottles and sells in the US three- ($20), five- ($29), and twelve-year ($45) expressions made by Foursquare. Dry, medium bodied, and spicy with plenty of wood-barrel notes on the finish, they are a good example of Bajan-style rum.

RHUM J.M.

One of the most prominent rhums agricoles available in the US, the sugarcane for the AOC rhums comes from the slopes of Martinique's Mount Pelée, the volcano famous for its turn-of-the-twentieth-century eruption that killed tens of thousands on the island. All the rhums in the range are good ($30–$70), though the particular standouts are the aged rhums, which have exceptionally long finishes, though with flavors of resin and a sugarcane flavor that disappears quickly, they might not be everyone's idea of a sipper. The younger rums are even bolder and call out, like so many of these spirits do, to be used in a cocktail or at least mixed up with bit of sugar and lime.

RICHLAND RUM

One of my favorite American craft rums, Richland Rum is produced in the tiny, tiny Georgia town of Richland by Karin and Erik Vonk, the latter of whom was introduced to rum by his Dutch grandfather, a connoisseur of rhums agricoles who held something of a disdain for molasses-based rum. From that experience, Erik, who moved to the US in 1979, always had in the back of his mind the thought that he might one day try to produce something in the style worthy of his grandfather's approval. In the mid-1990s, while he was living in Atlanta, he learned that south Georgia, though in no way a center of American sugar production, had land conducive to growing cane.

In 1999 he found a suitable plot of land, ironically called Sugar Hill Farm although it didn't produce any sugarcane, and bought it. Shortly thereafter he and Karin started a small test plot of sugarcane, which eventually grew into the basis for their distillery.

Today, the Vonks produce their rum entirely from estate-grown cane, which they press and turn into a sugarcane syrup, which is essentially sugarcane juice with much of the water boiled out of it, equivalent to the first step of producing sugar in a sugar refinery. They then ferment the sugarcane syrup; distill it on small, hammered copper pot stills, similar to cachaça stills; age it in new white oak barrels; and bottle it in numbered batches without additives. The result ($80) is something close to a rhum agricole, with an incredibly long profile of citrus fruit and spice that also includes a significant amount of oak I found to be very well integrated, rather than distracting, as it is in too many American craft rums.

SANTA TERESA

Santa Teresa 1796 ($40) is Venezuela's other prominent rum—besides Diplomático—on the international market, and its 1796 solera is a nice, complex sipping rum that's bold, lush, and, significantly drier than its compatriot. (Daniela Curiel, at the time the rum's brand manager in the US, told me it contains no additives.) Made from a blend of three types of rum—two that are column distilled (one at 95 percent alcohol with few congeners and another at about 85 percent with more congeners) and the third a high-congener pot-distilled rum, it is then aged in ex-bourbon barrels before being placed into a solera, which has been going since 1992, for further aging. The result is one of my favorite Spanish-style rums, especially for the price.

SMITH AND CROSS

This is aged Hampden Estate rum, and its lineage is apparent as soon as you pop open the bottle. Massive, flavorful, and funky, at 57 percent alcohol and $29 it performs fantastically in cocktails. But in a recent blind tasting of sipping rums I did, this one got slipped in. Its flavor and aroma are distinctive enough that it didn't remain incognito long, but with a splash of water to cool it down I was surprised at how sippable it is. You don't drink this seeking refinement, but with distinct cherry notes on the body and a finish that unspools and unspools and unspools flavor almost endlessly, it's a fun treat.

ST. GEORGE CALIFORNIA AGRICOLE RUM

There's a conundrum every reviewer faces eventually, which is that if you critically consume any type of thing—books, food, rum—for long enough, eventually your sense of approachability gets thrown all out of whack and the desire for pure novelty kicks in. For me and rum the St. George California Agricole Rum ($50) might represent my reviewer's Rubicon. I'm hesitant to recommend it to anyone, but I love it. Made by the brilliant American craft distiller Lance Winters at Alameda, California's St. George distillery from Imperial Valley sugarcane, this is an agricole-style rum that takes weirdness to the extreme. When I first popped off the cap and took a whiff, I was immediately taken back to the Augusts of my childhood in Iowa, when my mom would buy bushels of overripe sweet corn from my uncle and spend days boiling it, cutting it off the cob, and freezing it for winter, impressing me into the task of shucking, which I hated, as our farmhouse became increasingly laden with the odor. For this reason, I despise sweet corn and I thought I was going to despise this rum. But once I push that memory away, what's left is a tantalizing rum: wild and gamey with a clear finish of sugarcane that has little comparison with any other spirit. I use it almost exclusively for a variation on the Last Word cocktail.

THREE SHEETS

San Diego-based Cutwater Spirits, a spin-off of the Ballast Point brewery, makes white ($26), spiced ($29), aged ($40), and cask-strength ($90) rums under their Three Sheets brand. Each is made from a base of evaporated cane sugar fermented at a low temperature to create a very clean wash, Yuseff Cherney, the distillery's founder, told me. The result is very typical of many American craft-distilled rums, which is to say they are light and lack the funky, complex flavors that excite fans of Caribbean rums from places like Jamaica or Guyana. Overall, they, like so many of their compatriots, seem aimed at drinkers who are primarily used to light Spanish-style rums or even whiskey, and are willing to pay a premium for an American-made craft spirit. Whether you consider that a desirable quality or an undesirable one probably depends on your thoughts on the eternal "What is rum?" question, but the resonance seems intentional. Cherney told me he is a fan of both bourbon and Nicaraguan Flor de Cana rum. Cutwater's Three Sheets Barrel Aged Rum, which is aged for at least two years in heavily charred oak, will, I suspect, appeal to bourbon drinkers in particular thanks to its dominant oak flavors. The unaged rum, meanwhile, has an interesting bready nose and a light, almost neutral body that nonetheless does fine in cocktails typically made with other light rums.

YAGUARA

Yaguara means "Jaguar" in one of Brazil's indigenous languages, which would seem to be a strange name for these soft, refined cachaças, but perhaps there is something lost in translation here. As it is, these are great bottlings of artisanal cachaça from the distillery Weber Haus—yes, their heritage is German—in the southern state of Rio Grande do Sul. They are produced under the direction of Erwin Weimann, a chemistry professor specializing in cachaça, and imported into the US by brand co-founders and brothers Thyrso and Thiago Camargo. The bottles may seem gimmicky, with their undulations of raised glass, but I find them surprisingly ergonomic. Inside, the Blue ($38) is the standout. A blend of young, stainless steel-rested cachaça and aged cachaça at least five years old, it's fairly tame for cachaça, with a slightly grassy palate and long sugarcane finish. Meanwhile, the golden-hued Ouro ($44) is a blend of cachaças aged in Cabreúva, Amburana, and American Oak that's fuller bodied and slightly spicy and the brand also produces a Branca ($30), which hasn't seen any wood.

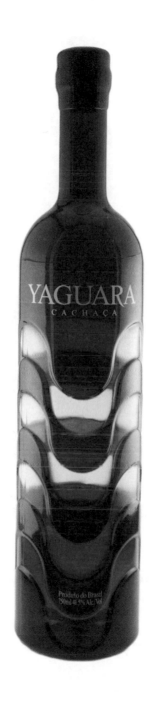

ZACAPA

Arguably rum's most polarizing mainstream brand, Zacapa has its lovers and its haters. It especially drew the ire of Caribbean rum purists for putting a "23" prominently on one of its labels, leading to the frequently repeated claim—in websites and liquor store shelf talkers—that it was a twenty-three-year-old rum. Instead, the Zacapa 23 is really a blend of rums aged six to twenty-three years. Furthermore, Zacapa's rums frequently come up high on internet lists for rums with added sweeteners. Nonetheless, this Diageo owned brand helped pioneer the way for high-end rum, becoming one of the first to stake out ultra-premium shelf space in the category. There are also plenty of fans of Spanish-style rums who rank it among their favorites. It clearly aims to be a sipping rum. The Edición Negra ($70), a blend of six- to twenty-four-year-old rums finished in ex-sherry casks, for example, is spicy, rich, and very full bodied, with a restrained sweetness.

ST. GEORGE CALIFORNIA AGRICOLE RUM LAST WORD

With their bright flavors and complex raciness, the most intense rhums agricoles can often act a little like gins in cocktails. In fact, sometimes I think they work even better, as the St. George California Agricole Rum does in that classic gin cocktail of four equal parts, the Last Word. In the Caribbean tradition, use lime instead of lemon.

0.75 ounce St. George California Agricole Rum

0.75 ounce Green Chartreuse

0.75 ounce Luxardo Maraschino Liqueur

0.75 ounce lime juice

Combine ingredients in a cocktail shaker, add ice, and shake vigorously until cold, about fifteen seconds. Strain into a cocktail glass.

Acknowledgments

First thanks go to my parents, who serve as a source of support and inspiration in everything I do. Thanks also to my aunt, Rita Auer, and uncle, Mike Crump, fellow travelers who provided invaluable advice before I ever left the States, and months of company when I was sequestered in Colorado, completing much of the work on this book.

In New York, I am grateful for Emily Pelleymounter and Victoria Kim, for dissuading me from heading off to the Caribbean with a wardrobe of New York black and for holding my place in the city until I returned; Rachel Lieff Axelbank, for providing a critical combination of advice, accountability, care, and a continual reality check; James Michel and Shauna Fitzmahan, for all their support and considerable forebearance and for making sure I get out of the city occasionally; David Burr Gerrard and Tyler Wetherall, for frequent consultation and professional commiseration; and Catherine Hull, for nearly a decade of friendship and evenings of garden wine.

Further afield, thanks to Margaret Poe, as always, and my cousins Alex Ryan Bauer and Andrea Bauer; also, Maggie Anderson, Emileigh Barnes, Danny Valentine, Seung Min Kim, Dan Manatt, and Kathy Manatt. Professionally, I'll forever owe David Schoenbaum, Jennifer Seter Wagner, Jo Ann Beard, Vijay Seshadri, and Rachel Cohen for helping me develop as a thinker and writer.

This book would also not have been possible without my agent, Adriann Ranta Zurhellen, who saw it through so many iterations well before it was even a book proposal; nor without my editor, Róisín Cameron, who is blessed with a tremendous amount of patience. Thanks also to Kathryn Flynn and everyone else who helped transform this from a manuscript to a book.

I also owe particular gratitude to Todd Oppenheimer, my editor at *Craftsmanship Quarterly*, for first encouraging me to take a look at the world of rum and for numerous rounds of editing advice on my work for him in all the years since.

Finally, this book took me on a journey of many, many weeks through many countries and it was one that would not have been possible without the assistance of countless people along the way. While I am especially grateful to those who appear in the interviews list, many of whom shared with me several hours to several days (to say nothing of months of follow-up emails), talking about rum and showing me around their distilleries, cane fields, aging warehouses, and countries, that list is just a fraction of everyone I encountered, from adept distillery public relations teams to amicable locals and fellow travels, who made the journey possible and profoundly meaningful. Thanks. Furthmore, I owe a debt to all of the authors and researchers whose work appears in the bibliography, without which I would never have been able to tackle a subject of such breadth.

Bibliography

Published Sources

Abbott, Elizabeth. *Sugar: A Bittersweet History*. New York: The Overlook Press, 2011.

Alcohol and Tobacco Tax and Trade Bureau. "Beverage Alcohol Manual." US Department of the Treasury. Vol. 2 (2007).

——. Certificate of Label Approval IDs#14190001000173; #15096001000093; #15338001000255. US Department of the Treasury.

——. "TTB Approves General-Use Formulas for Certain Distilled Spirits Produced Using Harmless Coloring, Flavoring, or Blending Materials." (TTB Ruling 2016-3). Department of the Treasury. September 29, 2016.

Aleman, Filadelfo. "Bootleg Liquor Kills 35 in Nicaragua." *Washington Post*. September 11, 2006. http://www.washingtonpost.com/wp-dyn/content/article/2006/09/11/AR2006091101067.html.

Annual Distillers' Resource Directory. Hayward, CA: American Distilling Institute, 2016.

Arroyo, Rafael. "Studies on Rum." *Research Bulletin*. University of Puerto Rico (Rio Piedras Campus): Agricultural Experiment Station (1945). Nb. This item doesn't seem to be cataloged in any standard manner. The call number for it at the New York Public Library is "VPG (Puerto Rico. Agricultural Experiment Station, Rio Piedras. Research bulletin) v. 1-5 (1941-45)." It is unfindable under title or author searches.

"Bacardi Takes Full Ownership of LEBLON® Cachaça." Bacardi Limited. July 8, 2015. https://www.bacardilimited.com/bacardi-takes-full-ownership-of-leblon-cachaca/.

Baiocchi, Talia. *Sherry: A Modern Guide to the Wine World's Best-Kept Secret, with Cocktails and Recipes*. Berkeley, CA: Ten Speed Press, 2014.

"Barbados' Rum Industry: An Analysis of the First Fourteen Years of the 21st Century." Barbados: Barbados Private Sector Association, July 30, 2015. http://tradeteam.bb/resources/barbados-rum-industry-an-analysis-of-the-first-fourteen-years-of-the-21st-c/.

Barclay, Eliza. "Are Women Better Tasters Than Men?" NPR. August 31, 2015. http://www.npr.org/sections/thesalt/2015/08/31/427735692/are-women -better-tasters-than-men.

Bauer, Bryce T. "The Fall and Rebirth of America's First Great Whiskey: Pennsylvania Rye." *PUNCH*. April 6 2015. https://punchdrink.com/articles/ the-fall-and-rebirth-of-americas-first-great-whiskey-pennsylvania-rye/.

Bauer, Bryce T. "Rum's Revenge." *Craftsmanship*. September 17, 2015. https:// craftsmanship.net/rums-revenge/.

Bettridge, Jack. "Appleton Estate Releases 50 Year Old Jamaica Rum - Jamaica Independence Reserve." *Cigar Aficionado*. June 22, 2012. https://www .cigaraficionado.com/article/appleton-estate-releases-50-year-old-jamaica -rum-jamaica-independence-reserve-16566.

Boyd, Pam. "Colorado rum flows from Stoneyard Distillery located at Dotsero." *Vail Daily*. August 17, 2015. http://www.vaildaily.com/news/colorado-rum -flows-from-stoneyard-distillery-located-at-dotsero/?show=comments.

Bruce-Gardyne, Tom. "Rum's renaissance a 'complex picture of growth.'" *The Spirits Business*. March 20, 2017. https://www.thespiritsbusiness. com/2017/03/rums-renaissance-is-a-complex-picture-of-growth/.

"Campari's 10-Year Courtship of Lascelles - New CEO Talks Priorities." Jamaica Gleaner. March 28, 2013. http://jamaica-gleaner.com/gleaner/20130328/ business/business1.html.

"Campari To Acquire Lascelles For US$414.75m." *Jamaica Gleaner*. September 4, 2012. http://jamaica-gleaner.com/gleaner/20120904/business/business1 .html.

Chandler, A. Russell, III. "Sitting Ducks over NORMANDY." *Aviation History* 14, no. 6 (July 2004,) 22–28. *EBSCOhost*.

Chatterjee, Rhitu. "Mysterious kidney disease goes global." *Science*. 31 March 31, 2016. http://www.sciencemag.org/news/2016/03/mysterious-kidney-disease -goes-global.

Chokshi, Niraj. "The United States of subsidies: The biggest corporate winners in each state." *Washington Post*. March 18, 2015. https://www.washingtonpost .com/blogs/govbeat/wp/2015/03/17/the-united-states-of-subsidies-the -biggest-corporate-winners-in-each-state/?utm_term=.339dd41cfe70.

Choi, Charles Q. "Origins of Human Alcohol Consumption Revealed." *Scientific*

American. December 2, 2014. https://www.scientificamerican.com/article/
origins-of-human-alcohol-consumption-revealed/.

Clammer, Paul, and Brendan Sainsbury. *Lonely Planet Jamaica*. Lonely Planet,
2014.

Clarke, Margaret A. "Sugar." *Encyclopædia Britannica, Inc.* December 13, 2016.
https://www.britannica.com/topic/sugar-chemical-compound.

Curtis, Wayne. *And A Bottle of Rum: A History of the New World in Ten Cocktails*.
New York: Crown Publishers, 2006.

———. "How the Rum-Soaked Royal Navy Sobered Up." *The Daily Beast*. July 29,
2016. https://www.thedailybeast.com/how-the-rum-soaked-royal-navy
-sobered-up.

———. "Making Sense of Sorghum Rum." *Distiller* 12, no. 1 (Summer 2016):
66–69.

de Aquino, Francisco Wendel Batista, et al. "Simultaneous determination of
aging markers in sugar cane spirits." *Food Chemistry* 98, no. 3 (2006):
569–574.

Department of City Planning. "NYC Population: Historical Population
Information." City of New York. https://www1.nyc.gov/site/planning/data
-maps/nyc-population/historical-population.page.

Dunn, Richard S. *Sugar and Slaves: The Rise of the Planter Class in the English
West Indies, 1624–1713*. Chapel Hill, NC: University of North Carolina Press,
2000.

Forero, Juan. "Brazil's ethanol sector, once thriving, is being buffeted by forces
both man made, natural." *Washington Post*. January 1, 2014.

Gallas, Daniel. "Brazil's Biofuel Industry Finds New Sweetspot." BBC. June, 23
2014. http://www.bbc.com/news/business-33114119.

Gibson, Carrie. *Empire's Crossroads: A History of the Caribbean from Columbus
to the Present Day*. New York: Atlantic Monthly Press, 2014.

Gilbert, Jo. "The Rise of Rum Part 2: Reaching a new generation." *Harpers
Wine and Spirits*. August, 17 2016. http://www.harpers.co.uk/news/
fullstory.php/aid/19701/The_Rise_of_Rum_Part_2:_Reaching_a_new_
generation.html.

Gjelten, Tom. *Bacardi and the Long Fight for Cuba: The Biography of a Cause*.
New York: Penguin, 2009.

Grannum, Guy. "African-Caribbean Genealogy." In *The Oxford Companion to Family and Local History*. Oxford University Press, 2008.

"Greenheart." *Wood Magazine*. http://www.woodmagazine.com/materials-guide/lumber/wood-species-2/greenheart.

Hansen-Bundy, Benjy. "Port Antonio: The Coolest Spot in Jamaica Right Now." *GQ*. May 17, 2016. https://www.gq.com/story/port-antonio-jamaica.

Hayes, Anne. "The world's best-selling regional specialty spirits brands." *The Spirits Business*. July 4, 2016. https://www.thespiritsbusiness.com/2016/07/the-worlds-best-selling-regional-speciality-spirits-brands/.

Heath, E. Rev. *A full account of the late dreadful earthquake at Port Royal in Jamaica*. London, 1692. Early English Books Online.

Hopkins, Amy. "The top 10 best-selling rum brands." *The Spirits Business*. June 28, 2017. https://www.thespiritsbusiness.com/2017/06/the-top-10-best-selling-rum-brands/.

"Hybrid Stills." Forsyth. http://www.forsyths.com/distillation/hybrid-stills/.

"The Hydrometer Method." Drecon. May 24, 2014. http://www.drecon.dk/index.php/16-the-hydrometer-method.

"An Interview with Johnny Drejer (Drecon.dk)." The Fat Rum Pirate. March 23, 2015. http://thefatrumpirate.com/an-interview-with-johnny-drejer-drecon-dk.

Jackson, Steven. "Fly Jamaica Weighs Tripling Fleet, Going Public." *Jamaica Gleaner*. January 27, 2017. http://jamaica-gleaner.com/article/business/20170127/fly-jamaica-weighs-tripling-fleet-going-public.

Jelly-Schapiro, Joshua. *Island People: The Caribbean and the World*. New York: Alfred A. Knopf, 2016.

"'JOY To The World' - Wray & Nephew's Special Run To Salute Female Master Blender Sold Out." *Jamaica Gleaner*. June 11, 2017. http://jamaica-gleaner.com/article/news/20170611/joy-world-wray-nephews-special-run-salute-female-master-blender-sold-out.

Lazarus, David. "L.A. business tries to make Fiji Water a star." *SFGate*. January 21, 2007. http://www.sfgate.com/business/article/L-A-business-tries-to-make-Fiji-Water-a-star-2622253.php.

Lender, Mark Edward. "Drinking In America: A History." New York: Free Press, 1987.

"Legalize Cachaça." Leblon. http://www.legalizecachaca.com.

Ligon, Richard. *A True and Exact Account of the Island of Barbadoes.* London. 1673. *Internet Archive*, www.archive.org.

"Long Pond Closure Devastating Clarke's Town." *Jamaica Gleaner.* March 16, 2017. http://jamaica-gleaner.com/article/lead-stories/20170316/long-pond -closure-devastating-clarkes-town.

Maccari, Roberto. "I nuovi Habitation Velier." Velier. July 10, 2017. http://www .velier.it/news/view/i-nuovi-habitation-velier.

Maguire, Steven and Jennifery Teefy. "The Rum Excise Tax Cover-Over: Legislative History and Current Issues." United States: Congressional Research Service. January 20, 2010.

Mann, Emily. "Story of cities #9: Kingston, Jamaica – a city born of 'wickedness' and disaster." *The Guardian.* March 24, 2016. https://www.theguardian.com/ cities/2016/mar/24/story-cities-9-kingston-jamaica-richest-wickedest-city -world.

McCartney, Karen. "Smart home: staying switched on from afar." *The Sydney Morning Herald.* August 17, 2016. http://www.smh.com.au/good-weekend/ smart-home-staying-switched-on-from-afar-20160804-gqkz69.html.

McDonough, Jeff. "Slave trade was Rhode Island's 'number one financial activity'." *The Jamestown Press.* March 19, 2009. http://www.jamestownpress .com/news/2009-03-19/front_page/003.html.

"Mercado Interno." Instituto Brasileiro da Cachaça – IBRAC. http://www.ibrac .net/index.php?option=com_content&view=article&id=46&Itemid=47.

"Mercado Externo." Instituto Brasileiro da Cachaça – IBRAC. http://www.ibrac .net/index.php/servicos/estatisticas/mercado-externo.

Mercer, David. "Chimpanzees found routinely drinking alcohol in wild." *Independent.* June 10, 2015. http://www.independent.co.uk/environment/ nature/chimpanzees-found-routinely-drinking-alcohol-in-wild-10309101 .html.

Mintz, Sidney Wilfred. *Sweetness and Power: The Place of Sugar in Modern History.* New York: Penguin, 1986.

"Morgan, Sir Henry." *The Oxford Companion to Ships and the Sea.* Eds. Dear, I. C. B., and Peter Kemp: Oxford University Press, 2006. Oxford Reference, 2007.

Mosedale, J. R., and J-L. Puech. "Wood maturation of distilled beverages." *Trends in Food Science & Technology* 9, no. 3 (March 1998): 95–101.

Naipaul, V.S. *The Middle Passage.* New York: Vintage, 2002.

"Necrology. Rafael Arroyo." *Chemical & Engineering News* 27, no. 49 (December 5, 1949): 36–43.

Newell-Hanson, Alice. "Port Antonio: Jamaica Unplugged." *New York Times.* September 18, 2015. https://www.nytimes.com/2015/09/18/t-magazine/port -antonio-jamaica-travel-guide.html.

Observatory of Economic Complexity. Massachusetts Institute of Technology. Internet Resource.

Office of the Federal Register. "Code of Federal Regulations. Title 27." National Archives and Records Administration. Revised January 1, 1970. Accessed via Google Books.

Owen, David. *Where the Water Goes: Life and Death Along the Colorado River.* New York: Riverhead Books, 2017.

Pachico, Elyssa. "Colombia's Illegal Booze Trade Causing Headaches." *InsightCrime.* October 7, 2011. http://www.insightcrime.org/news-analysis/ colombias-illegal-booze-trade-causing-headaches.

Pack, James. *Nelson's blood.* Annapolis, MD: Naval Institute Press, 1982.

Pardilla, Caroline. "Bars Toss Flor de Caña Rum Over Dire Worker Conditions." *Eater.* December 7, 2015. https://www.eater.com/drinks/2015/12/7/9838244/ bars-boycott-flor-de-cana-rum-over-its-dire-work-conditions.

Parker, Matthew. *The Sugar Barons: Family, Corruption, Empire, and War in the West Indies.* New York: Walker & Co., 2011.

Pieters, Janene. "'Component Failure' Caused Amsterdam Blackout; Power Utility Offers Cash to Those Hard Hit." *NL Times.* January 17, 2017 https:// nltimes.nl/2017/01/17/component-failure-caused-amsterdam-blackout- power-utility-offers-cash-hard-hit.

Pietrek, Matt. "Can Rum Survive Its Moment in the Sun?" *Cocktail Wonk.* January 3, 2016. http://cocktailwonk.com/2016/01/can-rum-survive-its -moment-in-the-sun.html.

Pine, Joseph. "What Consumers Want." TED, 2004. Video. https://www.ted.com/ talks/joseph_pine_on_what_consumers_want.

Pino, Jorge A., et al. "Characterisation of odour-active compounds in aged rum." *Food Chemistry* 132, no. 3. (June 1, 2012): 1436–1441.

Plutarch. *Theseus. The Internet Classics Archive*, Massachusetts Institute of Technology. http://classics.mit.edu/Plutarch/theseus.html.

"Report of the Outage Review Team." Jamaica: Office of Utilities Regulation. May 4, 2017.

Rodgers, Adam. *Proof: The Science of Booze*. Boston: Mariner Books, 2014.

"Rum industry" Statista. Accessed: 2017-08-11.

Sheridan, Richard B. "The Plantation Revolution and the Industrial Revolution." *Caribbean Studies* 9, no. 1 (October 1969): 5–25.

Smiley, Ian, and Eric Watson and Michael Delevante. *The Distiller's Guide to Rum*. Hayward, CA: White Mule Press, 2014.

Smith, Andrew F. and Garrett Oliver. *Savoring Gotham: A Food Lover's Companion to New York City*. New York: Oxford University Press, 2015.

Smith, Frederick H. *Caribbean Rum: A Social and Economic History*. Gainesville, FL: University Press of Florida, 2005.

Snell, Kelsey. "Virgin Islands Waits for Rum Subsidy." *Politico*. June 9, 2014. http://www.politico.com/story/2014/06/virgin-islands-rum-subsidy -107605.

"Sphere House 1 – Eduardo Longo." YouTube. Video.

Spender, Lily. "Brazil Finds Its Sweet Spot." CNH Industrial. http:// cnhindustrial.com/en-us/top_stories/Pages/brazil_sugar.aspx.

Stern, Marcus. "Lobbyists Help Smooth the Way for a Tax Break for Foreign Rum Maker." *ProPublica*. February 3, 2010. https://www.propublica.org/article/ lobbyists-help-smooth-the-way-for-a-tax-break-for-foreign-rum-maker- 203#fortuno_correx.

Thomson, Ian. *The Dead Yard: A Story of Modern Jamaica*. New York: Nation Books, 2011.

UN Comtrade. United Nations. Internet Resource.

"US-Based Company to Inject US$38m Into Long Pond Sugar Factory." *Jamaica Gleaner*. May 22, 2017. http://jamaica-gleaner.com/article/news/20170522/us -based-company-inject-us38m-long-pond-sugar-factory.

VanderMey, Anne. "What shipping can tell us about the global economy."

Fortune. September 18, 2014. http://fortune.com/2014/09/18/global-trade
-economic-indicator/.

Vazquez, Javiar. "Setting the record straight on the rum issue." *The Hill.* June 25,
2010. http://thehill.com/blogs/congress-blog/economy-a-budget/105627
-setting-the-record-straight-on-the-rum-issue.

Verhoog, Jeroen. trans. DBF Communicatie, Alphen aan den Rijn. "Walking on
Gold." E&A Scheer. 2013. Private Publication.

Ward, Edward. *A collection of the writings of Mr. Edward Ward.* ... vol. 2. The
fifth edition. London, 1717. *Eighteenth Century Collections Online. Gale.*

Wetherall, Tyler. "Female distillers prove women know their alcohol – and
always have." *The Guardian.* April 20, 2015. https://www.theguardian.com/
society/2015/apr/20/women-distillery-industry-alcohol.

Williams, Ian. *Rum: A Social and Sociable History of the Real Spirit of 1776.* New
York: Nation Books, 2005.

———. *Tequila: A Global History.* London: Reaktion Books, 2015.

"When is a Rum Not a Rum." Tales of the Cocktail. Video. https://vimeo
.com/195983006.

Woodard, Colin. *The Republic of Pirates: Being the True and Surprising Story
of the Caribbean Pirates and the Man Who Brought Them Down.* Orlando:
Harcourt, 2007.

Wondrich, David. *Punch: The Delights (and Dangers) of the Flowing Bowl.* New
York: Perigee, 2010.

Work, Henry. *Wood, Whiskey and Wine: A History of Barrels.* London: Reaktion
Books, 2014.

"The World's Biggest Public Companies." *Forbes.* https://www.forbes.com/
global2000/list/#industry:Beverages.

Interviews Conducted by the Author

Dragos Axinte; Sharon Sue-Hang Baksh; Alex Dupuy Barceló; Jeff Berry; Michael Booth; Gilberto Briceño; Lennox Shaun Caleb; Thiago Camargo; Thyrso Camargo; Juan Cartagena; David Cid; Gordon Clarke; Thomas Collins; Mike Daigle; Arthur Dawe; Dani DeLuna; Puran Dhanraj; Kevin Farmer; Otto Flores; Lloyd Forbes; Marcello Gaya; Pepe Grant; Raphael Grisoni; Edward Hamilton; Christelle Harris; Andrew Hassell; Karen Hoskin; Felipe Jannuzzi; Mike Kelly; Adrian Keogh; Alexander Kong; Jason Kosmas; Brandon Lieb; Steve Luttmann; Darryl Manichand; Catherine Mcdonald; James Michalopoulos; Luigi Moroni; Shannon Mustipher; Patrícia Neres; Carlos Oliveira; Pedro Ramon López-Oliver; Mario E. Pujols Ortiz; Franklyn Parris; Bailey Pryor; Vaughn Renwick; Richard Seale; Eric Seed; Allen Smith; Joy Spence; Jassil Villanueva; Carsten E. Vlierboom; Max Vogelman; Erik Vonk; Karin Vonk; Evandro Weber; Erwin Weimann; Vivian Wisdom.

Index

French West Indies, 133, 187, 217, 255
fructose, 195
fruit flavors, 80, 93–94, 97–98, 119–
120, 122–24, 220

G

Gabriel, Alexandre, 198, 206, 295
Gargano, Luca, 209, 211–12
Gaya, Marcello, 156
gender inequality, 120
geographic indication, 208, 212–13
Georgetown, 42, 44–45
gin still, 66
"Global Rum Club" Facebook page,
205
Golden Jubilee, 46
Grant, Pepe, 80–81, 85–86, 89–92, 98,
220
greenheart wood, 61
Grisoni, Raphael, 21, 38, 113
Gruppo Campari, 107
Guyana, 41–72
Guyana Sugar Corporation (Guy-
SuCo), 46

H

Haiti, 21, 148
Hamilton, *270*, 271
Hamilton, Ed, 214
Hampden Estate, 78–86, *82–84*,
89–102, 210–11, 272, *273*
Harris, Christelle, 90–93
Harvest Rum, 185
Hassell, Andrew, 63, 65, 69, 89, 112,
114, 117–18, 196–97
heat exchanger, 145
high-ester rums, 80, 93–96, 97–100

Hinton, John, *23*
Hispaniola, 21
hogo quality, 80
humidity, 111–12, 115
Hussey family, 90
hybrid stills, 58
hydrometer sugar testing method,
194–95, 205

I

indentureship, 44
industrial cachaça, 134–35, 156
industrial processing, 25, 59
Industrial Revolution, 34
intermediate blends, 167
intermediate bulk containers (IBC),
150
isoamyl acetate, 94
IWSR (International Wines and Spirits Record), 134

J

Jamaica, 31, 78–102, 105–29, 166–67,
171–72, 174–75, 197, 210, 220
Jamaican rum, 11–12, 78–102, 212–13,
220–22, 223
Jannuzzi, Felipe, 152–56
Jones, Ben, 206
Jonestown, 44
Joy signature cocktail, 129
J. Wray and Nephew, 107, 118, 122–23,
171

K

Kelly, Mike, *126*
Keogh, Adrian, 240